45194

Touching History

The Untold Story of the Drama That Unfolded
in the Skies over America on 9/11

LYNN SPENCER

FREE PRESS
New York   London   Toronto   Sydney

To Caroline, Brigitte, and Chase

and

To those who responded with enormous conviction and courage—
whether in the air or on the ground—and to those who perished

Free Press
A Division of Simon & Schuster, Inc.
1230 Avenue of the Americas
New York, NY 10020

First Free Press hardcover edition June 2008

FREE PRESS and colophon are trademarks of Simon & Schuster, Inc.

For information about special discounts for bulk purchases,
please contact Simon & Schuster Special Sales at 1-800-456-6798
or business@simonandschuster.com.

Manufactured in the United States of America

1   3   5   7   9   10   8   6   4   2

Library of Congress Cataloging-in-Publication Data
Spencer, Lynn.
Touching history : the untold story of the drama that unfolded
in the skies over America on 9/11 / by Lynn Spencer.
p.   cm.
Includes bibliographical references and index.
1. September 11 Terrorist Attacks, 2001. 2. American Airlines Flight 11
Hijacking Incident, 2001. 3. United Airlines Flight 93 Hijacking Incident, 2001.
4. American Airlines Flight 77 Hijacking Incident, 2001. I. Title.
HV6432.7.S687   2008
973.931—dc22   2008004266
ISBN-13: 978-1-4165-5925-2
ISBN-10:   1-4165-5925-6

CONTENTS

FOREWORD

September 11, 2001, began benignly, with the most beautiful sunrise heralding soft winds and the clearest of blue skies. The entire East Coast of the United States was bathed in sunshine, signaling a high-volume day of few delays for the busy airspace of Boston, New York, and D.C. No ground delays were in the offing; normalcy reigned. Then the attacks began.

Through the shocking course of the series of events that started at approximately 8:15 a.m. and culminated at 10:03 in the lonely countryside of Pennsylvania, our aviation and military communities strove mightily to comprehend the meaning of the events that were unfolding. I was on my first day of a new job as the National Operations Manager of the Federal Aviation Administration that morning, overseeing the agency's Command Center. The live television image of United Airlines Flight 175 streaking into the World Trade Center's South Tower told all of us in aviation immediately that we were under planned attack; no pilot of any commercial airliner would deliberately fly an aircraft into a building. These exquisitely prepared professionals would sacrifice all to avoid loss of life on the ground. This is the pilot's long and storied credo.

From the first notification of the possible hijacking of American Airlines Flight 11, we in air traffic control worked furiously to gain precisely that, control over an unprecedented and bewildering series of shocks to the system. A mere few minutes, from 8:56 until 9:03, elapsed between notification that United 175 was a possible hijack and the time it struck the South Tower. More than

Foreword

4,000 aircraft were flying over the country that hour, and every one suddenly became a potential missile.

While some stories of that day have been told in great depth, we have read comparatively little of the drama in the skies. The consummate professionalism and skill displayed in responding to apparent chaos, while the military simultaneously improvised a complete defensive shield around U.S. airspace, is unparalleled. Pilots, crews, controllers, and the military collaborated in a magnificent effort, and it is this inspiring story that Lynn Spencer brings us.

Only when the last aircraft touched down that day did we allow ourselves to believe that the terror was over. Only now, thanks to Lynn Spencer, do we know the full story of the extraordinary and heroic actions of so many who confronted the challenges on the front lines that fateful day.

—Ben Sliney
FAA National Operations Manager on 9/11/2001

PREFACE

September 11, 2001, was our nation's second Pearl Harbor. When the smoke cleared, the loss of life was actually greater, and the shock to our country equally palpable.

Years later, the *9/11 Commission Report* gave us the explanations we sought. Finally, the inside story. I was one of the seven million citizens who flocked to the nearest bookstore to buy a copy. I wanted answers. I needed an understanding. As an airline pilot, the tragedy had been gut wrenchingly personal, and collectively, aircrews seemed to have a more difficult time leaving the tragedy behind.

When I finished reading the commission's findings, I was much better informed, but I couldn't shake the feeling that the story was incomplete. Something was missing. I felt compelled to dig deeper, so I began a journey to meet with the people behind the headlines: those who found themselves on the front lines that day in the cockpits of airliners and fighters, and in the control towers and military battle cabs. I went to their homes and their offices. I met their families. I listened intently as they shared their stories, and I experienced their pride, their sadness, their furor, and their unresolved emotions.

I also discovered that the *9/11 Commission Report* did not even begin to tell the full story; that it did not convey the heroism, confusion, anger, bravery, and sacrifice that are an inextricable part of this tragedy. I invite you to reconsider what you know about the events of 9/11, and to experience 9/11 through the eyes and minds of those who were there. In talking with them, I was moved, comforted, astounded, and proud, and felt as though I had somehow touched history. I hope you will feel the same.

Skies Severe Clear

Federal Aviation Administration Command Center, Herndon, Virginia, the Morning of September 11, 2001

Ben Sliney arrives early for his first day on the job as the national operations manager at the FAA Command Center in Herndon, Virginia, 25 miles outside of Washington. He feels invigorated, even eager to be taking charge, responsible for the hands-on management of the entire national airspace system.

With nearly 5,000 planes in the sky during peak hours and approximately 50,000 flights operating on any given day, the work of the Command Center keeps nearly 50 specialists intensely busy at their posts, around the clock, planning and monitoring the flow of air traffic over the United States. The Center is a communications powerhouse, modeled after NASA's Mission Control. The Operations floor is 50 feet wide and 120 feet long, packed with tiered rows of computer stations, and at the front, seven enormous display screens show flight trajectories and weather patterns. The specialists work with airlines and air traffic control facilities to fix congestion problems and contend with weather systems. The job is demanding, and as Sliney makes his way through the tiers of desks, the center pulses with an energy so strong that he feels he can almost touch it.

Having spent many years with the FAA as a controller and then a manager, Sliney is intimately familiar with the workings of the agency. Originally he had trained to be a lawyer; he returned to the agency only six months ago after many years of working in a law partnership he started with a friend from law school. He hadn't thought much about rejoining the agency until his friend, Jack Kies, the FAA's manager of tactical operations, approached him with a tantalizing offer.

Kies wanted him to take the position of national operations manager, but thinking things over, Sliney asked instead for a job first as a specialist. He preferred to develop a comfort level with all the operational details of the Command Center from the ground up. Becoming a traffic management specialist, he was responsible for reroutings for weather, airspace congestion, ground stops, and all other traffic management issues for the entire East Coast.

After just six months, though, Kies again approached him about the job of national operations manager, in charge of supervising all activities on the Operations floor, overseeing the entire air traffic control system, and wielding the power to resolve all disputes arising among the 22 air traffic control zones, or "centers," across the United States. This time, Sliney felt ready.

Another style of manager might sit back at his desk and start his first morning by asking for briefings from the center supervisors. Sliney instead makes the rounds.

"Class pictures today?" a weather specialist teases Sliney as he makes his way across the Operations floor wearing a conspicuous blue suit that matches his striking blue eyes.[1]

Sliney flashes back a bright smile. Having battled in the pits with the specialists, he knows the ribbing is good-natured. He owns at least a dozen suits, but he never wore one as a specialist, and he's not surprised by the attention he's getting.

"Masquerade party today?" ribs another of his former peers as he walks by.

Sliney pauses to make an exaggeratedly slow study of the guy's own outfit before responding in his most formal courtroom manner. "I chose my attire carefully so as to reflect all of my readiness, willingness, and ability to manage the complexities of the National Airspace System. Your disguise, by the way, is perfect."

The nearby specialists snicker, and Sliney hasn't taken many steps before another of them calls out, "Hey, are we still allowed to talk to you? Do we need to address you as 'Your Honor?' "

Sliney doesn't miss a beat. "No, you may still address me as Ben. However, henceforth you may not approach me without permission." Sliney is feeling good, confident that his team is on his side.

With picture-perfect weather across the nation—"severe clear" conditions in pilot-speak—nearly 50,000 flights are scheduled for the day, and over 3,000 of them are already airborne. It's shaping up to be a great first day on the job.

Northeast Air Defense Sector, Rome, New York

For the first few days of a big training exercise, it's always fun to bring in something fattening. Apple fritters are Bob Marr's favorite morning treat, and he was happy to stop by the Price Chopper this morning on his way to the Northeast Air Defense Sector (NEADS) to pick up a few dozen. The gesture would be good for morale, he figured, as his troops head into what promises to be 10 grueling training days of 12-hour shifts that will test their preparedness.

Now at the command post, Marr stares out from the glass-enclosed battle cab at the rows of workstations where his staff are at the ready at their computer consoles, radars screens, and communications equipment. They are awaiting the kickoff of the first big event of Operation Vigilant Guardian, the annual simulated exercise, or "simex," run by North American Aerospace Defense Command (NORAD), which oversees NEADS.

Although the military bases scattered around the country might give the impression that our soldiers and aircraft sit armed and ready to defend the nation at a moment's notice, in fact the vast majority of troops train to deploy only overseas. NORAD alone is responsible for the detection of and response to an attack against the mainland United States. To accomplish this critically important mission, NORAD command is divided among three subordinate regional headquarters: Alaska, Canada, and the continental United States (CONR). CONR is further divided into three regions: the Western Air Defense Sector (WADS), the Southeast Air Defense Sector (SEADS), and the Northeast Air Defense Sector (NEADS). All report to the CONR commander at Tyndall Air Force Base in Florida, who, in turn, reports to the NORAD commander at Peterson Air Force Base in Colorado.

The air defense of the continental United States is charged to the military branch known as 1st Air Force, which at the height of the cold war boasted 175 jets on alert, meaning fully armed and ready 24/7 to launch at a moment's notice. On this day, the number of alert jets has dwindled to 14 due to post–cold war budget cuts. The 1st Air Force deals regularly with search-and-rescue operations for planes that have crashed, assists the FAA in locating lost civilian aircraft, participates in drug interdiction operations, and is tasked with responding to hijackings, which are very rare. Critics have argued for years that the fighters are unnecessary, little more than babysitters.

Because 1st Air Force was transferred from active duty to the Air National Guard in 1993, the 14 jets are stationed at seven Air National Guard fighter squadrons across the United States. Two of those squadrons fall under Bob Marr's jurisdiction: a detachment of four F-16s at Langley Air Force Base in Virginia and a larger unit of 18 F-15s at Otis Air National Guard Base on Cape Cod. Both facilities keep two jets scramble-ready at all times, armed, fueled, and ready to launch.

NORAD training exercises of one kind or another go on almost any given week, ranging from table-top drills, in which commanders sit in conference rooms and contemplate attack-and-response scenarios, to comprehensive, live-fly exercises. In these, fighters are positioned all across the skies of North America, engaged in mock air battles. These live-fly exercises were much more common during the cold war, when preparation for responding to a Soviet attack was the cornerstone of U.S. military defense. In those days, F-106 and F-4 fighter aircraft intercepted and engaged huge forces of B-52s in simulated attacks. The exercises have been scaled down in recent years.

The current exercise is taking place off the shores of the northeastern United States and Canada. Yesterday was consumed by simulated intelligence briefings and meetings setting the stage for the mock engagements to come. The actual exercise will kick off today. It is the kind of war game that the Russians usually respond to, even in this post–cold war ear, and Marr's not surprised that they have announced plans to deploy aircraft today to several of their "Northern Tier" bases. The Russians are still eager, Marr knows, to show that they too have military capabilities. During previous NORAD exercises, Russian jets have penetrated North American airspace, and Marr is prepared for them to do so today as well. If they do come down the coast during today's exercise, armed fighters will greet them and escort them back to their own territory. He has ordered additional fuel and weapons loaded on his alert aircraft, just in case. The jets typically carry only "hot guns," meaning six-barrel 20 mm guns capable of firing 6,000 rounds per minute, with the exception of Florida's Homestead fighters, which, due to their close proximity to Cuba, carry live missiles as well. Today all of the alert fighters are loaded with live missiles in anticipation of any show of force that might be needed to respond to the Russians.

Marr has gotten a jump on today's work and has finished his first status briefing. He wanted to get it out of the way early so that he could plan for the surprises he knows the simex guys are concocting. Scanning the five 15-foot screens that line the front wall of the Operations floor, he thinks, *Any time now.* An edgy excitement runs through the highly secure facility.

Marr is well suited for command, nearly impossible to fluster, and boasts a long history in aviation and the military. He flew on active duty for nearly 18 years, until 1994, protecting America in an F-15. Then, when he left active duty, he became captain of a Lear

36 that was contracted as part of a simulated "target force" hired to stage attacks on the United States. That job was an enjoyable turnaround given all the time he'd spent on the other side of that equation, but after 20 months he returned to the Air National Guard as the director of exercises. He was soon promoted to vice commander and, in 1999, to NEADS commander. Standing in the battle cab—a raised glass-enclosed room at the rear of the Ops floor, jokingly referred to by the Ops staff as the "fish tank"—Marr surveys his troops as they prepare for the tricks to be thrown at them. He is fully confident in their ability to contend with whatever comes their way today.

Boston Center, Nashua, New Hampshire

In a darkened, screen-filled room in Nashua, New Hampshire, air traffic controller Pete Zalewski is seated at his high-resolution computer screen in the Boston Regional Enroute Center, one of the 22 FAA air traffic control centers responsible for handling long-distance, high-altitude flights in the United States. His shift began at 6:30. A controller's job is so stressful that nearly 20 to 30 minutes of each hour worked is spent on required breaks, but Zalewski thrives on the pressure, and he's enjoying another frenetic, no-margin-for-error morning.

He is one of the 260 controllers at Boston Center who are responsible for flight separation—keeping airliners well away from one another—in the 165,000 square miles of airspace over Connecticut, Vermont, Massachusetts, Rhode Island, Maine, New Hampshire, New York, and northeast Pennsylvania, including the major metropolitan areas of Boston and New York.

Today he is responsible for aircraft at altitudes over 20,000 feet in an area just west of Boston. He's monitoring many of the westbound departures out of Boston Logan, New England's busiest airport, which logs one takeoff every two minutes. As flights depart the airport toward the west, they quickly enter his airspace on their climbs toward their final cruising altitudes. He monitors each aircraft and gives instructions to the pilots to keep them on course, away from other planes, and clear of any severe weather. This is busy airspace, and keeping the airplanes apart is a finely choreographed group effort.

When a plane flies into a controller's sector, the pilot—who's been "handed off" by the previous sector's controller—calls up to announce his presence on the new controller's radio frequency. Each controller has a discrete frequency, and all planes flying into a controller's sector are told to tune into that particular frequency. While they are flying through that air space, all planes on that frequency hear all of the communications between all of the pilots and the controller managing that frequency. Zalewski's job is to make note of each aircraft on his radar screen as it enters his airspace, acknowledge the flight, manage its course, and then monitor it, along with all of the other planes in his sector, until it leaves his section of the sky, handing it off to the next controller.

In high-altitude airspace like that Zalewski is controlling, there are only fast-moving aircraft, and each is required to "squawk" a certain transponder code assigned by air traffic control. Every aircraft is equipped with a transponder, which emits a coded signal during flight, and this transmitted code assists in identifying flights on the controller's crowded radar screens. The transponder code also shows up on the collision-avoidance systems of other aircraft, alerting pilots about planes near them. Ground-based radar equipment picks up the transmitted information and sends it to the controller's screen, so that, on his screen, Zalewski sees all the aircraft in his sector along with a tag, or data block, that accompanies it. The tag tells him the plane's call sign, which refers to the airline and flight number, as well as its ground speed and altitude. If a pilot enters an incorrect code, or a special code to signify a radio failure or other emergency, that number will flash where the ground speed normally displays, alerting the controller right away.

Zalewski has had no such problems to contend with this morning. The weather is great, and at Boston Center things are moving along nicely.

Boston Logan Airport

In the stark lower level of Boston's Logan Airport, United Airlines Capt. Rick Johnson can't help but feel as though he is running on five cylinders as he finishes up his flight planning at Operations. Passengers are not allowed to venture into these mostly windowless, less finished, linoleum-lined hallways in the lower level of all airports. They're like basements, with long sterile hallways connecting crew lounges, airline operations offices, and, in hub airports, employee stores, chief pilot/inflight offices, and employee cafeterias. The areas are well secured and can be entered only through coded and alarmed doors because from this area, flight crews and ground personnel have direct access to the tarmac, where the planes are parked.

Johnson's wake-up call came far too early on this last day of a four-day trip, and he is waiting for the caffeine to kick in from a second cup of freshly brewed lobby coffee. Pilots can live anywhere they want and commute by plane or car to their assigned base. Johnson is based in Chicago but lives in Denver. Each week, he flies to Chicago, flies his three- or four-day schedule, then returns home for his time off. He's enjoying this flight schedule so far. The weather's gorgeous and he's getting along well with his first officer, Tony Stella, who is an all-around great guy.

Johnson arrived in Ops to find it vacant. Unlike United's hub airports Chicago and Denver, each boasting expansive and busy employee areas, Boston is considered an "out station." Only a small number of United flights arrive and depart each day, so the area is small and generally quiet. Crews come here to pick up their flight plan, use the computer, check the weather, and make calls to Dispatch, if necessary, before heading out to the aircraft.

When he arrived he took a quick look at the weather radar: severe clear. *Won't take much to earn my pay today,* he thought as he grabbed his bags to head out to the smoking area and a lone picnic table.

He is sitting atop the table resting his feet on the bench and taking a drag from his Marlboro Red when a quick glance at his watch tells him it's 7:55, time to get to work. Backtracking past Operations and toward the flight side of the airport, he walks out onto the tarmac and toward his waiting aircraft, passing in front of a United Boeing 767. That flight, United Flight 175, is just getting ready to push back from the gate. When Johnson passes in front of the towering wide-body, he glances up at the pilots and can see the first officer is drinking a cup of coffee. Figuring the pilots are from the West Coast and are also feeling the effects of an early morning wake-up, he offers a quick wave. The first officer nods back with a warm smile and a toast of his coffee cup. Just then Johnson feels a strange hair-standing-up-on-the-back-of-your-neck sensation.

Meanwhile, just across the ramp at Gate 67B, Delta First Officer Dave Dunlap enters the cockpit of his Boeing 767. Taking off his pilot's hat, he glances at the small photo of his wife and their 2-month-old son that he has tucked into the lining and smiles at them. Then he props the hat up on the ledge next to him, as he always does, so that he can see them at any time during the flight. He misses them terribly when he's gone, but he loves his job. After all, he's at the top of his game, flying a wide-body aircraft for one of the best-paying and most sought after airlines in the industry.

As with so many other pilots, his identity is closely tied to his job, and when he meets people for the first time he can't help but let them know that he's an airline pilot. Sometimes he can even be fairly obnoxious about it. "I'm a pilot and YOU are not" is his less than subtle message. He can't help it, he is proud of his skills. Not everyone can fly a 40-ton airliner and react to wind shear, rejected landings, engine fires, and hydraulic failures like they're everyday occurrences. Pilots are forced to stay sharp. Every six months they need to prove their skills on a check-ride—or find another job.

Dunlap knows that if he loses an engine just after takeoff, his passengers will hardly detect any change in the plane's flight because of his precise and expertly trained response. He'll do what it takes to keep that plane within 5 degrees of the assigned heading, not losing a single knot of airspeed or even a foot of altitude. And he'll remain methodical and perfectly calm while he's doing it.

Unlike many of his colleagues who resent being the number 2 guy in the cockpit, doing the lion's share of the work while earning half the captain's pay, Dunlap is happy for now with the goal of being the best first officer that any of the Delta captains he works with has ever flown with.

This morning Dunlap is feeling optimistic. He's looking forward to getting back home to southern California and four days off. The weather for the whole route is forecast as severe clear, and he's been told by clearance delivery that they are looking at an on-time departure.

Finished early with all his preflight checks, Dunlap is able to shoot the breeze a bit with the captain, Paul Werner. They discover they are both big fans of *The Simpsons,* and Dunlap recounts the episode in which two male characters both sense that death is imminent. They are facing a nuclear meltdown because Homer, who works at a nuclear reactor, put his jelly donut down on the control panel, setting off a spill. They look at one another, facing their final moments, and one says, "Sir, there may never be another time to say . . . I love you, sir!" Taken aback, the other responds, "Well, thank you for making my last moments on earth socially awkward."

The two pilots chuckle.

"So if anything happens to us today," Dunlap announces, "I'm going tell you I love you, and the rest is up to you!"

Werner just laughs.

Just then, an American Airlines Boeing 767, Flight 11, is pushed back off its gate. Their flight, Delta 1989, is next. Scheduled just behind them is United 175.

CHAPTER 1

American 11,
Do You Hear Me?

Boston Center, Nashua, New Hampshire, 7:59 a.m.

American Flight 11 receives takeoff clearance at 7:59 and is handed over from the controllers at Logan to the FAA's Boston Center after reaching 11,000 feet. The plane appears on Pete Zalewski's radar screen just after passing through 20,000 feet, and he radios the flight crew climb and course instructions.

"American 11, turn 20 degrees right."

"20 right. American 11," comes the prompt reply from the cockpit.

"American 11, now climb/maintain flight level 3-5-0," Zalewski continues, instructing them to head up to 35,000 feet.

He receives no response.

"American 11," he repeats, "climb/maintain flight level 3-5-0."

Still nothing.

"American 11, Boston," he radios, requesting a call back from the pilots. "American 11, uh, the American on the frequency, how do you hear me?" [1]

Again, there is no response. When a crew is handed off to a new controller, they're given a new frequency and are expected to check in right away. In this case, either the pilots aren't paying attention, Zalewski thinks, or, more likely, there is something wrong with their radios or perhaps with the frequency. Airliners have two primary radios for communicating; each can transmit on two frequencies, one that is active and another that is normally inactive. The pilot simply has to flip a switch to go between the two radios, or between the inactive and active frequencies. They usually listen to just one frequency at a time, and they can hear all the communications between the controller and other aircraft on that frequency. They can also listen to both active frequencies available to them simultaneously, although that gets confusing, like having a phone to each ear.

If a crew doesn't check in right away, it's usually because they've accidentally tuned to the wrong frequency or because they got the frequency information wrong. In that case, they just go back to the previous frequency and ask for a clarification. Such mishaps are not uncommon, and it usually doesn't take a crew much time to get onto the correct frequency.

Zalewski wonders if the pilots have returned to the frequency of their last sector, so he calls them on that frequency, but they're not there. Next he tries them on the emergency or "Guard" frequency, 121.5. This frequency is reserved for emergency communications with aircraft in distress, and airline crews usually monitor it continuously on their secondary radios. Zalewski figures the American 11 pilots should hear him if he calls them on that. But again he gets no response. He then tries several more times on the normal frequency, but to no avail. Zalewski is getting concerned, but not overly so. His radar tells him that the plane is still on course and the pilots have not yet changed their transponder to the "loss of radio" code, 7600. They may not yet realize that they have fallen out of the loop. If they *are* aware, Zalewski is confident that the crew is working on the problem.

"American 11, this is Boston Center. How do you read?" he repeats again and again. "American 11, if you hear Boston Center . . . please acknowledge." [2]

He begins systematically running through a checklist in his mind, trying to recall all the eventualities that might account for the loss of communication.[3] The crew may be significantly distracted or dealing with some problem on the aircraft. In a worst-case scenario, he figures, they may have experienced a failure in their avionics equipment or some other electrical problem. There doesn't seem to be any issue on his side of the equation; his other flights are hearing him just fine.

He reports to his supervisor that American 11 is not responding, and then, at 8:14, just as the flight is officially labeled "NORDO," no radio contact, the plane's transponder signal is turned off. This is rare, and not a good indication at all. No pilot would turn off his or her transponder, so this indicates a serious electrical failure on board the aircraft.

American 11 is no longer transmitting any signal to other aircraft or to air traffic control, and the plane's altitude is now a matter of sheer guesswork. The flight has become a simple blip on Zalewski's screen, with no data tag, what's called a primary radar return. The radar picks up the plane only because of its large mass, but no additional information is transmitted. Zalewski keeps his eyes riveted on the blip, afraid to lose it in the sea of returns that fill his monitor.

"Would you please come over here?" he calls out urgently to his supervisor. "I think something is seriously wrong with this plane. I don't know what. It's either mechanical or electrical, I think, but I'm not sure."[4]

When his supervisor asks him if he suspects a hijacking, though, Zalewski replies without hesitation, "Absolutely not. No way."

Hijacking is completely out of the realm of his experience. Hijackings are a thing of the past, a concern of the '60s and '70s. The operating manuals provided to controllers and pilots, which outline every imaginable procedure and regulation dictating pilot and controller actions, have only three or four pages dedicated to hijacking procedures. They're just not relevant these days.

At their peak in 1969, hijackings were committed by refugees or criminals and were nearly always headed to Cuba. As a precaution airliners carried navigating data, known as approach plates, for the

Havana airport. Diplomatic procedures were in place to ensure the return of planes and passengers, and most incidents were resolved without violence. In subsequent years, extortion-centered hijackings increased, in which hijackers commandeered aircraft for political purposes or monetary gain all around the globe, from Egypt to Pakistan, Singapore to Ethiopia. Yet as hijackers increasingly ended up dead at the hands of highly trained teams of negotiators and commandos, hijackings became less and less common. Zalewski can't imagine what is going on; but it's not *that*.

His supervisor instructs him to use standard operating procedures for handling a "no radio" aircraft, which includes calling back to the last sector that worked the flight and asking the aircraft to "ident," meaning to press a button on their transponder that makes their data tag light up on the controller's screen. If the pilot presses the Ident button, this lets the controller know that although the pilot cannot communicate, the crew is at least hearing controller instructions. Controllers can also ask the dispatcher of the airline company to try to reach the pilot, or enlist the help of other company flights. All airlines have a staff of dispatchers who also monitor their flights and can communicate directly with their pilots via various methods. Pilots of the same airline can communicate with each other on special company frequencies. Nearby flight controller Tom Roberts, who is working another American flight on his frequency calls to another American flight he is working on his frequency. He asks that pilot to attempt to contact the pilots of American 11, and within moments the pilot reports back that he's tried without success.

Zalewski is becoming increasingly anxious. He's never lost communication for this long—or to this degree—with one of his flights, and he is desperately continuing to try get through.

"American 11, Boston."

"American 11, if you hear Boston Center, ident."

"American 11, if you hear Boston Center, ident please or acknowledge."

He keeps his eyes glued to the flight's radar blip on his screen, and now, to his amazement, he sees the target making an abrupt turn toward the south, taking it significantly off course. He is shocked. Standard operating procedures dictate that, in the event of loss of radio communication, a flight continue along its planned route. The last thing a pilot would do when out of radio contact is to divert from the flight plan, leaving controllers with no clue as to where the plane is going.

With no way now to predict the aircraft's course and no altitude information for the flight, Boston Center controllers have no choice but to clear, or "sterilize," the entire airspace around the plane to create a buffer zone. They cannot have other aircraft coming into its proximity. Aircraft separation is urgent if a crash is to be averted. Working at a frenzied pace, the controllers call every aircraft between zero and 35,000 feet—and between New York, Albany, and Syracuse—to keep them out of the way. At least 20 flights are at immediate risk.

Meanwhile, planes have continued taking off from Logan and are heading into the danger zone. One of them is United 175. It is 8:23 when the cockpit crew checks in with Boston Center. They had taken off out of Boston at the same time that American Flight 11 turned off its transponder. The Boeing 767, under the command of Capt. Victor Saracini, is climbing toward its initial cruise altitude of 23,000 feet, and the cabin crew is beginning preparations for the meal service.

"Boston, morning, United 175's out of 19 for 2-3-0," Saracini announces when he checks onto Zalewski's frequency.

"United 175, Boston, uh, Center, roger," Zalewski responds. But he is quickly distracted by an odd transmission he has just heard on the frequency.

"We have some planes. Just stay quiet, and you'll be okay. We are returning to the airport."

"Uh, who's trying to call me here?" Zalewski calls out to the voice. "American 11, are you trying to call?" The voice is heavily accented and he can't readily understand the nonstandard phraseology he's hearing.

15

He is sure that the transmission is coming from the wayward flight. *Are they heading back to Boston?* he wonders.

The ominous voice continues, as if the speaker is unaware that Zalewski is even addressing him. "Nobody move. Everything will be okay. If you try to make any moves, you'll endanger yourself and the airplane. Just stay quiet."

Clearly the speaker is using the handheld radio in the cockpit, which he must think transmits only to the passengers, when in fact that radio transmits out to whatever active frequency the pilot is using. Only once the pilot flips a switch on the radio panel is its transmission restricted to the cabin of the plane.

There is now no doubt that American 11 is being hijacked. Zalewski calls out to his supervisor, "John, get over here immediately! Right now!"[5] and immediately starts to hand off his other flights to a neighboring controller's frequency so that he can concentrate on American 11.

"Delta 351, Boston Center on 125.57," he calls, giving the flight that frequency to switch to.

"2-5-5-7, Delta 351," the pilot parrots back.

"Flexjet 420, Boston Center 125.57," he says to the next.

Not only is this a hijacking, but it's no normal hijacking. Pilots would always find a way to let air traffic control know that they are dealing with a hijacker, and hijackers don't know how to turn off transponders or use radios!

Stunned by the urgency in his voice, the other controllers up and down his aisle stop to stare at Zalewski.

"This is really scary," a controller two positions down comments.

Zalewski calls to an assistant to pull the tapes that are automatically recorded of all transmissions to and from the center and to listen to the troubling transmissions he's just heard. He isn't sure he has made out clearly exactly what was said, and he knows that those transmissions will be critical in evaluating what's happening.

Supervisor Dan Bueno immediately calls the FAA's Command Center to notify them, and Zalewski continues to hand off his flights while keeping his eyes intently on the small blip that is the only identifier of the hijacked plane.

"United 175, contact the, um, Boston Center on 133.42," he directs.

"Okay, 3-4-2. United 175, so long." [6]

Though Zalewski has not been able to get through to American 11, a remarkable communication is about to be made from the flight: a courageous call is placed from the cabin of the plane.

American Airlines Reservations Office, Cary, North Carolina, 8:19 a.m.

Nydia Gonzales is on duty in American's Southeastern Reservations Office in Cary, North Carolina. As an operations specialist, her responsibilities include monitoring any emergency situations with American flights and forwarding information to American System Operations Control at headquarters in Dallas. At 8:19, one of the reservation agents receives an alarming call from a woman claiming to be a flight attendant on a hijacked American plane, and the agent immediately patches the call through to Gonzales.

When Gonzales picks up her phone, the caller calmly identifies herself as the number three flight attendant on American Flight 11, out of Boston. She is calling from one of the seatback Airfones in the cabin. She hurriedly relays that two flight attendants have been wounded and one passenger fatally stabbed, and she believes her aircraft is being hijacked. The passengers cannot breathe; something's been sprayed in the cabin. The flight attendants have tried to communicate with the cockpit but have been unable to.

Gonzales is stunned. She knows that someone at headquarters needs to be hearing this call, *now*. But her telephone system is not set up to transfer calls, so she holds the phone to her ear and grabs another phone to dial the airline's emergency line to the operations center in Dallas.

When the American Airlines' operations center emergency hotline rings at 8:27, manager Craig Marquis picks up. Gonzales excitedly explains that she is on the phone with a caller claiming to be a flight attendant on a hijacked plane. With a phone to each ear, Gonzales hurriedly relays that the caller says her name is Betty Ong, on American 11, a Boeing 767 en route from Boston to Los Angeles.[7]

Marquis is not sure what to think. *Could this be a hoax?* Remaining calm, he pulls up the personnel record for Betty Ong and asks Gonzales to have the flight attendant verify her employee number. His face drains of color when the information Gonzales relays matches the record on his screen. He then looks further in the record to see that Betty Ong is indeed listed as a flight attendant working American Flight 11 today. *Okay,* he thinks, *so I'm dealing with something real. But could this be an incident of air rage that the flight attendant is misinterpreting?*[8]

In his 20-something years at American, Marquis has faced his share of multimillion-dollar, airline-impacting decisions. He stays calm.

"I'm assuming they've declared an emergency," he tells Gonzales, figuring that the pilots must have reported the hijacking to the air traffic controller whose airspace they're in. "Let me get ATC on here. Stand by." He initiates a call to air traffic control at Boston Center. "Okay, we're contacting the flight crew now and we're . . . also contacting ATC."[9]

Betty Ong continues to talk to Gonzales. She relays that the hijackers are in the cockpit with the pilots, that the first-class passengers have been moved to the back, and the plane is now flying erratically. Gonzales focuses on providing reassurance, working to keep her voice calm. She is stunned that somehow Ong is managing to maintain such composure.

"We've contacted air traffic control," Marquis quickly reports back to Gonzales. "They are going to handle this as a confirmed hijacking, so they are moving all of the traffic out of this aircraft's way."[10] Then he asks Gonzales to find out if there is a doctor on board.

"No, no doctor," she reports back moments later.[11]

Ong then fills Gonzales in that the hijackers came from first-class seats 2A, 2B, 9A, and 9B. Marquis directs one of his staff to look up the flight and see who was assigned those seats. Meanwhile Marquis is informed by Boston Center that controllers there have heard radio transmissions from the plane indicating arguing in the cockpit. What they've actually heard is the transmission instructing the passengers to remain in their seats, but the information is relayed inaccurately. He also learns, correctly, that the plane has made an unauthorized southerly turn over Albany. Following protocol, Marquis calls out to an aide to notify the FAA Command Center that the airline has a confirmed hijacking.

FAA Command Center, Herndon, Virginia, 8:30 a.m.

Ben Sliney is making his way among the tiered rows of computer stations in the Command Center toward the glass-enclosed conference room at the far side of the Ops floor for the daily 8:30 meeting. The meeting is convened among all department heads and is a forum for briefings about the status of things in all sections: training, plans and procedures, computer operations, international operations, and system efficiency. As the National Operations Manager, Sliney is expected to present an outlook for the coming days' operations and expectations. Delays and what they did or will do about them are naturally the focus, as well as anything that may be newsworthy, like a huge backup at some airport. A staff member from FAA headquarters in downtown Washington, D.C., attends telephonically and reports to the highest echelons of the FAA as needed.

Sliney has thoroughly reviewed yesterday's operational log entries and delay summaries, which each air traffic control center must submit every day, and he's prepared to brief further up the chain as to any elements of the previous day's operations that may be called into question. He will also discuss the weather outlook, airport and route congestion, and any staffing shortages affecting operations. He is well prepared, but what he's not prepared for is what happens next.

As he strides toward the conference room, one of the supervisors calls to him, "We may have a hijacking out of Boston."

Sliney is startled. As far as he can recall, it's been years since the last hijacking in the United States.

"American Flight 11—a 767 out of Boston for Los Angeles," the line supervisor continues.

Sliney flashes back to the routine for dealing with hijackings from the days when they were more common. Keep other aircraft away from the errant plane. Give the pilots what they need. The plane will land somewhere, passengers will be traded for fuel, and difficult negotiations with authorities will begin. The incident should resolve itself peacefully, although the ones in the Middle East, he recalls, often had a more violent outcome.

"When was the last time we had a hijacking?" he asks. The supervisor shrugs, and Sliney continues into the conference room, thinking *So much for a quiet first day on the job!*

It has, indeed, been many years since the last hijacking of a U.S. airliner. In 1987, a fired USAir employee used his invalidated credentials to board an aircraft with a pistol. He hijacked the flight and killed the pilots. The plane crashed. More recently, in 1993, a Lufthansa flight that was hijacked in Europe flew into JFK Airport in New York. In that case, the hijacker surrendered.

Sliney begins the meeting by announcing the news of the apparent hijacking and then commences with his briefing. The weather is clear across the nation and they have no current equipment, staffing, or airspace restrictions. The volume of air traffic will necessitate some spacing restrictions between aircraft to smooth the flow in some congested sectors. They might need to order some short-duration ground stops at airports that have too many arrivals scheduled in order to prevent a bottleneck—and then holding—for incoming flights.

His briefing is interrupted when the same supervisor comes in and whispers into his ear that the situation with the hijacking is developing. American Airlines has just called and there's a report that a flight attendant may have been stabbed.

Sliney decides his place is on the Operations floor, and he excuses himself, announcing to the room, "Look, this hijack situation has seriously escalated and I need to get back to the floor. There is an unconfirmed report indicating that a flight attendant may have been stabbed."

The others quickly clear the room, heading to their posts. On the floor, the supervisor reports to Sliney on the rest of the call from American Airlines headquarters and the information from Betty Ong. He also reports that the plane's transponder has been turned off so that no flight data is showing on controller screens. The latest information from Boston Center is that the aircraft has turned south and is now 35 miles north of New York City.

Sliney looks up at one of the large screens at the front of the Command Center and sees that what *was* the track for American 11 is in "ghost," meaning that no transponder data is being received. Instead, the computer is giving track information based on the previously stored track data.

Sliney directs his staff to query facilities on the north-south line the flight appeared to be on when it was last seen and determine if anyone was talking to or tracking the flight. The plane is somewhere, and they need to find it. He then requests a teleconference between the FAA's Boston Center, New York Center, and headquarters so that all parties can get caught up and can share information in real time. The higher echelons at headquarters in Washington will make the determination as to the necessity of military assistance in dealing with the hijacking.

The standard hijacking protocol calls for the air traffic facility that first becomes aware of the incident to pass the information up the FAA chain of command, from the facility to the Command Center to FAA headquarters. There, a hijack coordinator contacts the National Military Command Center, or NMCC, to officially request fighter assistance. Once the NMCC receives authorization from the secretary of defense, orders are transmitted down the military command chain, in this instance to NORAD, then CONR, and then to NEADS, to issue a scramble order, getting fighter jets in the air to intercept the hijacked plane and follow it. The nearest alert aircraft in this instance are at Otis Air National Guard Base on Cape Cod.

Boston Center, Nashua, New Hampshire, 8:30 a.m.

Back at Boston Center, supervisor Dan Bueno has just hung up with the FAA Command Center in Herndon. His next move is to request military assistance from the 102nd Fighter Wing at Otis Air National Guard Base on Cape Cod. He knows it's not standard operating procedure to call the military directly—that's supposed to be done by FAA headquarters—but he's checked the FAA regulation manual, and in the back under section FAAO 7610.4J. Appendix 16, it states that fighters can be launched directly at FAA request, so he is going to make that happen. He may not be FAA headquarters, but he *is* FAA!

When he reaches tower control at Otis, though, the controller tells him to contact NEADS, under Bob Marr's command. That's the protocol.

"You've got to go through the proper channels," the controller says. "They're the only ones with the authority to initiate a scramble order." So much for the back page of the regulations manual.

Despite the emergency situation with American 11, controllers still need to take breaks in order to stay alert, and Tom Roberts is now relieved from duty for a scheduled coffee break. *Forget the coffee!* Roberts thinks, and instead he hurries over to controller John Hartling's desk, whose airspace American 11 is heading for. Just as he gets there, American 11 blips onto Hartling's screen. Hartling hasn't heard the word yet about the hijacking. The concentration required for the job is so intense that controllers operate on a need-to-know basis. They don't need to know what's happening in other controllers' sectors unless it might affect their own airspace, and distractions are rigorously kept to a minimum.

"You see this target here?" Roberts says to Hartling. "This—this aircraft we believe is hijacked, and he's last reported at 29,000 feet."

Hartling stares incredulously at the blip on his screen. It's bad enough that he has no access to the flight data or identifying information for the plane, that he's just got a primary radar return with no data tag—but it's a real shocker hearing the plane could be hijacked.

With no altitude data for the plane, he turns to another flight that has just moved into his airspace, United 175, to ask for assistance getting a read on American 11's altitude. The United pilot has just checked onto his frequency, after being handed off from Zalewski's sector.

"Do you have traffic?" Hartling asks the United pilot. "Look at, uh, your 12 to 1 o'clock at about, uh, 10 miles southbound to see if you can see an American 767 out there please."

"Okay, we're looking," Captain Saracini responds. Then moments later, "Negative contact, United 175 Heavy." He has added the "Heavy" tag to his call sign to indicate that he is a wide-body aircraft.

Hartling tries to give him a better description in hopes that the crew can spot the aircraft. He really wants to know its altitude and he knows that it's not easy for a pilot to spot another aircraft in the vast sky unless he knows exactly where to look.

"Okay, United 175, do you have him at your 12 o'clock now and five, 10 miles?" Hartling offers.

"Affirmative," the pilot now responds, "we have him, uh, he looks, uh about 20, yeah, about 29, 28,000."

"Okay, thank you."

Considering that airliners typically fly between 450 and 500 miles per hour, and because their flight paths are converging,

Hartling chooses to err on the side of caution and move United 175 away from American 11.

"United 175," he directs, "turn 30 degrees to the right. I want to keep you away from this traffic." [12]

"Thirty degrees to the right, United 175 Heavy," the pilot responds, and the 767 compliantly rolls into a gentle right bank.

With United 175 out of American 11's flight path, Hartling passes the United plane on to the next link in the air traffic control chain, Dave Bottiglia at the New York Center in Islip, Long Island. Hartling then continues to track American 11 as it approaches New York. He can tell that it is flying much faster than the 450 mph it should be moving.

Meanwhile, per Supervisor Dan Bueno's instructions, Boston controller Joseph Cooper has gotten through to the NEADS facility in Upstate New York to request fighter assistance.

NEADS, Rome, New York, 8:37 a.m.

Bob Marr is in the battle cab expecting the Vigilant Guardian exercise to commence at any moment. Today's training exercise runs a number of scenarios, including a simulated hijacking in which the perpetrators overtake an aircraft for political purposes, directing it to an island in order to seek asylum.

There's no way to know exactly when the exercise will begin— it just will—so the NEADS staff go about their normal business of monitoring until something different happens. When it does, each section will do what they've been trained in order to respond to the challenge or threat. The three operational groups—Surveillance, Identification, and Weapons—are interdependent. The Surveillance technicians find targets and pass on their coordinates to Identification, who determine what the target is and if it is friend or foe. The ID techs then hand off the target to Weapons, who give scramble orders to fighter jets and direct them to their target.

At 8:37, Tech Sgt. Jeremy Powell, who works on the Ops floor in support of the senior director in charge of the Weapons section, receives the phone call from the FAA's Boston Center controller Joseph Cooper.

"Hey Huntress," Cooper says, using the NEADS call sign, "we have a problem here. We have a hijacked aircraft headed toward New York, and we need you guys to scramble some F-16s or something up there, help us out." [13]

"Is this real-world or exercise?" Powell asks, looking across the Operations floor to the simulations team, to see if he can discern whether this may be one of their tricks for the morning.

"No, this is not an exercise, not a test," Cooper responds urgently.

Powell bolts up and turns toward the ID section behind him on the Ops floor. "We've got a hijack going on!"

Assuming that the exercise has begun, the leader of the ID section directs her team into action.

"We have a hijack going on. Get your checklists. The exercise is on."

"No," Powell urges, "you don't understand. We have a no-shit hijack!"

The ID supervisor raises her eyebrows. *Okay*, she figures, taken somewhat off guard. Quickly shifting gears, she thinks, *I know this routine.* Sitting just next to her is the mission crew commander technician, whose job it is to support the mission crew commander, or MCC. The MCC is in charge of the entire Ops floor, and if there is anything at all happening, he needs to know about it. The MCC tech gets on the building's paging system and calls for the mission crew commander, Maj. Kevin Nasypany, to return to the Ops floor immediately. The loudspeakers in the building crackle as the call to Nasypany goes out.

The technician then bellies up to his console, which shows the entire northeast sector, to look for an aircraft squawking the universal hijack code. Pilots have three special transponder codes that they can dial in: 7500 for hijacking, 7600 for loss of radio, and 7700 for other emergencies. Any of them will cause the airplane's tag to light up on his radar screen, but he doesn't see any such tag.

Nasypany arrives on the Ops floor moments later to talk of a hijacking. *No, that can't be right,* he thinks, *the hijacking simulation doesn't start until later. Who screwed up?*

"The hijack's not supposed to be for another hour!" he snarls, clearly not happy with this early mistake.

In the battle cab overlooking the Ops floor, Marr and his staff make note of a huddle of people gathering. Sergeant Powell, who took the call from Boston Center, is up on his feet and mouthing something to Marr that Marr can't make out. Since only the MCC has a hotline into the battle cab, Powell doesn't have any other way of communicating directly with the commander. It's not his job.

Marr has participated in enough training missions to know this is something out of the ordinary. Clearly, he thinks, the simex is kicking off with a lively, unexpected twist. Marr sends one of his officers to check out what's going on. His bet is that his simulations team has started off the exercise by throwing out a "heart attack card" to see how the troops respond to a first-aid call from a fellow soldier, testing their first responder training.

The officer Marr sent to the Ops floor rushes back into the battle cab after a brief conversation with the Boston Center controller, still on the line on Powell's telephone. "It's a hijacking, and this is real life," she reports to Marr, "not part of the exercise. And it appears that the plane is heading toward New York City."

This is an interesting start to the exercise, Marr thinks. This "real-world" mixed in with today's simex will keep them on their toes. A direct call from a regional FAA facility is not the customary means for requesting military assistance with a hijacking. The 1993 Lufthansa hijacking had been textbook in terms of FAA-military coordination. On that day in 1993, Marr spoke directly with his counterpart at the FAA and explained that they needed to start a request up their chain of command, or the military would not be able to respond quickly enough if the hijacking, which took place in Europe, came to the United States, which it did. Then he went up the same route of his own chain of command, letting them know that they should be prepared for a request for military assistance from the FAA. Several hours later, Marr received notification that military assistance was authorized, and the Otis F-15s, and later the Atlantic City F-16s, were scrambled.

Proper request or not, Marr decides to act first and ask questions later. At 8:37 he directs Mission Crew Commander Nasypany to order the two F-15 alert aircraft at Otis Air National Guard Base to battle stations. A battle stations order requires the pilots to suit up into their full flight gear and get into their jets. There, they're ready to start their engines and taxi out should a scramble order follow.

Otis Air National Guard Base, Cape Cod, Massachusetts, 8:34 a.m.

Though the Otis tower controller had directed Dan Bueno from the FAA's Boston Center to call NEADS, he decides that he should also go ahead and alert the Otis Operations Center that a call from NEADS might be coming. If the information Bueno was giving about a hijacked flight was accurate, he figures a call will be coming from NEADS soon and a scramble order is likely. He knows the fighter pilots will appreciate the heads-up.

MSgt. Mark Rose is on duty at the Operations desk when the phone rings. As the superintendent of aviation management, he is in charge of flight records and currency for the Wing's pilots. He's not sure what to make of the call.

"What do you have available?" the tower controller asks. He has not taken the time to first identify himself, and Rose has no idea where the call is coming in from.

"What are you talking about?" he responds. He knows what the caller is asking, but you just don't blurt out that kind of information: "Yeah, I've got 24 F-15s armed with AIM-120 Amraam missiles capable of locking onto targets at 50 nautical miles . . ." For all he knows, this could be a wrong number or a crank call.

The tower controller then identifies himself and offers a quick explanation that he's had a report of a hijacking. Rose knows it's time to forward the call to someone better suited to respond. The director of operations for the fighter squadron, Lt. Col. Timothy "Duff" Duffy, is standing next to him, chatting with some pilots who are getting ready to depart for a routine training flight.

"Duff, you got a phone call," Rose says.

When he left home this morning, Duff couldn't help but think that it was a perfect day to fly—it felt like the first day of autumn. The chances were slim, though, of his getting up in the air, because he was scheduled to sit alert for the next three days, and alert scrambles were few and far between.

"Who is it?" Duff asks, looking over at Rose and thinking that the only person who knows he is here this early in the morning is his wife.

"Otis tower—something about an apparent hijacking under way: American 11, a 767, out of Boston and headed for California."

Well, it's not my wife, he thinks. At an alert site such as Otis, the word "hijacking" is not used casually. Scramble orders involving a commercial airliner are not all that uncommon; often enough a flight loses radio contact or carelessly dials in an incorrect transponder frequency, or gets off course and flies a little too close to someplace it ought not to be. Jets are scrambled to investigate and report back. But a hijacking? That's a whole different matter, and for Duff, whose primary job is as a commercial pilot and who is part time with the Guard, the word hits very close to home. He fully expects that he and the other alert pilot on duty, his wingman, Maj. Dan "Nasty" Nash, will be getting a scramble call, so he grabs his handheld radio and calls for Nash to suit up.

Duff is betting that they're going to at least be ordered to go to battle stations. It's a fairly rushed process, so if there's even a chance of that call, Duff would just as soon have a head start.

Wingman Nasty Nash is a full-time National Guard F-15 pilot. Muscular, and in extremely good physical condition, he is a classic fighter pilot: all business. A man of few words, he comes across as not just serious but borderline offensive, and that's when he's not speaking. When he does speak, he uses the fewest possible words. He does have a sensitive and reflective side—he just doesn't often show it.

Nasty wasn't scheduled to sit alert this week, but the pilot who was is part of the training mission flying this morning. So by a twist of fate, Nasty has been left covering the guy's alert shift, "holding the alert packet" for him.

"Have you ever done a hijacking?" Duff asks Nasty as he fastens his G suit.

"No," Nasty responds with his hallmark brevity.

"I have," Duff says, and he recounts his experience with the 1993 hijacked Lufthansa flight. Since the FAA and law enforcement have primary responsibility for dealing with hijackings, the military is brought in only to give "safety of flight" support. There are very clear rules about the use of the military, and their presence is strictly to monitor and report back—nothing more. If something happens to the hijacked aircraft—maybe there is an explosion on board—the fighters are able to report to the pilots on the extent of the damage.

In 1993, Duff explains, the Otis F-15s, and later the Atlantic City F-16s, were scrambled. The fighters intercepted the aircraft off the coast of eastern Canada and initially stayed at a distance of about 10 miles in trail. As the hijacked plane approached JFK Airport, the fighters moved in closer, to around 5 miles, and stayed a bit above the aircraft and out of sight. They did a low fly-by as the plane landed, then circled overhead while the hijacking played out on the ground, finally returning to their bases when the crisis was resolved. No one was injured, and the hijacker surrendered.

In light of Duff's experience, Nasty tells him, "You've got the lead."

But Nasty had been designated lead in the alert roster, so after strapping into this G suit, Duff makes a quick trip across the hall into the Command Post to report the switch.

As he enters the Command Post, the supervisor of flying has a phone to each ear, talking to Otis tower on one phone and NEADS on the other.

"I'm 1, Nasty's 2, and we're going to the jets," Duff reports, and the supervisor calls back to him.

"It's an American 767 from Boston to California—American Flight 11—and it looks like the real thing."

"Okay, we're going to the jets," Duff responds, heading out the door before finishing his sentence.

He sprints out to the alert truck to join Nasty, and within minutes the pilots are being driven across the ramp to the alert hangar, where their fully fueled and armed F-15s await. Duff can't help but think about his sister, who is a flight attendant for American. She often flies the Boston–L.A. route. He forces the thought out of his mind, reminding himself to remain focused on his mission. *If I can't effect change, I have to let it go,* he tells himself.

When they are halfway across the tarmac, the claxon blares, indicating an order to battle stations. The radio in Duff's hand crackles to life: "Alpha-Kilo 1-2, Battle Stations!"

He and Nasty are way ahead of the game, and Duff is glad he made the decision to suit up right after getting that call from the control tower. It has saved precious time. His pulse quickens while the truck speeds across the ramp, and he can't help but think about the troubled flight. Being a commercial pilot, he pictures the scene in that cockpit and imagines what those pilots must be going through.

CHAPTER 2

No Ordinary Hijacking

NEADS, Rome, New York, 8:38 a.m.

Although Bob Marr took the initiative and ordered the Otis alert aircraft to battle stations within a minute of learning about the hijacking, he does not have the authority to scramble fighters to intercept a hijacked airliner. That approval must come from the secretary of defense. He reports up his chain of command to his boss, Maj. Gen. Larry Arnold, at Tyndall Air Force Base in Florida, who will then seek the higher authorization through the rest of the chain of command. Arnold is the commander of the whole continental U.S. NORAD Region, the CONR, as well as commander of its air component, 1st Air Force. In that capacity, he's in charge of all 14 alert NEADS fighters around the country. When Marr calls Arnold, it has been 14 minutes since American 11 took its turn south.

The general is on a teleconference with senior NORAD staff, so Marr leaves an urgent message that he's dealing with a hijacking and requesting a call back. Meanwhile, down on the NEADS Ops floor, the three operational groups are furiously going through their hijack checklists. With the Otis jets prepped to scramble, the Surveillance techs know they've got to locate American 11 fast, otherwise the Weapons Team has no instructions to pass on to the fighters.

But the NEADS radar equipment is different from that used by air traffic controllers. It's much older, developed in the 1970s and brought into use by NEADS in the early 1980s. The system was designed to monitor the shoreline for incoming high-altitude threats: missiles coming from across the ocean. Slow and cumbersome, and not nearly as user friendly as more modern equipment, the NEADS monochromic radar displays are not designed to take internal FAA radar data or to identify radar tracks originating from inside the United States. The system offers little, if any, such low-level coverage over the country.

To identify American 11, the surveillance and ID techs must go through a grueling process. Their radar scopes are filled with hundreds of radar returns not just from aircraft but from weather systems, ground interference, and what's called anomalous propagation—false returns caused by conditions in the atmosphere, or by such obstructions as flocks of birds. The technicians must first determine which radar data on their screens is for aircraft, which they do by monitoring its movement, which is distinctive for planes. The technician must observe for at least 36 seconds to a minute just to confirm that a blip is in fact an aircraft track. The tech must attach what's called a tactical display number to it, which tells the computer to start tracking and identifying the target. If the target is in fact a plane, then over a period of 12–20 seconds, the computer will start to generate information on the track: heading, speed, altitude, latitude, longitude, and the identifying information being transmitted by the transponder. Of all the blips on their screens, American 11 will be the target that gives no flight information, since the transponder has been turned off. With the hundreds of pieces of radar data filling their screens, and little information as to the location of the flight, the task is daunting.

At approximately 8:38, another call comes in from Boston Center, this time from controller Colin Scoggins, who has just arrived at work. A large, jolly man, with a thick head of light brown wavy hair, a full mustache, and smiling brown eyes, Scoggins's huge size hints at his 22 years as a power lifter, where his efforts earned him state records for the squat and bench presses. An experienced controller, he specializes in airspace, procedures, and military operations, and is currently working in Boston Center's airspace section. He manages operating agreements between Boston Center and other air traffic control facilities, and also the military. His responsibilities include generating the military schedules that keep the FAA facilities in sync with military airspace requirements, and because of this, he has personal relationships with most military units in the region.

When a colleague told him of the hijacking as he entered the building a few minutes ago, he made his way to the Traffic Management Unit and the desk of Dan Bueno, the supervisor. "It sounds real," Bueno said. "We heard a Mideastern or Arabic voice on radio. They've also turned off the transponder to prevent the hijack code from appearing."

Scoggins could feel the edginess rising up in him as Bueno filled him in on the details. This was bad, highly unusual. The controllers were still tracking the primary radar return for the flight, but they lacked altitude information. It occurred to Scoggins that NEADS might be able to provide that, because the FAA radar system filters out certain altitude information that NEADS gets. Having the altitude would sure make it easier for Boston Center to keep all the planes in the vicinity of American 11 out of danger. As soon as he got to his station, Scoggins got on the phone to NEADS.

"Have you identified the radar target for American 11?" he asks the NEADS ID tech who answers.

The tech tells him that they're still searching.

"It's 50 miles south of Albany," Scoggins offers.

That information won't be of much help to NEADS Surveillance, though. Their monochromic displays aren't even capable of showing the outline of states, much less those of cities like Albany or New York.

Since NEADS has no information for him, Scoggins hangs up fast. He doesn't want to waste their time. A few minutes later, when he sees that the Otis fighters aren't yet airborne, he calls back to suggest that they try to scramble Atlantic City. He knows that

Atlantic City is no longer an alert facility, but he also knows that they launch F-16s for training flights every morning at nine. He figures that the pilots are probably already in their planes and ready to go. They're unarmed, but they're a lot closer to New York City than the Otis fighters on Cape Cod, and the military serves only a monitoring purpose in hijacking anyway. Unarmed fighters are better than no fighters, he thinks. The NEADS tech takes his advice and dials the only number he has for Atlantic City, the one they used to scramble Atlantic City's F-16s before the unit was removed from the shrinking Air Defense Mission in 1997. The number connects him directly to the highly secured Command Post. But these days, the Command Post is more of a highly secured storage area, opened just once a month for drill weekends. The phone rings and rings.

Meanwhile, just a minute after Scoggins's last call, one of the NEADS ID techs calls him back. She wants to make sure she has all the information that's available.

"He's being hijacked," Scoggins explains. "The pilot's having a hard time talking to the . . . I mean, we don't know." He catches himself. He was going to say that the pilots are having a hard time talking to air traffic control, but that's not exactly true. They're simply not talking! He continues, sticking to the facts. "We don't know where he's goin'. He's heading towards Kennedy. He's . . . 35 miles north of Kennedy now at 367 knots." That's about 422 miles per hour, which means that the plane will be over New York in less than 5 minutes. "We have no idea where he's goin' or what his intentions are," Scoggins finishes.

"If you could please give us a call and let us know—you know—any information, that'd be great," the tech asks.

"Okay. Right now, I guess we're trying to work on . . . I guess there's been some threats in the cockpit. The pilot . . ."

"There's been what?!" she responds, shocked.

"We'll call you right back as soon as we know more info," he answers.

As the news of the reports of threats made in the cockpit ripples around the Ops floor, the stress level at NEADS ratchets up. This is clearly no traditional hijacking.

American Airlines Headquarters, Fort Worth, Texas, 8:38 a.m. (EST)

On the large radar-tracking screen at the front of the room at American's System Operations Control, the radar blip of American 11 has been specially tagged so that it is readily identifiable. Managers and dispatchers alike stare at the screen. They've watched it turn off course and head for New York. The call from flight attendant Betty Ong is ongoing, and Nydia Gonzales continues to forward information over the hotline to Craig Marquis. Ong has managed to stay calm and professional, reporting that two flight attendants have been stabbed and one is on oxygen. A first-class passenger has had his throat slashed and appears dead, and the hijackers are in the cockpit.

In response to requests from Boston Center, the flight's dispatcher has tried several times to contact the flight using ACARS, the Aircraft Communications and Reporting System, a data link that allows direct, typed correspondence between each airline's dispatch center and the cockpit. Under FAA rules, dispatchers at each airline are responsible for monitoring aircraft in flight: following every flight's progress, relaying safety information, and handling any problems. The dispatcher's first message to American 11, sent at 8:23, was simple: "Good morning . . . ATC looking for you on 135.32." The subsequent one, sent several minutes later, was more urgent: "Plz contact Boston Center ASAP . . . They have lost radio contact and your transponder signal." [1]

When the vice president of operations, Gerard Arpey, received news of the hijacking, he sped over to the Operations Center from the airline's headquarters. By the time he arrived, the managers had already opened up the airline's crisis command center. While managers there are busy monitoring the progress of the flight via calls to the FAA Command Center and air traffic facilities, they receive regular updates regarding the phone call from Betty Ong.

Suddenly, Ong exclaims into the phone, "We're starting to descend!"

"They're going to New York!" Marquis shouts out across the Operations Center. "Call Newark and JFK and tell them to expect a hijacking!"[2] He doesn't consider LaGuardia for the simple reason that wide-body aircraft don't usually land there.

**New York Air Route Traffic Control Center,
Islip, Long Island, 8:41 a.m.**

When New York Center controller Dave Bottiglia takes the hand-off for United 175 from Boston Center's John Hartling, the flight waits nearly 45 seconds to check in with him. That's rather long, and Bottiglia is just about to call the plane.

"New York, United 175 Heavy," Captain Saracini finally transmits, requesting a callback from Bottiglia.

"United 175, go ahead," Bottiglia responds.

"Yeah, we figured we'd wait to go to your center," Saracini continues. "We heard a suspicious transmission on our departure out of Boston with someone, ah, it sounded like someone keyed the mike and said 'Everyone ah stay in your seats.' "

Saracini is referring to the most recent transmission made by the hijackers, at 8:33, nine minutes after their first. The speaker again pressed the transmit button on the handheld microphone—still thinking that it transmitted to the passenger cabin—and said, "Nobody move. Please. We are going back to the airport. Don't try to make any stupid moves." Every pilot on the frequency heard it, and it didn't take a rocket scientist to figure out that it wasn't the pilot talking. Saracini had stayed on the frequency hoping to hear more, but no further transmission was made, so he finally switched to his newly assigned frequency to check in.

"Oh, okay," Bottiglia responds, "I'll pass that along," He's surprised to hear that there's trouble brewing in one of Boston's sectors. Because controllers are given information only on a need-to-know basis and American 11 is not in his airspace, he hasn't heard anything about the problem until now.

"It cut out," the pilot continues, referring to the fact that there was no further transmission, but Bottiglia is no longer listening. He has already touched his computer screen to connect to the hotline for his sector controller.

"UAL 175 just came on my frequency and he said he heard a suspicious transmission when they were leaving Boston Center. 'Everybody stay in your seats'—that's what he heard . . . just to let you know." [3]

Just then, Bottiglia sees an unidentified radar blip move onto the edge of his screen. The controller next to him comes over and points to the blip.

"You see this target here?" he says. "This is American 11. Boston Center thinks it's a hijack." [4]

Bottiglia has no altitude information for the plane, but he can tell from the radar that it appears to be descending. Even without a transponder, controller radars calculate ground speed for all radar targets, and when a plane is descending, the ground speed decreases. The flight had been "grounding" 600 knots, and now it has decreased to 320. After watching the blip for a few moments, it disappears from his screen. The plane has dipped below his radar's coverage area—below 2,000 feet.

"Well, we know he's not high altitude anymore," he comments. He surmises that it's going in to land at one of the New York area airports, although it's going much faster than is normal for landing.

As he has been watching American 11 on the center of his screen, the transponder code for the flight he had just been talking to, United 175, has changed and quickly changed again. This is the only indication controllers might have gotten that the flight is, at that moment, being hijacked. But due to the distraction of American 11, Bottiglia hasn't noticed.

CONR Headquarters, Florida / NEADS, Rome, New York, 8:42 a.m.

As CONR Commander General Arnold finishes up his teleconference, his assistant hands him the urgent message from Bob Marr. Given that a hijacking is part of the day's simulated exercise, he asks the obvious question on the way to his office: "Is this part of the exercise?" Even as NORAD's commander for the continental United States, Arnold is not privy to everything concerning the exercise. The simex is meant to test commanders also, to make sure that their war machine is operating as it should.

His assistant tells him it's real world, and the thought occurs to Arnold that it's been many years since NORAD has handled a hijacking. He's relieved that he recently reviewed the protocol.

He gets through to Bob Marr right away, who quickly fills him in. "Boss, Boston Center is reporting a possible hijacked aircraft, real world, somewhere north of JFK Airport. I've got Otis going battle stations, and I'd like to scramble them to military airspace while we try to get approval for an intercept."

"Confirm this is real world?" Arnold asks.

"That's affirm, real world," Marr replies.

"Where is the hijacked aircraft?" he asks.

"We don't have a good location," Marr explains. "The FAA says they don't have it on their scopes, but had it west of Boston and thought it was now heading to New York."

There is a momentary silence on the other end of the line.

"Even if we find it," Marr continues, "I don't think we'll get there in time if it's going to JFK, so the best we can do is get as close as possible while we try to find it and get clearance from the FAA."

"Do we have any other information, type, tail, number of souls on board?" Arnold asks.

"I don't have all the particulars yet, but we'll pass them on as we get them."

This is a lot less information than Arnold would like, and a call from Boston Center hardly constitutes the standard protocol to request military assistance. Such requests customarily come from FAA headquarters. But he knows that the protocol is based on assumptions: that the hijacked aircraft is readily identifiable and trackable and that there is time to coordinate an appropriate military response. Most important, perhaps, it assumes that the hijacking is taking the "traditional" form.

But today they have nothing more than a call from an air traffic control facility. American 11 is not easily identifiable. It's already in U.S. airspace, and the hijackers have made no demands. Especially disturbing is a lack of communication from the cockpit crew.

The bottom line is that one of his battle commanders has asked for assistance in getting the authorizations he feels he needs. Arnold's instincts tell him to act first and seek authorizations later. He'll give Marr what he's asking for.

"Go ahead and scramble and I'll take care of the authorities," Arnold assures Marr. Such a command should be coming from the secretary of defense, but Arnold isn't going to wait on that.

"Let me know when the jets get airborne," he says in closing. "I'll run this up the chain."

"Thanks, sir," Marr replies. "I'll get back to you when we have an update."

Arnold hangs up and immediately puts through a call to the NORAD Command Post deep inside Cheyenne Mountain in Colorado Springs. The operations commander, Major General Rick Findlay, concurs with Arnold's assessment and decision to scramble the fighters.

"I'll call the Pentagon for the clearances," he promises Arnold. Rather than waiting on directives from the top, the commanders are working in reverse. The situation seems to require it.

At NEADS, Bob Marr is directing his mission crew commander, Kevin Nasypany, to issue the scramble order. Marr is taking decisive action, but he isn't actually anticipating much military participation. He figures that by the time the fighters are airborne, the plane will have already landed at JFK or Newark. The last information Nasypany forwarded to the battle cab indicated that the aircraft was already descending. *Still*, he thinks, *we should get up there and show our support.*

On the Ops floor, after Nasypany issues the scramble order, the Weapons director urgently calls to him: "I don't know where I am scrambling these guys to. I need a direction, a destination."[5] Those fighters will be racing through the skies and yet he still has no specific target for them to intercept.

The Surveillance techs have continued to search for American 11 among hundreds of blips for airliners and dozens of smaller planes filling their screens, but it's an excruciatingly slow job. Nonetheless, the jets have to have some target information.

"Okay, I'm going to give you the Z-point," Nasypany tells the Weapons director, referring to a set of coordinates techs can use to create a tag on their monitor to help them identify the location of New York City. He calls out the coordinates. "It's just north of New York City. . . . Head 'em in that direction."

Still on the phone with Boston Center controller Colin Scoggins, MSgt. Joe McCain, the mission crew commander technician, makes note of a particular blip. McCain is not a controller, but he knows that planes tend to fly very specific routes, like highways in the sky, and this particular target seems not to be on any of those regular routes. It's also very fast moving.

"I've got a search target that seems to be on an odd heading here," he says to Scoggins, then describes its location. It's about 20 miles north of Manhattan.

"Yeah, I see that one," Scoggins responds, noting the target he's referring to, which is not American 11, but an aircraft just next to it on the radar. But he realizes that American 11 is right behind the target McCain has identified. "There's a target 4 miles behind it," he yells to McCain, "*that*'s the one! That's American 11!"

"I've got it!" McCain shouts, hanging up the phone and calling out the coordinates to the whole Ops floor.

The blip is 16 miles north of JFK, heading down the Hudson River valley. They still have no altitude, but the plane is clearly traveling very fast. McCain continues to track the flight as it heads south. Then suddenly, inexplicably, less than a minute after he had finally located the track, the blip disappears. It is 8:46, and American Flight 11 has just flown into the North Tower of the World Trade Center flying 530 mph. McCain doesn't know that, though; he knows only that the blip he has struggled so mightily to locate has now vanished. He figures that the plane has descended below his radar coverage area to land at JFK. The fact that the plane was flying much too fast for landing does not hit him; the concept that the plane might have been intentionally crashed is simply too far outside his realm of experience. McCain also doesn't know that there is another hijacked airliner flying at high speed toward New York. United 175 has not yet raised the concern of air traffic control.

Newark Control Tower, 8:41 a.m.

At 8:41, Newark Tower controller Greg Callahan is just sending another United flight on its way. "United 93, wind 3-3-0 at seven, runway four left, cleared for takeoff."

"Cleared takeoff, four left, United 93," the pilot repeats. A minute later, Callahan directs the flight to contact departure control.

"Going to departure, United 93. Good day," the pilot answers before switching over to the next frequency. Callahan moves on to the next aircraft.

A couple minutes later, the controller next to him, Rick Tepper, glances out the window of the tower and sees a huge mushroom cloud of smoke billowing out of the World Trade Center. He taps Callahan's shoulder, pointing the smoke out to him.

They comment to each other that they can't imagine how anyone is going to put out that fire, and after watching for a moment, Callahan catches himself and refocuses on his screen.

At the opposite side of the tower cab—the side farthest from the runways—calls reporting that a small plane has crashed into the World Trade Center begin flooding into the office of Traffic Management Coordinator Bob Varcadapane, the supervisor in the tower. The assumption is that only a small plane could have gone so badly off course. The tower controllers who aren't currently handling aircraft start calling around to JFK, LaGuardia, Teterboro, and other area air traffic facilities to see if any of them have lost an aircraft. But all are reporting "operations normal." They haven't heard word of the crash yet and they're stunned at what they see when told to look out their windows at the World Trade Center, now engulfed in flames.

Varcadapane calls the FAA's New York Center on Long Island to find out if they have any idea whose plane just crashed into the Twin Towers.

"No, but Boston Center lost an airplane. They lost an American 767," comes the answer.

Varcadapane is shaken by what he's just heard. What if it was that 767 that just hit the Trade Center? He prays he's wrong. The damage an airliner would do on impact with those towers is unthinkable.

"I have a burning building and you have a missing airplane," he says back. "This is VERY coincidental!" [6]

Otis Air National Guard Base, Cape Cod, 8:46 a.m.

Lt. Col. Duff Duffy is strapping into his ejection seat when the scramble siren blares. He and Nasty Nash start their engines and taxi out of the hangar.

Duff radios to Operations for mission guidance. "Do you have words?" he asks urgently.

"Possible hijack, American Flight 11, 737, flight level 290 [29,000 feet], over JFK," comes the response from the Command Post. The NEADS controller had the flight information wrong; the plane was a 767.

As Duff and Nasty roll onto Otis's Runway 5, they have every reason to feel confident they'll achieve their mission, whatever it may entail. The F-15 is an extremely sophisticated, maneuverable tactical fighter. Loaded with classified tactical electronic-warfare systems and weaponry able to detect, track, and attack enemy aircraft at distances beyond visual range and down to treetop level, the radar is able to automatically home in on enemy aircraft and project this information onto a heads-up display. Chances are, they figure, that they won't need all that fancy equipment today; they'll just locate and track the hijacked aircraft. It still feels good, though, to have such amazing capabilities.

As Duff pushes the throttles full forward, the rapid acceleration presses him back into his seat. The tower controller instructs him to fly a heading of 280 at flight level 290—almost due west at 29,000 feet. Taking off right behind him, Nasty rejoins to fly in tactical formation: line abreast and about 2 miles apart. This formation provides maximum lookout for enemy attack and in-cockpit scans of necessary equipment, but fighters can only fly this way in wartime or for an air sovereignty interception. The broad swathe of airspace it requires presents a spacing challenge for air traffic control that is otherwise unacceptable.

Even if it's not a hijack, Duff thinks, *something is very wrong because it's a beautiful day and the plane is off course and not talking to anybody*. The whole scenario just feels wrong, and he wants to be there *now*. So, against regulations, he takes his plane supersonic, breaking the sound barrier as he passes through 18,000 feet. This is a violation that can get a pilot into a good deal of trouble since the sonic boom tends to break windows in the homes down below.

Nasty feels compelled to check in with Duff. A pilot can't hear the sonic boom his own plane makes—because the plane is traveling faster than the sound it's making—and Nasty figures it's just possible that Duff hasn't noticed.

"You're supersonic," he radios.

"Yeah, I know, don't worry about it," Duff responds. If there's an airliner in trouble out there, he's going to get to it just as fast as he can. Without hesitation, Nasty follows his lead. At this speed, they'll reach New York airspace in less than 15 minutes.

CHAPTER 3

Another

FAA Command Center, Herndon, Virginia, 8:48 a.m.

Ben Sliney is on the Operations floor trying to gather and disseminate the bits and pieces of information coming his way regarding American 11. He has initiated a teleconference between the Command Center, FAA headquarters, Boston Center, and New York Center so that all parties are being kept apprised of developments simultaneously. The hijacking protocol specifically calls for FAA-military coordination to originate at the headquarters level, and Sliney assumes that that is already in the works. He can't help but notice that the "rules" as they apply to hijackings don't seem to apply today. There are many ways for a pilot to inform authorities that an aircraft has been commandeered, but this morning none of those are happening. He is having trouble confirming that this flight is even hijacked. *Why isn't the pilot letting us know that he is hijacked, either by words or by actions? Why has this plane disappeared from the radar screens, and why aren't they talking? What do the hijackers want?*

At 8:48, a New York Center manager—unaware that American 11 has crashed—gives an update on the teleconference. "Okay. This is New York Center. We're watching the airplane. I also had conversation with American Airlines, and they've told us that they believe that one of their stewardesses was stabbed and that there are people in the cockpit that have control of the aircraft, and that's all the information they have right now." [1] Clearly, this is old news by the time it has worked its way from the controllers to a manager to the teleconference. But this is the information that Sliney is getting. The latest information from American is that the flight is descending.

The Command Center's military liaison, a colonel who is not part of the NORAD chain of command and whose job entails handling military airspace reservations, approaches Sliney. "You may want to put CNN up on one of the screens," he says. "They are reporting that a small plane has hit the World Trade Center."

Jesus, something else? Sliney thinks.

"Give me CNN on screens 2 and 7!" he orders. Two huge pictures of the World Trade Center in the brilliant sunlight against the backdrop of clear blue skies obediently appear on the 10-by-12-foot screens on the front wall of the Command Center. The staff is shocked to see the billows of black smoke mushroom from the side of the North Tower. Sliney is completely mystified. He stares intently at the image, trying to make sense of it.

"That's a lot of smoke for a small plane," he comments. "I've *worked* New York airspace. Why would you be right over the World Trade Center on a clear, bright day?"

The notion that it is actually American 11 that has hit the tower doesn't cross his mind; the idea that the hijacking they've been tracking might have flown into that building, especially on such a clear day, is simply unfathomable.

United Airlines Headquarters, Chicago, 8:50 a.m. (EST)

At United Airlines' Operations Center in Chicago, the manager of the Center, Rich "Doc" Miles, receives a phone call at 8:50 from an airline maintenance center in San Francisco. The center was set up to receive in-flight calls from flight attendants wishing to report problems with planes, such as broken ovens and seat backs.

The distraught caller announces that he just received a call from a male flight attendant on a United Airlines B-757 exclaiming,

"Oh my God. The crew has been killed; a flight attendant has been stabbed. We've been hijacked. The hijackers are flying the plane." The line then went dead, and the caller hasn't been able to reestablish contact.

"No," Miles explains, sure that this is a simple misunderstanding, "the information we're getting is that it is an American 737." [2]

But the caller insists that the call he took was from a United flight—more specifically, from United 175.

Miles figures the issue won't take long to resolve. He calls the dispatcher for the flight, who immediately sends an ACARS message to the plane's cockpit.

To his consternation, he receives no answer.

New York Center, 8:51 a.m.

At New York Center, air traffic controller Dave Bottiglia, who watched American 11 dip below his radar coverage, now discovers he's got another unexpected problem on his hands. Having been preoccupied watching the blip of American 11, he has just noticed that United 175 is no longer appearing on his screen. Before he can call up the flight crew to advise them that he is not picking up their transponder, he is interrupted by a report from another aircraft.

"Anybody know what that smoke is in lower Manhattan?" queries Delta 1489.

"I'm sorry, say again," Bottiglia responds.

"There's a lot of smoke in lower Manhattan coming out of the top of the World Trade Center building. A major fire." [3]

What now? Whatever it is, Bottiglia thinks, he can't afford to worry about it. Too much is happening at once and he's got to focus on first things first. Two aircraft in his airspace are now out of contact, and his stomach is in knots at the thought that the two incidents are related. The controller next to him, Curt Applegate, has just spotted an "intruder" on his screen—an aircraft transmitting an unauthorized transponder code—about 90 miles west of New

York. Not knowing anything about United 175, he thinks that maybe he has found American 11.

"Look!" he shouts. "There's an intruder over Allentown."[4] Bottiglia immediately locates the aircraft. He's pretty sure that he's looking at United 175 and that the crew has inadvertently changed their transponder.

"United 175, recycle transponder," he instructs. "Squawk code 1-4-7-0."

The pilot doesn't respond, so Bottiglia repeats himself.

"United 175, do you read New York?" Nothing.

Is it my radio? he wonders. It seemed to be working fine, but that's one thing he can easily check by querying another aircraft on the frequency.

"Delta 1489, do you read New York?"

"Delta 1489, go ahead," the flight promptly answers.

"Okay," Bottiglia replies. "Just wanted to make sure you were reading New York. United, United 175, do you read New York?" Again he gets no answer.

Feeling a gut-tightening dread, he calls out to a neighboring controller.

"We may have a hijack. We have some problems over here right now, . . . I can't get a hold of United 175 at all right now and I don't know where he went to." He cannot assume that the intruder is United 175, but the aircraft has started to descend and turn toward the south. He has little doubt that he is watching a second hijacked airliner, and the plane is on a direct collision course with one of his northbound Delta flights!

"Traffic 2 o'clock, 10 miles!" he urgently calls to the Delta pilot. "I think he's been hijacked. I don't know his intentions. Take any evasive action necessary!"

Just then, Colin Scoggins in Boston calls New York Center to notify them that American 11 appears to be descending toward New York, most likely to land at JFK.

"We're too busy to talk," snaps the New York Center controller who answers, overwhelmed with this new emergency. "We're working a hijack."

The controller hangs up quickly, and Scoggins just figures that he's talking about American 11. He has no idea that a second airliner is in crisis.

Just then, at 8:52, Scoggins gets a call from Tech Sgt. Jeremy Powell at NEADS letting him know that the Otis fighters are airborne. Scoggins is talking to supervisor Dan Bueno about the strange loss of the primary radar track for American 11 when Powell's call comes in. They're discussing whether American 11 has descended beneath their radar coverage, which bottoms out at about 1,500 feet. Since Boston Center tracks high-level air traffic, their radar information doesn't need to pick up the lowest flying aircraft.

Filling Powell in that the target has disappeared from their screens, Scoggins tells him, "Last known position we have is 8 nautical miles northeast of JFK." Those were the last data the radar sweep provided before the blip dropped from their coverage area. He gives Powell the specific lat-long coordinates and hangs up.

Back in New York Center, the magnitude of the unfolding emergency becomes clearer to Bottiglia just moments later, when an aircraft on his frequency calls in.

"We're getting reports over the [AM] radio of a commuter hitting the World Trade Center. Is that NORDO 7-6 still in the air?"

Not my flight! Bottiglia thinks. With two aircraft hijacked and now reports of an aircraft hitting the World Trade Center, Bottiglia, his voice shaking, cries out to the other controllers, "Please . . . just take everything and don't ask any questions!"[5] He begins frantically handing off his flights to them so that he can concentrate on United 175. Continuing to call up the plane, he gets no response.

Several hundred miles away, where Scoggins is trying to get the tail number of American 11 so that the Weapons controller at

NEADS can pass it on to the Otis fighters, he hears yelling at the system engineer's desk across the room. They have turned on CNN after hearing from the center's manager in charge that a plane has crashed into the World Trade Center, and are reacting to the footage.

Scoggins walks over and listens while the newscaster explains that it was a small aircraft that hit the building. His initial thought is that some controller must have really screwed up. Yet the more he thinks about it, the less that makes sense. It's a clear day with unlimited visibility, and planes don't just fly into buildings. Still unable to pick up a radar track for American 11, Scoggins and Bueno scurry to find out more. They contact other facilities, several of which are picking up an aircraft's emergency locator transmitter, designed to begin transmitting when a plane crashes. But Boston Center doesn't have the direction-finding equipment needed to pinpoint the location the signal is coming from.

Taking another look at the television coverage and the gaping hole in the side of the Trade Center tower, the horrible realization occurs to Scoggins that perhaps they have found American Flight 11. "Call American and confirm if their aircraft is down!" he yells to Bueno.

Just then, controller Joe Cooper comes over with the tail number for American 11, and Scoggins picks up the phone to dial NEADS. "They can't confirm that the plane that has hit the Trade Center is American 11," Bueno interrupts. "They've lost their radar track on the plane and cannot confirm where it is."

At NEADS, ID technicians are still furiously working to relocate American 11 when ID tech Stacia Rountree picks up a call from Scoggins and receives his startling report.

She yells out to the Ops floor, "A plane just hit the World Trade Center." She then asks Scoggins, "Was it American 11?" and he tells her that's unconfirmed.

"Hit what?" MCC tech Joe McCain calls back at her, not certain of what he has just heard.

"The World Trade Center," another ID tech repeats with astonishment.

"Oh my God. Oh my God. Oh my God," one of the ID techs prayerfully murmurs.[6]

Just then, a computer maintenance technician comes running into the Command Post to report that CNN is broadcasting that a 737 has struck the World Trade Center. The floor staff is stunned. The idea that an airliner could crash into the Towers is unfathomable. Is that plane in the North Tower the hijacked flight? How could a hijacking have gone so wrong? And if it's not the hijacked flight, whose aircraft is it?

Snapping back to focus on the intercept operation, the Weapons director calls out, "What do I do with the fighters?"

"Send 'em to New York City still. Continue! Go!" Mission Crew Commander Kevin Nasypany orders emphatically.

"This is what I got," Nasypany urgently briefs his troops. "Possible news that a 737 just hit the World Trade Center. This is a real-world and we're trying to confirm this. . . . Continue taking the fighters down to the New York City area, JFK area if you can. Make sure that the FAA clears it—your route—all the way through. Do what we gotta do, okay? Let's press with this."

Nasypany then reports to Bob Marr in the battle cab, where the million-dollar question is: Did American Flight 11 really just fly into the World Trade Center? Nasypany's instincts tell him that must be true. The loss of the radar track for American 11 and the crash into the Trade Center is just too much of a coincidence otherwise. Marr agrees. He guesses that something has gone terribly wrong with the hijacking. Perhaps the distracted pilot flew too low and lost control while coming in to land at JFK. *What a freak accident*, he thinks.

One of the techs finally manages to display the live CNN coverage on one of the large screens at the front of the room. As the 15-foot screen flashes to life with the scene of the burning World Trade Center tower, a stunned silence grips the room.

American Airlines Headquarters, Fort Worth, Texas, 8:51 a.m. (EST)

American Airlines operations has lost all contact with Betty Ong and has been unable to reestablish contact. The last thing she reported was that the flight was descending.

At 8:51, a call comes in from an American Airlines ramp supervisor at JFK Airport reporting that a plane has flown into one of the World Trade Center towers. The supervisor taking the call shouts across the room for someone to turn on CNN.[7]

As the coverage flashes onto the screen, the room fills with the horrible dread that this is what has happened to their missing plane. The media is conjecturing that the plane was a smaller aircraft, but they fear they know better. Boston Center has just called to ask if it is their plane, but they can't confirm anything.

At home, American Airlines CEO Don Carty is stunned to receive a disturbing message on his pager. Although sent several minutes earlier, it has just arrived. "Confirmed hijacking Flight 11." He calls for his wife to turn on the television and picks up the phone to call his vice president of operations, Gerald Arpey. On the television, newscasters are reporting breaking news of an aircraft hitting the World Trade Center. Arpey answers his phone to an immediate question from the CEO.

"The press is reporting an airplane hit the World Trade Center. Is that our plane?" Carty asks.

"I don't know, Don," Arpey replies. "We confirmed it was hijacked and was heading south from Boston."

His mind racing, Carty heads for the door, sickeningly aware that his worst nightmare is unfolding.

"Could that be your airplane?" his wife asks him.

"No, of course not," Carty responds with reassurance. "It couldn't be."

Yet inside, he knows it is. He just can't bring himself to say it.[8] He's out the door and racing toward headquarters within minutes, his mind reeling from the news.

New York Center, 8:52 a.m.

"United 175, do you read New York?" controller Dave Bottiglia continues to call. "United, United 175, do you read New York? United 175, New York."

At 8:55, the Center supervisor notifies the Center manager that she believes that United 175 has also been hijacked. The Center manager, in turn, tries to relay the information to the regional FAA office, but when he gets through he is advised that managers there are not able to take the call because they are discussing a hijacking.[9]

Meanwhile, eastbound over central New Jersey, United 175 makes a northerly turn and is now aimed directly at New York City.

CHAPTER 4

Confusion in the Cockpits

Midwest Express Airlines Flight 7, Milwaukee–LaGuardia, 8:51 a.m.

While New York Center controller Dave Bottiglia continues to try to make contact with United 175, controllers and pilots across the New York region struggle to contend with the confusion caused by the impact of American 11 crashing into the North Tower.

Capt. Gerald Earwood and his first officer, Eric Fjelstad, are being vectored to land on Runway 31 at New York's LaGuardia after an uneventful, albeit early, flight from Milwaukee. Their flight plan has them filed for the Milton Seven Arrival, which means they will fly over Allentown, Pennsylvania, turn southeast for about 20 miles, head northeast toward JFK, and then turn northeast toward LaGuardia, flying over New York City and the Verrazano-Narrows Bridge, with Manhattan passing about 4 miles to their left.

Such preplanned arrivals, known as STARS (standard terminal arrivals), are customary at large airports. The thinking is that if the pilots know exactly where to go, then the already busy controllers have less talking to do. This particular STAR doesn't list any altitudes. Instead, the pilot is expected to descend at the controller's discretion. That's great, and Earwood has done it many times before, but to descend at controller's discretion you must be talking to a controller, and this seems to be getting increasingly difficult this morning.

It had been an early wake-up for the crew of Midwest Express (Midex) 7: a 5:30 check-in with a 6:30 scheduled departure. When Earwood met Fjelstad and the rest of the crew in the ready lounge, even though it was ungodly early, they were all in good spirits, trading jokes among themselves while Earwood collected the paperwork and made one last check of the weather radar.

They shut the main cabin door just in time for an on-time departure. It was Fjelstad's turn to fly, and as he took off, heading east over Lake Michigan toward Grand Rapids, they witnessed the sunrise.

The traffic and radio chatter were normal until they got in the vicinity of New York. Now, after an otherwise easy flight, Earwood wonders if he has a broken airplane on his hands. The radio frequency has become much quieter than usual, and the controllers aren't answering some of his calls. He's wondering if his radios are malfunctioning when a controller calls and directs him. "Midex 7, contact New York Center on 128.57."

He immediately responds, "128.57, Midex 7. Good morning," and dials in the new frequency.

"Center, Midex 7 is flight level 3-3-0," Earwood calls, letting the new sector controller know that he is flying at 33,000 feet.

But he gets no response. After waiting a few moments, he repeats the call.

"New York Center, Midex 7 is checking in with you level at 3-3-0."

"Ah . . . Midex 7, I got your check-in at flight level 3-3-0," the controller finally responds.

Having to repeat his call and then getting a tardy response concerns Earwood. New York controllers don't miss radio calls. They operate in the busiest airspace in the world and are some of the best controllers in the industry. They expect the flight crews to listen up and follow instructions and they don't like to repeat themselves. They certainly aren't going to be the ones missing radio calls.

"What is up with these controllers?" Earwood exclaims to his copilot, hoping that it's them and not his radio that has a problem.

"They're missing our calls, and I'm thinking we might be dealing with a radio problem."

The last thing he needs is a radio malfunction in the busy skies over New York.

US Airways Flight 6805, Boston–LaGuardia

US Airways pilot Stephen Miller reaches his assigned cruising altitude and is enjoying some light conversation with the captain while the New York City skyline comes into view.

"USAir 6805, stand by for holding instructions," comes the unexpected radio call.

So much for the quick flight to New York, Miller thinks.

The day was off to a good start. Flying the shuttle route back and forth between New York's LaGuardia and Boston's Logan this week, it had been an early morning for Miller, who got on the road before sunlight while his wife and two small daughters slept in their Pennsylvania home.

Like many airline pilots, Miller's a reservist for the Air National Guard. Although his full-time job is flying for US Airways, he's also an F-16 fighter pilot assigned to the 177th Fighter Wing in Atlantic City. It's a great part-time job with good benefits, and it gives him a nice backup in the uncertain airline industry. It also feeds his "need for speed," which has managed to earn him the call sign "Speedy," but that's just a side benefit.

On their 6 a.m. inbound flight into Boston, it was the captain's leg to fly, so Miller handled the nonflying pilot duties: working the radios, doing the checklists, and programming course changes into the flight computer, the busier but more mundane job. He and Capt. Ron Maxwell enjoyed watching the sun come up, and even the flight attendants had it easy since most of the passengers were trying to get a little sleep to offset their indecently early wake-ups.

After their short stint on the ground, Miller was ready to fly the aircraft back to New York and looking forward to his opportunity to enjoy the more favored and relaxing job of actually flying the airplane. On the taxi-out in Boston, they waited at the runway's hold-short line, where Miller looked up to watch a United Boeing 767 take off, United Flight 175.

The final weight and balance calculations from dispatch came over the ACARS at 8:05, and with that in hand, the crew was ready to fly. Wide-body aircraft produce especially powerful wingtip vortices—horizontal, tornado-like winds off the ends of the wings—which require time to dissipate before other aircraft can take off, so he waited the required three minutes after United 175 departed before he received his takeoff clearance. He had expected the flight to New York would be short and uneventful. But now this request to enter a holding pattern has come in from New York Center.

As he directs the airliner toward the holding coordinates he's just been given, he notices a plume of dark smoke rising out of the New York skyline to his south. It looks like the kind of smoke or steam one would see rising from a power plant or cooling tower: rising vertically for a short distance, then carried horizontally by the winds. But this smoke is thick-black and too voluminous to be from a power plant.

"Hey, get a glimpse of that!" he calls to the captain, pointing out the smoke.

After several minutes of conjecturing as to the source, the pilots give up. They cannot come up with any explanation for what might produce so much smoke.

177th Fighter Wing, Atlantic City, New Jersey

As word of the crash into the World Trade Center ripples throughout the region, some know more quickly than others that the plane that hit the North Tower was no small craft, and that the crash was no accident.

Col. James Haye sits back at the supervisor of flying (SOF) desk at Atlantic City's 177th Fighter Wing, chatting with one of his sergeants between frequent communications with maintenance regarding the readiness of the unit's F-16s. He's finished briefing for a four-aircraft training flight to Fort Drum in Upstate New York, and the pilots have all gone to the flight line to get under way. There's not much more for Haye to do now but monitor the radios in case there's a problem. Then the direct hotline from the Maintenance Operations Center rings.

"Hey, an airplane just hit the World Trade Center! Go look at a TV," the caller tells Haye.

There's a television in the break room just adjacent to the SOF desk, and Haye quickly goes to check it out.

Astonished by the image on the screen, he calls out to fellow pilot Lt. Col. Randall "Vandal" King, who is in the break room waiting to fly a midday mission, "Hey, Vandal, come and see this!"

Walking over to get a closer look at the breaking news and hearing the commentary about a small aircraft having accidentally crashed into the World Trade Center, Vandal takes issue with the news coverage.

"Whoever was at the controls did that on purpose," he says. "That is *no* accidental crash! And that was no small airplane!"

Having worked for many years as a commercial pilot, he knows the crash had to be intentional, and the size of the hole in the Tower tells him the plane wasn't small. After several minutes taking in the coverage, news reports seem to confirm Vandal's thinking, and Haye makes a beeline for the door.

Sticking his head into a room down the hall where two pilots are just finishing their briefing for the morning's training mission, he gives a heads-up. "Hold on," he announces. "Things have just changed. An airliner has just struck the World Trade Center." Then he ducks back out the door as quickly as he came.

The pilots exchange curious glances, then bolt out of their seats and into the break room, where they join several others who are congregating in front of the television. One thinks back to the military bomber that ran into the Empire State Building in bad weather in the 1930s or '40s. *But this isn't bad weather today*, he says to himself.

US Airways Flight 6805, Boston–LaGuardia

When US Airways pilot Speedy Miller gets closer to New York City, he realizes that the smoke he has been watching is coming from Manhattan—more specifically, the World Trade Center. He calls New York Center and asks if they are aware of something going on in Manhattan.

"We just tracked a target descending through 10,000 feet at 500 knots," the controller blurts out.

Damn! Every airline pilot is aware that you cannot exceed 250 knots below 10,000 feet without drawing significant attention to yourself, so Miller knows this pilot is sure to get busted. *500 knots?* That will certainly get him a message to "call the FAA upon landing." And when he does, Miller knows, there'll be some FAA inspector on the other end of the telephone line committed to revoking his pilot's license.

Although news of an airliner exceeding the airspace speed limit by a whopping 250 knots is certainly noteworthy, it doesn't answer Miller's question: What is going on with all of that smoke over Manhattan? The connection is so implausible that it doesn't occur to him.

Before he has the opportunity to inquire further of New York Center, he hears on the radio that an aircraft has hit one of the Twin Towers. *Impossible!* he thinks. How could a plane have hit a Manhattan skyscraper on such a clear day? Not even the most inexperienced pilot could simply stray so badly, and commercial aircraft shouldn't be anywhere near that vicinity. True, one approach to LaGuardia, which is for traffic arriving from the south and landing to the east, does take planes fairly close to the city, but Miller knows it's not in use this morning. Aircraft should be nowhere near the World Trade Center.

He struggles to make sense of the information and is unable to come up with any plausible explanation. It's an impossible mental leap to conclude that flying a wide-body jet into the World Trade Center could be an intentional act.

Midex 7, Milwaukee–LaGuardia

When New York Center misses yet another radio call from Midex 7, Captain Earwood becomes seriously concerned that he is experiencing radio difficulties. Then he looks up at the Manhattan skyline and sees the smoke billowing off the roof of one of the World Trade Center towers.

"Look at the World Trade Center," he comments to his first officer, Eric Fjelstad. "There is smoke coming off the roof."

"What *is* that?" wonders Fjelstad. "It looks too thick to be steam. You don't think there's a fire, do you?"

The best Earwood can figure is that there are boilers on the roof and they are letting off steam or something.

A few moments later, New York Center instructs the crew to descend to 18,000 feet, and Fjelstad pulls back the thrust levers to initiate the descent. As the pilots look toward the Towers again, they can see that the plume of smoke is getting larger and thicker, developing into a mushroom cloud.

"Midex 7, contact New York approach on 124.45," comes a call from New York Center.

Earwood checks in with the approach controller and, much to his relief, receives an immediate response.

"Midex 7, continue the arrival and expect the Expressway visual approach to Runway 31."

Good, they heard me this time, he thinks. He reads back the clearance for the approach that will direct them over the Long

Island Expressway to Shea Stadium, and then left toward the airport. This is a visual approach, rather than one based on flight instruments and navigational aids. But with the dense smoke now coming from the World Trade Center, Earwood has serious doubts about their ability to keep the airport in sight.

When they are cleared out of 7,000 feet for 4,000 feet, he can see that it's a losing battle. It's not going to happen.

"I'm gonna let this guy know that we won't be able to keep a visual on Runway 31," Earwood tells Fjelstad.

"Approach, Midex 7," he calls to ATC.

But there is no reply.

"Approach, Midex 7," he offers again.

He waits, but there is still no reply.

"What is *wrong* with these controllers this morning?" he growls, finally losing his cool.

Earwood has no idea that air traffic control is confronting a situation unlike any they've ever encountered, and soon his own aircraft will be drawn into the unfolding nightmare.

Indianapolis Center, 8:54 a.m.

Far away from the confusion reigning in the skies over New York, yet another flight now becomes a cause for concern.

American Flight 77, although 10 minutes late when it departed Washington's Dulles Airport for Los Angeles at 8:20, enjoyed a routine first 30 minutes of flight. It has traveled nearly 300 miles across West Virginia and is over the southern tip of Ohio. The wide-body Boeing 757, under the command of Capt. Chic Burlingame, a Naval Academy graduate, and First Officer Dave Charlebois is relatively empty. It's carrying only 53 passengers despite its capacity of over 220. At 8:50, a controller at the FAA's Indianapolis Center calls the flight crew. "American 77, cleared direct Falmouth," he says, indicating that they should go directly to one of the navigational waypoints farther along their route of flight.

"Uh, direct Falmouth. American 77, thank you," Captain Burlingame acknowledges.[1] This innocuous transmission is the flight's last. At 8:54, the aircraft begins to deviate from its flight plan with a slight turn toward the south. Just after the controller notices the deviation, the cockpit transponder on board American 77 is turned off and the flight disappears completely from the Indy Center's radar screens. The controller searches in vain for any trace—even a primary radar return—but can find nothing. A technical failure in the radar software, combined with poor radar coverage in the area, prevent the primary return from showing up on his screen.[2]

"American 77, Indy," he calls to the flight.

"American 77, Indy," he repeats a few seconds later. After four additional attempts to communicate with the aircraft, a sector radar associate, whose job it is to help with hand-offs and coordinate with other sectors and facilities, puts through a call at 8:58 to American's Dispatch in Dallas to request assistance in contacting the flight.

"American Dispatch, Jim McDonnell," the dispatcher on duty answers.

"This is Indianapolis Center trying to get a hold of American 77," the controller begins.

"Uh . . . Indy, hang on one second please," the dispatcher interrupts, distracted by the airline's crisis with Flight 11. The headquarters' staff is desperately trying to determine if it's really their plane that hit the World Trade Center.

"What?" the controller asks.

"Hang on one second please."

"All right."

"Who you trying to get a hold of?" the dispatcher asks just two seconds later.

"American 77."

"Okay."

"On frequency 120.27."

"One-two-zero."

"Point two seven," the controller repeats. "We were talking to him and all of a sudden it just, uh . . ." The dispatcher has heard enough.

"Okay, all right," he interjects. "We'll get a hold of him for you."

"All right," the controller responds, somewhat taken aback by the dispatcher's curtness. He then continues to try to raise American 77.

"American 77, Indy Center, how do you read?"

"American 77, Indy. Radio check. How do you read?"

Another American flight on the frequency, Flight 2493, radios in to offer assistance. The pilot has heard the controller's repeated attempts to communicate with Flight 77 and he's well aware that missing several radio calls indicates a possible radio malfunction. He has already separately notified American headquarters of the communication problem.

"Center, American 2493," he calls to the Indy controller.

"American 2493, go ahead," the controller responds.

"Yeah we, uh, sent a message to Dispatch to have him come up on 120.27. Is that what you want 'em to do?" the Flight 2493 pilot asks.

"Yeah," the controller replies. "We had 'em on west side of our airspace and they went into coast and we don't have a track on 'em and now he's not talking to me so we don't know exactly what happened to him. We're trying to get a hold of him. We also contacted your company, so thanks for the help."

"All right," the pilot says, clearly concerned.

The controller doesn't know it, but American 77 has turned 180 degrees and is now flying directly toward the nation's capital.

American Airlines Headquarters, Fort Worth, Texas, 9:00 a.m. (EST)

American Airlines' Crisis Command Center is working to determine whether American 11 is the plane that crashed into the World

Trade Center when the vice president of operations, Gerard Arpey, is notified of the call from Indianapolis Center.[3]

Shocked looks fire questioningly across the Crisis Center at the news that Flight 77 is not responding to calls. The questions ripple through the room: Is this more than a single hijacking? Could this be a coordinated attack on American's fleet?[4]

Arpey isn't going to take any chances. He issues an immediate ground-stop order for all American and American Eagle flights in the northeast quarter of the United States. No flights will be allowed to take off. The order is unprecedented.

CHAPTER 5

The Unfathomable

FAA Command Center, Herndon, Virginia, 8:53 a.m.

The North Tower of the World Trade Center engulfed in flames presents a paradox for Ben Sliney. He is trying to gather and disseminate what little information there is. Although none of the air traffic control facilities in the area is reporting any communications or radar contact with American 11, the airline will still not confirm that it's their aircraft that crashed into the World Trade Center. Watching the television coverage, he just can't imagine how a small plane could torch off such a furious fire.

The longer he watches the news coverage and hears nothing of the hijacked flight, the more convinced Sliney becomes that the "small plane" that has struck the World Trade Center has to be American 11. It was believed hijacked, even though they couldn't confirm that. It disappeared heading southward toward New York City, and now they can't seem to find the aircraft anywhere.

"Jesus, I can't believe that a pilot . . . *an airline pilot* . . . would fly that plane into a building," he moans to one of the assistants. "I just can't believe it. I don't care if they had a gun to their heads. The pilots would dunk their plane into the Hudson or the East River. They would not take out lives on the ground." Given everything he understands of pilots, Sliney knows that, even in the most calamitous and catastrophic circumstances, pilots would sacrifice them-

67

selves to avoid killing people on the ground. It's one of the most basic tenets of their training.

While he continues to monitor the news footage filling the 11-foot screens, a specialist notifies him of a call from a New York Center supervisor. "New York Center is requesting ATC Zero," the specialist reports. "They want to speak to you."

Sliney is puzzled. ATC Zero is designed for situations in which an air traffic facility is completely incapable of handling aircraft due to a massive computer failure, power outage, or even a large enough weather system. The declaration pushes all their aircraft onto neighboring sectors, and any new airplanes from adjacent sectors are turned back, at the sector boundaries if necessary.

The New York Center supervisor has just been notified that United 175 has shut off its transponder and has made a hard left turn back toward the east. Several controllers are still trying to communicate with the cockpit. Although the transponder code changed twice, it is still transmitting, and controllers are still tracking the flight.

"It's escalating big, big time," the agitated supervisor exclaims when Sliney picks up the line. "We need to get the military involved with us. . . . We're, we're involved with something else. We have other aircraft that may have a similar situation going on here. We have several situations going on here."[1]

Sliney senses the extreme tension in the supervisor's voice. "You take care of matters in your center and we will provide all the assistance necessary by stopping any further aircraft from entering your airspace," he assures. But the supervisor seems almost too distracted to hear what he is saying. "Take care of business in your house and we'll take of business here," Sliney encourages before the supervisor hangs up.

"Give 'em everything they need!" he shouts to his staff after hanging up the phone. Whatever the Center is dealing with, they're being very creative in declaring ATC Zero as a means of preventing additional overload, and Sliney is going to do what he can to assist. If that means diverting everything heading toward New York's sector, then that's what he'll do.

One thing Sliney urgently needs is more information. He calls for the airlines to be brought into the teleconference with area air traffic control facilities, then relays this latest information, that United 175 appears also to be hijacked, to Manager John White, who is manning the open line to the conference room at FAA headquarters in downtown Washington, D.C., where FAA Administrator Jane Garvey is just arriving in the building.

Several minutes earlier, Garvey had been in Transportation Secretary Norman Mineta's conference room at the Transportation Department, where she was engaged in a cordial, though challenging, breakfast meeting with a commissioner from the European Union. They were preparing for a midmonth International Civil Aviation Organization conference, discussing environmental issues and trying to find some common ground in their very divergent positions.

In the midst of their discussion, the door of Mineta's office burst open and Transportation Department Chief of Staff John Flaherty uncharacteristically barged in. "Secretary and Madame Administrator," he blurted out, "we need you right away!" He nearly pulled them into the secretary's office, where the television was showing the World Trade Center engulfed in flames.

Almost immediately, Garvey's phone had rung. It was her deputy administrator, Monte Belger. "We have a potential hijacking," the manager reported.

"I'm coming right over," she replied. "But what about the plane in the World Trade Center?"

"We know about that, but at this point we are focusing on this hijacking." She immediately excused herself and exited the building, walking briskly up 7th Street toward FAA headquarters, just a quarter of a mile away on Independence Avenue.

In the final year of her 5-year term, Garvey had thought that things were calming down. Just the previous weekend, at her high school class reunion, she had told people that she was looking forward to her last 11 months but also looking forward to the experience ending. She had taken the helm of the FAA on the heels of the Valujet and TWA 800 crashes, at a time of tremendous congressional and White House concern about airline safety. Then she had dealt with the Y2K issue and then the terrible summer flight delays of 2000 and 2001. All that now seemed like a distant memory.

She steps off the elevator at FAA headquarters just as John White forwards the new information about United 175 looking like a second hijack.

Meanwhile, Sliney contemplates the incongruence between what he knows to be true and what he is seeing and hearing. It's not adding up. The United States has never had multiple hijackings. How does that happen? And pilots don't stop communicating with controllers, and they would never turn off their transponders. Even hijacked flights want to avoid midair collisions! And airplanes don't fly into buildings. He is beginning to process just how out of bounds the events of this morning are becoming.

Midwest Express Airlines Flight 270, Milwaukee–Newark, 8:57 a.m.

With the issuance of ATC Zero in New York Center's airspace, controllers across the Northeast begin issuing sweeping holding instructions to flights approaching New York. Most flight crews still have no knowledge of the crash into the North Tower, and the controllers are not forthcoming about the reason for the holds. Midwest Airlines' Capt. Chuck Savall has been enjoying an uneventful early morning flight from Milwaukee to Newark and is preparing for landing when he is interrupted with a call to go into an indefinite hold.

A bit of a maverick in the piloting profession, Savall looks at flying airplanes as another one of his passions. He is no conservative, married-with-children kind of guy. When he's not flying airplanes, he is taking advantage of his travel benefits on adventures all over the world. He spent his summer in a training regimen for an around-the-world yacht race, hang gliding in Utah, hiking the Dolomites of Austria, and scuba diving in St. Lucia. When it comes to work, he's the guy in the chief pilot's office questioning why the airline does things a certain way, constantly pushing to be safer and more efficient. Without a doubt, he is Midwest Airlines' squeaky wheel. He likes to have fun at work, but he also expects his coworkers to be professional and know their jobs well.

On a beautiful morning like this, he's frustrated to be delayed. *And after such a good start to a day of flying!* he thinks as he puts down his stack of instrument approaches for Newark and looks over at his first officer.

"A beautiful day like this?" he frets, clearly disappointed. "It's way too early for the usual traffic delays. Something must be going on."

He figures it's just a simple problem, like a runway change slowing down traffic or, worst case, a disabled aircraft on one of the runways.

"It's New York!" his first officer says and shrugs.

The flight deck gets quiet while the first officer sets up and enters a holding pattern and Savall calculates fuel requirements. As the captain, fuel management is one of his critical responsibilities. Scribbling on his flight release, he computes his "bingo fuel." He will be able to stay in the hold until he reaches that fuel level; if he hasn't been cleared for an approach by then, he'll have to divert to an alternate airport. The federal aviation regulations require that he have enough fuel to fly to an alternate destination and still land with a specific amount of reserve fuel on board, just in case of an emergency.

After his work is done, Savall's curiosity gets the better of him. "Why the holding pattern?" he radios to the air traffic controller.

"We can't tell you at this time," comes the answer.

Baffled, Savall frowns at his first officer. "Okay, this is really odd!

They *always* tell us when something is happening, even when it's something we don't want to hear!"

Other airline crews on the frequency that are also in holding patterns start to ask the same question. After several inquiries from impatient pilots, the controller finally gives in. "There is some kind of emergency in the New York area," he announces.

Savall's first speculation is that there has been some catastrophe, maybe a gas explosion, that has required the firefighters from Newark Airport to go to assist elsewhere and that the airport will be closed until they can return. He knows he doesn't have the fuel to wait forever for the problem to clear up, so he begins to plan for a possible diversion to LaGuardia. It's time to bring his dispatcher at Midwest headquarters into the loop.

Dispatchers at airline headquarters take guardianship of each company aircraft in the sky. They are assigned to a certain number of aircraft and know all there is to know about each: who is flying, who is working the cabin, how many pounds of fuel are onboard, the flight plan, the alternate plan, and anything at all relevant to that flight. If there is a glitch in the system, the pilot talks to the dispatcher, and together they formulate a plan of action.

Since his DC-9 is not ACARS-equipped, Savall can't simply communicate via text messages back and forth to his dispatcher. He must rely on the antiquated communication method known as selective calling, or Selcal. He uses one of the airplane's secondary VHF radios to contact a ground-based radio handler. These radio handlers, stationed at sites around the world, work for the worldwide air-ground radio communications company ARINC, which contracts with the airlines to provide communications relay services between airborne aircraft and each airline's dispatch center.

The frequency is unusually busy, though, and communication is slow. While listening simultaneously to both his main and secondary radios—hearing both air traffic control and the ARINC radio frequency—Savall is distracted by a conversation on the main ATC frequency. Someone mentions an aircraft hitting the World Trade Center.

He immediately glances in the direction of New York, now 35 miles in front of him, and is startled to see a plume of black smoke hovering over the Twin Towers.

His brain moves into overdrive. How could an airplane hit the World Trade Center? *Even if a plane had somehow lost control on departure from or approach into New York*, he thinks, *what are the odds of it hitting the World Trade Center? It has to be a small plane or helicopter with unbelievably bad luck,* he thinks, *or perhaps a crazy suicidal pilot. But why so much smoke?* The same worried questions are being asked by hosts of those just getting the news in the aviation industry, the military, the media, and millions of Americans watching the live coverage on CNN.

"You think it's been bombed again?" his first officer asks.

"If so, they did a pretty good job of it this time!" Savall exclaims.

New York Center, Islip, Long Island, 9:00 a.m.

At New York Center, although hijackers aboard United 175 have changed the transponder code so the data tag connected to the radar blip is no longer labeling the flight "UAL175," the controllers are still able to track the aircraft. It is showing as an intruder on their displays, with the incorrect transponder code alternating with the airspeed readout in its data box. One of the controllers realizes that the flight is descending out of New York Center's airspace and into the region controlled by New York Approach, the regional air traffic control facility that handles the departures and arrivals into the various New York airports. He gets on the phone to New York Approach and references the target. "It looks like he's going into one of the small airports down there," he says. Maybe Philadelphia?

"We're just picking him up now," the Approach controller reports, spotting the flight as it descends out of 9,000 feet.

"All right," Center responds. "Heads up, man, it looks like another one coming in."[2]

The news sends New York Approach controllers into critical mode. The plane, which had been flying eastward over central New Jersey, has now turned northeast and is heading toward New York City, and directly into the paths of several aircraft. The New York Center controllers watch in horror as the flight continues its steep descent, Bottiglia calling off the altitudes as the aircraft dives down toward New York City. The Approach controllers scramble to prevent a midair collision. They begin frantically firing off alerts to the various flights in the path of the errant plane. One of the flights into whose path United 175 has just turned is Capt. Gerald Earwood's Midwest Express Flight 7.

Midex 7, Milwaukee–LaGuardia

As Midex 7 approaches New York, Captain Earwood's frustration level with air traffic control has been rising. He has called twice for landing instructions with no reply and now tries a third time.

"New York Approach, do you read Midex 7?"

There is a long 10 seconds of silence on the frequency before the voice of a panicked controller barks out, "Midex 7, are you with me? *Midex 7, Midex 7, are you with me?*" He sees that a midair collision is imminent. Unknown to Earwood, United 175 is now flying directly at his plane at over 500 miles per hour.

"Midex 7 is with you out of 7 for 4,000," Earwood replies, thoroughly flustered, yet sticking to protocol that requires him to give his current and assigned altitude when checking in with a new controller. He has just passed through 7,000 feet in his descent to his assigned altitude of 4,000.

"Roger, Midex 7, turn left now!" the controller responds. "Head two-four-zero degrees now, as quick as you can!"

The clearance is rather odd, with that "quick as you can" tacked onto the end, but First Officer Fjelstad doesn't think too much about it and simply complies, rolling the DC-9 into a standard 30-degrees-of-bank turn.

"Left turn, Midex, *left turn*!" the controller orders.

"Roger. Midex 7 is rolling left," Earwood replies, wondering why the controller seems so agitated when they're doing exactly as instructed.

After several more seconds, the controller comes back with an unequivocal command. "Midex 7, tighten it up! *Roll left! Now! Now! Now!*"

Most pilots will spend an entire career without hearing that kind of command. It means *You are in imminent danger. Screw procedure and move that plane!* With a surge of adrenaline, Fjelstad rolls the aircraft into a much steeper bank, pulling on the yoke with increasing pressure to keep the aircraft's nose from dropping as the laws of physics come into play. When an aircraft turns, some of the vertical lift generated by the wing is lost, and the pilot must compensate for the loss by pulling back on the yoke, which forces the wing's relative angle to the wind to increase, thereby generating more lift. The steeper the turn, the more force the pilot must use to prevent the aircraft's nose from dropping.

Earwood sees that Fjelstad is straining to keep the nose up and grabs his own flight controls to assist. Both pilots now pull back hard, and the startled first officer is still increasing the bank.

"Keep it at 45 degrees!" Earwood bellows, concerned that they'll overbank and cause a high-speed stall. A high-speed stall occurs when the pilots pull back too much on the wing, forcing the wing's relative angle to the wind to become too steep. When a critical angle is surpassed, the airflow over the wing becomes turbulent and separates from the wing surface, causing the wing to stall, or stop producing lift, and the aircraft to dive. To recover from the stall, the pilot must release pressure on the controls and allow the nose (and the plane) to drop so that the wings can once again generate lift. Then the pilot can initiate a recovery and gradually come out of the dive. If a stall occurs too close to the ground, there may be insufficient altitude to recover.

Earwood looks frantically out the window to see what he is about to hit, but he can't see anything. After several moments, confident that their steep turn has averted a collision, Fjelstad starts to roll out of the turn, and Earwood takes his hands off the flight controls. But almost immediately, the controller is back on the radio, more panicked than ever.

"Roll right, Midex! Roll right as hard as you can!"

Shit! Earwood thinks. He has never experienced anything like this.

"Midex 7 is coming right," he calls.

"Keep it tight, Midex. Roll hard right! *Now! Now!*"

"Where *is* this guy?" Earwood fumes.

As they roll into a hard right turn, the cockpit chime rings, indicating that one of the flight attendants wants to talk with them.

Very bad timing! If a pilot is making extreme maneuvers, he or she isn't doing so out of boredom and isn't going to want to chat.

Flight attendants are usually attuned to such emergency handling of an aircraft. They know that the pilots must adhere to the adage "aviate–navigate–communicate"—strictly in that order. First, they fly the plane. Second, they figure out where they are and where they're going. Third, and only if the other two allow, they communicate with air traffic control, their cabin crew, and their passengers.

Even so, Earwood, almost instinctively, picks up his handset to respond. The piqued flight attendant wastes no time sharing her thoughts.

"What in God's name is going on up there?" she asks. "You are tossing us all over the place! Is everything all right?"

"Can't talk right now!" he manages to respond and then quickly hangs up. Everything is *not* all right. They are being vectored all over the place by a highly agitated air traffic controller who is doing everything in his power to prevent a midair collision.

While the Approach controllers try to get other flights away from the diving aircraft, controllers at New York Center—who can still see the track on their screens—watch in horror while the radar returns for the two planes move so close that they seem to merge on their screens, but then United 175 barrels on toward New York. A collision has been avoided by the narrowest margin.

United 175 is now rapidly descending, and it appears to be lining up to land at Newark, just across the Hudson River from downtown Manhattan, except that it's descending far too fast for a landing. A supervisor grabs a hotline to the Newark control tower, urgently asking if they see an incoming aircraft.

Newark Control Tower, 9:02 a.m.

The network news and police helicopters are buzzing over Manhattan like bees around a hive when Newark controller Rick Tepper answers a call from New York Center.

"Can you see any planes over Manhattan?" the controller urgently asks.

Tepper looks carefully out over the skyline.

"I don't see anything over the city that shouldn't be there," he responds. "Nothing except for a whole lot of smoke coming from the World Trade Center."

"I'll call you back!" the New York Center controller fires back before the line goes dead.

Tepper is puzzled. None of this is making any sense to him. New York Center works high-altitude aircraft, above 18,000 feet. Newark tower handles aircraft only up to an altitude of 2,000 feet in an 8-mile radius around Newark Airport. *Why would Center be calling us to ask about one of their aircraft?* This simply doesn't happen.

Nearby in the Newark tower, controller Bob Varcadapane is also on the phone with New York Center. He is learning that a second plane has been hijacked and that it's nearly on top of them.

"Do you see that target coming over the Verrazano Bridge?" the Center controller asks desperately.[3] Varcadapane looks down at his radar, which depicts the bridge just a few miles south of the control tower. He immediately sees the target.

"I have a target in sight," he calls. "He's descending rapidly."

Tepper's phone rings again. It's the same New York Center controller who just hung up on him. He says that there is another airliner possibly inbound toward Manhattan.

"Can you see him?" he asks anxiously. "We think he's down to the southeast."

Tepper shifts his glance to the right, down the Hudson River toward the majestic Verrazano-Narrows Bridge.

"Hey, who's that by the Verrazano Bridge?" a third controller demands, just noticing the airliner.[4]

"What in the world?" Tepper gasps. He sees the airplane all right! And it is much faster—and descending at a steeper angle—than he has ever seen before. It appears to be out of control, leveling off over the river, then rolling wildly into alternating 90-degree left and right banks. Varcadapane starts to call out altitudes: "4,700 . . . 3,600 . . . 2,700."

Tepper gives a blow-by-blow account over the phone of the plane's erratic behavior and controllers watch in horror as United 175 approaches Manhattan.

"I can see him at the Verrazano Bridge," Tepper reports. "He's real fast. He's coming down . . . fast! He's down low now." The plane is now heading across the Hudson River, heading toward Manhattan at 590 miles per hour. "He's moving up the Hudson," Tepper continues, "and OH MY GOD! He just hit the tower!"

It's 9:03. United 175 has slammed into the South Tower of the World Trade Center with such force that it looks to the controllers as if the airplane has gone in one side and out the other. A wave of profanity erupts in the control tower.

Standing stunned at his station, tower controller Greg Callahan looks down at the long line of planes awaiting their takeoff clearances. He keys his mike and chooses his words carefully.

"Something terrible has just happened over New York City," he mutters heavily. "It appears an aircraft has struck a building. It looks like we may not be going anywhere for a while."[5]

CHAPTER 6

A Nation Under Attack

FAA Command Center, Herndon, Virginia, 9:02 a.m.

It has been one minute since Sliney reassured the New York Center manager that he would do his part to keep all aircraft out of that sector. The manager had reported that the center was dealing with several situations and that the crisis was expanding "big time." He was too frazzled to give any more details, and Sliney needs access to this information to fill in the missing pieces. *What exactly is happening there? What other situations?* He already has a hijacking and a plane crash into a building!

The Command Center has the ability to rapidly connect with any air traffic control facility or airline. Specialists quickly call up the airlines to hook them into the teleconference call. All parties will be readily available to provide and access critical information. Sliney has already briefed manager John White, who is monitoring the call from the conference room.

At Boston Center, Operations Manager Terry Biggio has been relaying all the information he has about American 11 to the Command Center's teleconference. When one of his specialists reports that they have deciphered the odd radio transmissions from American 11, he returns to his phone to make another report.

"Hey . . . you still there?" he asks, establishing first that he's still connected to the teleconference.

"Yes, I am," White answers.

"I'm gonna reconfirm with, with downstairs," Biggio reports, "but as far as the tape . . . seemed to think the guy said that 'We have planes.' Now, I don't know if it was because it was the accent, or if there's more than one, but I'm gonna, I'm gonna reconfirm that for you, and I'll get back to you real quick. Okay?"

"Appreciate it."

"They have *what*?" another participant in the teleconference queries.

"Planes, as in plural," Biggio responds. "It sounds like—we're talking to New York—that there's another one aimed at the World Trade Center."

"There's another aircraft?" someone gasps.

Then, yelling into the phone, Biggio cries, "A second one just hit the Trade Center!"[1]

At the Command Center, 50 feet away from the conference room where John White is monitoring the conference call, Sliney looks up at CNN's live coverage on Screen 7 just in time to witness United 175 crashing into the South Tower. All around the room people gasp at the sight. Sliney knows he has lost control. *Damn it! Not in my airspace . . . not on my watch!* he thinks.

With imposing concentration, Sliney crosses the screen-filled room, now deafening with the panicked voices of controllers and specialists, each seeking explanations and trying to process what they have just seen. White hurriedly dispatches a manager to report to Sliney about the foreboding radio transmissions deciphered by Boston Center.

" 'Some planes'?" Sliney demands. The words take on a sickening significance after what he has just observed. They will echo in his mind all day. His whole understanding of hijackings now seems useless as his mind goes into high gear, reaching outside of the box to find a solution. *How many planes?*

"Give me a first-tier ground stop!" his powerful voice thunders across the room. The order stops all aircraft departing, arriving, or flying through New York Center's airspace, effectively closing down the nation's busiest skies. The advisory is immediately fired off to every air traffic control facility in the nation, and the skies over New York are now officially closed. A flurry of holding instructions for flights both in the air and getting ready to take off follow.

The disturbing footage is vividly repeated on the 11-foot screen across the front of the room, and it becomes sickeningly obvious to all watching that the plane was a large commercial airliner. And it was no accident.

Sliney decides that he must expand the teleconference to include the secretary of transportation. Something more sinister than a hijacking is going on here, and they all need to figure out what the hell it is and what they're going to do about it. Sliney seeks out the military liaison for more information, but it's clear that the lieutenant colonel's job has nothing to do with NORAD or the air defense interceptors. He is military, but his job duties at the Command Center are focused on military airspace usage. He has no place in the military chain of command that is relevant this morning. Sliney can only assume that people much higher up than both of them are dealing with the military response. The fighters *must* be on their way.

Linda Schuessler, the deputy director of systems operations, can see that Sliney has his hands full. She is uncomfortable with the uncertainty of the developing situation and decides to secure the Center, directing all non-FAA staff to leave the premises immediately. She has come to the Command Center after working at headquarters and she lacks operation-level experience, so she focuses on staying out of Sliney's way and taking care of administrative items.

Sliney is standing up in the middle of the Command Center floor, and he glances up at the repeating footage. *Who the hell is flying these planes?* he asks himself. *How in God's name are terrorists doing this? Did they infiltrate our pilot ranks?* He cannot conceive that hijackers can fly sophisticated aircraft like these. None of this is rational, and he cannot conceptualize what is taking place. It just doesn't make sense!

NEADS, Rome, New York, 9:02 a.m.

Moments before United 175 crashes into the South Tower, Boston Center controller Scoggins calls NEADS to fill them in about the flight also being a hijack. He was stunned to hear on the FAA headquarter's hijack teleconference that there was a second hijacked airliner. When he called New York Center, he heard that they were dealing with a hijack, but he had assumed that they were referring to American 11. He was certain that NEADS was also getting the information. *Aren't they on the teleconference also?* They're not. The FAA headquarters' teleconference is between air traffic control facilities, the Command Center, the Defense Department, and several other agencies; NORAD is not looped in.

Although Scoggins had just hung up from NEADS minutes before, he sensed that he should call them back with this latest information. He doesn't want to be a pest, and imagines that he must be one of dozens of FAA facilities flooding them with phone calls. What he doesn't know is that he is in fact the *only* one giving them information about the flights this morning, other than the coverage on CNN. Despite his hesitations, his instinct to call is too strong, and he picks up his phone.

No sooner has his report of the second hijacking arrived at NEADS and ID technician Stacia Rountree, who took his call, yelled out, "They have a second possible hijack!" than the troops look up to the screen at the front of the Ops floor just in time to witness United 175 slamming into the South Tower. A shocked silence fills the room. Rountree's supervisor looks away from the screen at the stunned faces around her, glancing back at the battle cab to see Bob Marr's face frozen in shock. Other battle staff members stand similarly frozen, staring at the screen.

The supervisor shifts her gaze back to her crew and sees that Rountree is looking back at her, her eyes brimming with tears.

"We don't have time for that," the supervisor directs, willing Rountree to assume a military mind-set. And she immediately does.

In the center of the room, Mission Crew Commander Kevin Nasypany grabs the shout line to the battle cab to brief Marr.

"Sir, we got—we've got an unconfirmed second hit from another aircraft. Fighters are south of—just south of Long Island, sir."

Seeing the image of the second impact, there is no lingering doubt in Marr's mind that New York is under attack. But by whom?

"Whose fighters?" he demands, the fog of war settling in. He mind is racing with the realization that the nation is under attack, flashing to the fact that this morning he had ordered his fighters uploaded with extra weapons in case the Russians came too close. Is Nasypany possibly referring to incoming enemy fighters?

"Our fighters," Nasypany clarifies. Otis alert pilots Duff and Nasty were scrambled at 8:46 and they have been flying supersonic toward New York for approximately 15 minutes. Even if they had arrived over New York before United 175 entered the airspace, they would not have shot the plane down. Before the plane's impact, the notion that American 11 had flown intentionally into the North Tower, and that the country was under an unprecedented kind of attack, was unfathomable. To shoot down a commercial airliner over a major metropolitan center would simply have been beyond the pale. Now, with the second impact, it is clear that the military is confronting a horrifying, unheard of challenge.

Marr immediately gets on the phone to General Arnold. He knows one thing for sure: he needs authorization for his fighters to engage any hijacked aircraft. It's the law. That the protocol for authorization is cumbersome and sluggish is becoming glaringly apparent, but without official authorization, his hands are tied. Arnold assures Marr that if authorizations are not quickly forthcoming, they will take matters into their own hands. They cannot and will not stand by and do nothing.

Unlike the FAA's Command Center, which is a huge communication center with enormous conferencing capabilities and instant access to every component of the national airspace system, neither Marr nor Arnold have such resources, and there is no protocol for them to directly communicate with the FAA, or the secretary of defense, or even with fighter units outside of the few Air National Guard units under their command and assigned to air defense. Although the Command Center has established and expanded its teleconference, the highest levels of government have not yet made provisions for putting all necessary decision makers into direct communication. Information is making its way up to the higher levels at the FAA, the Defense Department, and the Executive Branch, but the high-level officials are still simply trying to comprehend what is happening. At the operational level, Marr is going to wait only so long. He *will* defend.

Across the NEADS Ops floor, the staff attempts to grasp unfolding events. Several have decided that they do not believe that this is "real-life."

"I think this is a damn input, to be honest," hisses one tech.

"Then this is a damned messed-up input!" comes a gruff reply.

At the Weapons station, a radio query comes in from Otis F-15 pilot Duff. Supersonic over Long Island, he is heads down in his cockpit looking at his scope and trying to find his target in a sea of dozens of flights over JFK, where American 11 was last reported. He wants his target information, his "bogey dope," in fighter lingo.

"The second aircraft just hit the World Trade Center," the Weapons controller excitedly responds.

Duff and Nasty are shocked by what they've just heard. *What second plane? What about American 11?*

Until now, they've known only that there is an airliner in distress and they need to get to it quickly, analyze the situation, and help in any way they can. They were still expecting to intercept a hijacked American 11 and tail it as it landed at either Newark or JFK. They look toward Manhattan and are stunned by what they see.

"Tell me that's a cloud," Duff begs.

"No, that's smoke," Nasty retorts with his usual stoic brevity.

To prepare for their missions in support of NORAD, the Air National Guard pilots—some of the finest pilots in the world—

often use hijacking scenarios to train for intercept tactics. Duff and Nasty know the rules and procedures, and they can fly their missions extremely well. But nothing they are now experiencing fits into any hijacking scenario they've trained for. They comprehend instantly that this is not just about a hijacking; this is a coordinated attack against their country.

Okay, people are dying now, Duff thinks as he gapes at the smoke spewing from the burning towers. He instantly shifts into a combat mind-set.

"Huntress, Panta 4–5, say mission!" he impatiently calls to the Weapons controller at NEADS. "What do you want me to do next? What do you need from me *right this second*?"

"Uhhhhhhh . . . ," comes the hesitant response. The controller, staring up at the shocking CNN coverage, has no idea what to tell the fighters.

With no clear mission and no target information, Duff knows he has few options available. It would hardly be helpful or prudent to simply rocket into the crowded skies over Manhattan. He would be putting other aircraft in jeopardy. And what would he do? He has no authorizations, just who is the enemy?

"Okay, tell you what," he says, remaining calm and pulling his F-15 out of afterburner, bringing its speed down from supersonic, "we have Whiskey 105 reserved this morning," referring to a military airspace training area over the Atlantic just south of Long Island. "How about we just jump in there and I'll stay at the northwest corner so that we're protected from airliners and out of your way. If you need us, we're just 40 miles from the city."

"Yeah, okay," the bewildered Weapons controller responds, not knowing what else to tell them. "Go do that."

Any sense of invincibility that the fighter pilots felt has turned to roiling feelings of anger, horrible frustration, and impotence. They glare at the smoke in the distance over Lower Manhattan, ready and willing but unable to do anything about it. His heart pounding, Duff takes a deep breath and reluctantly turns his F-15 away from the city.

With two aircraft now imbedded in the World Trade Center, Mission Crew Commander Nasypany wants the Otis F-15s closer to New York City, but NEADS has not yet received any official FAA authorization to intercept any hijacked aircraft. He can't just bust his fighters into the dense airspace over New York City. Their actions must be coordinated with the FAA—there are simply too many commercial planes in New York airspace—and Nasypany wants that coordination *now*.

Fuming, he calls out to his senior director, Major James "Foxy" Fox, "Okay, Foxy. Plug in. I want to make sure this is on tape. . . . This is what I foresee that we probably need to do. We need to talk to FAA. We need to tell 'em if this stuff is gonna keep on going, we need to take those fighters, put 'em over Manhattan. That's the best thing, that's the best play right now. So coordinate with the FAA. Tell 'em if there's more out there, which we don't know, let's get 'em over Manhattan. At least we got some kind of play."

He gets on the shout line to update Marr in the battle cab. "We need to get those fighters over Manhattan because we don't know how many guys are out of Boston. Could be these two, could be more. We just need to get someone there . . . not down to Whiskey 105, where FAA wants to hold 'em. We need to be more proactive on this."

The phone calls start flying between the various NORAD command centers. General Arnold calls Maj. Gen. Rick Findlay at NORAD headquarters to give him the latest information and have him withdraw all forces from the simulated exercise. Today he will have his hands full dealing with the real world. Arnold is quickly back on the secured line to Marr in the NEADS battle cab, and the two commanders agree that the NEADS mission is now, clearly, to protect New York City. Marr is running out of patience. He's no longer comfortable waiting for the formal authorizations from the FAA.

"I want those fighters closer in!" he orders on the shout line to Mission Crew Commander Nasypany. To hell with the formalities. The United States is under attack.

Otis Air National Guard Base, Cape Cod

The first of the base's regular Tuesday morning meetings had ended at 8:55 and the next was slated to begin at 9:00. The senior commanders took a few minutes to check in with their assistants and grab another cup of coffee.

Lt. Col. Paul Worcester, the Logistics Group commander, was distracted when he walked past the break room and noticed that the group inside was fixated on the television mounted in the corner. Glancing in to see what had them so transfixed, he got his first glimpse of the footage of the burning World Trade Center. He knew that the base's two F-15s had been scrambled to intercept a possible hijack, but when he saw the footage he made no immediate connection between the scramble order and the image on the screen. All that occurred to him was how odd it was that a plane could have crashed into one of the Twin Towers.

On such a clear day, planes don't just go astray, he thought to himself. *That just doesn't happen.*

More senior commanders soon crowded into the room, and they stared in disbelief as a second airliner hurtled violently into the South Tower. Immediately they all knew that these crashes were no accidents, that the nation was under attack. "We need to go to battle staff!" one of the commanders barked out immediately, and the officers dispersed to reconvene one building over, in the battle cab of the Command Post.

"The commander has ordered the 102nd core battle staff to assemble," a voice now blares over the base's loudspeakers. "Please report to the Operations building immediately."

The squadron has already dispatched their two alert aircraft, flown by pilots Duff and Nasty, which are now responding directly to NEADS. But now the senior command staff must assess their entire operation to make sure that they are prepared for what might come next.

Under the leadership of the Wing commander, the various subordinate group commanders cross-brief on scramble activity, training flight issues, available munitions, personnel available to begin uploading more fighters to combat-ready status, security force increases, and more. In short, they begin to mobilize the wing for war, keeping NEADS in the loop on their preparations.

FAA Headquarters, Washington, D.C., 9:04 a.m.

FAA Administrator Jane Garvey had been at the Transportation Department in a meeting with commissioners from the European Union when she received news of the hijacking and the first crash. She excused herself and hurried on foot back to the FAA headquarters, several blocks away, talking on her cell phone to Deputy Administrator Monte Belger. "What do we know?" she had asked. At that point, it wasn't much; initial reports were very unclear. What little information they were getting was coming out of Boston Center via the teleconference set up by the Command Center in Herndon. After hanging up with Garvey, Belger put a call through to the office of the secretary of transportation, Norman Mineta, hopefully to glean more information.

When Garvey arrives at her office on the tenth floor of the FAA headquarters only minutes later, she quickly finds Belger. "What do we know?" she asks again.

He steps outside the room with her. "This is something . . . this is something beyond a hijacking. This is not an accident. There is something here. Defense is going to be taking the lead." He informs her that just before her arrival, when he was on the phone with Transportation Secretary Mineta, a second aircraft struck the South Tower of the World Trade Center.

The news arrives like a sucker punch to her gut. Garvey immediately turns to enter the Ops room across the hall, where security personnel have already established a "hijacking net," or teleconference, with several agencies, including the Defense Department. She understands that it will be her job to pull information from the

Command Center in Herndon and forward that information as quickly as possible up the chain, to the Department of Transportation and any other agencies requiring it.

She returns to her office as a call comes in from American Airlines CEO Don Carty, who doesn't know if it's one of his planes in the World Trade Center.

"Is that our plane, Jane?" he grieves. "We lost contact! Is that our plane?"

Next comes a call from United.

Jane hangs up the phone and immediately heads to the Ops room. Her mind reeling, she recalls the bombing of the Federal Office Building in Oklahoma City. Remembering that there are children in the day care center this morning several floors below her, her heart pounding, she hurries down to the Center, stopping along the way to tell parents to pick up their kids and get them out of there. If this is an attack on aviation, the national FAA headquarters is an obvious target. The loss of dozens of children is a loss she cannot risk.

Across Washington, in the West Wing of the White House, Richard Clarke, the chair of the Counterterrorism Security Group, has just learned of the second crash and has ordered a videoconference. The conference will connect the FBI, CIA, the Presidential Emergency Operations Center, and the highest-level officials from the State, Defense, and Transportation Departments. He wants the FAA—Jane Garvey—on it too. As the highest levels of the government and military begin to coordinate, those on the front lines of the unfolding events must improvise a moment-to-moment response that will call upon all of their mental energy and intensive training. They are fighting a new kind of war, with no rules.

CHAPTER 7

Secure the Cockpit!

Midex 7, Milwaukee–LaGuardia, 9:05 a.m.

After the several intense seconds of extreme maneuvering Capt. Gerald Earwood and his copilot Eric Fjelstad were instructed to do by the panicked New York Approach controller, saving them from a collision with United 175, no explanation has been forthcoming, and they have simply resumed normal flying, continuing on a southerly heading away from Manhattan. Things seem oddly calm, but the pilots are on edge. The next communication they receive from the controller is strangely matter-of-fact: "Midex 7, turn right and proceed direct LaGuardia," he instructs, as if nothing has happened.

What am I missing here? Earwood thinks, flustered. He inputs the course change into the computer while First Officer Fjelstad banks the aircraft to the right. Just as they roll out of the turn, they hear another aircraft calling up ATC.

"Approach, we just saw an aircraft hit the World Trade Center."

"Roger," the controller responds with a complete lack of emotion, as if he hears that kind of news every day.

Earwood and Fjelstad are stunned by what they've heard and look out the cockpit to see the fireball rising into the sky above the tower. *Oh my god! What is going on here?* Earwood thinks. Neither pilot says a word. Their stunned silence is broken moments later by a call from New York Approach.

"Midex 7, New York, are you with us?"

"Roger. Midex 7 is with you," Earwood responds. He has figured out that the controller doesn't want to alarm them, so he doesn't ask for clarification; he just tries to piece together what's going on. He and Fjelstad quietly focus on flying.

Every few minutes they receive the same query from New York Approach: "Midex 7, are you still with us?"

They are feeling intense stress, and even the most basic flight procedures require powerful concentration. *Just get this plane on the ground!* Earwood tells himself repeatedly, like a mantra, intensely aware that he cannot afford to lose his focus. Unlike takeoffs and cruise flights, approaches and landings require significant pilot input. This landing has *all* their attention.

They notice that all of the controller clearances on the frequency have become markedly brusque and succinct, and other planes are being asked repeatedly to verify that they're still in contact. Clearly, the controllers have become suspicious of every aircraft in the sky.

Earwood decides to take some precautions and calls his lead flight attendant.

"Keep everyone seated for the remainder of the flight," he instructs. "Absolutely no exceptions!"

Meanwhile, with the heavy smoke billowing from the Twin Towers, it's getting increasingly difficult to keep LaGuardia in sight. *This is just not going to work*, Earwood thinks, realizing he will not be able to make the visual approach landing they have been assigned.

"New York Approach, Midex 7 is unable to maintain visual contact with LaGuardia," he reports.

The controller gives them instructions for flying over the airport, and Earwood looks down to see what appears to be a traffic jam of airplanes on the ramp. The controller then sends them west for almost 15 miles, where the flight is turned back toward the airport and is cleared for a visual approach to Runway 31.

Earwood and Fjelstad manage a smooth landing, immensely relieved when they touch down.

"Midex 7, pull up on taxiway Bravo and hold short of Echo," the ground controller instructs when they turn off the runway. Every taxiway is referred to by a phonetic letter name, and the "hold short" instruction lets the pilots know that they are to stop just before taxiway Echo.

As they arrive there, the controller calls back with additional instructions.

"Midex 7, you may want to shut down your engines because you're not going anywhere for a while."

The pilots don't ask questions, they just follow the orders. Clearly something extremely serious is happening, but at least now they're on the ground. Earwood does not have much information to share, but he knows he has to say something to his nervous passengers. By now, he suspects, they have all made pacts to travel on Amtrak next time.

"Ladies and gentlemen, there appears to be some kind of emergency in New York and all air traffic has been grounded," he announces. "We will get you to a gate as soon as one becomes available, but it is out of our hands at this point. Please stay in your seats, and feel free to use your cell phones."

Earwood looks out the cockpit to see huge black holes in the World Trade Center towers and large pieces of glass and debris falling off. A dark orange flame is growing larger, creating billows of dense, black smoke.

After several minutes of staring at the inferno, Earwood comments to Fjelstad, who has remained totally silent, "I am sure they are getting everyone out of there." The comment sounds more like a question than a reassuring conviction.

"Yeah, but the damage is too high," Fjelstad responds. "That tower will burn for days before they can get that fire under control."

Newark Control Tower, 9:05 a.m.

For several minutes, all hell breaks loose in the control tower. There are at least 25 airliners on the ramp at Newark Airport either taxiing or waiting to take off. The controllers snap into action, improvising management of the developing chaos. They do not have the option to take a moment to process what they have just witnessed. Airplanes in midair cannot simply stand by. They're moving and moving *fast*. To make matters worse, the airport is in the midst of the hectic early morning arrival and departure push. Planes are lined up on final approach, preparing to land; others that have just taken off are waiting for hand-offs to Departure control. Those on runways are ready for takeoff clearances; still more are taxiing out for departure, and now some are requesting to return to their gates.

Greg Callahan starts to field throngs of radio calls from aircraft. Some of their passengers are distraught after having watched the impact of United 175, which they could see all too clearly through the cabin windows. Feeling his knees quake, Callahan struggles to retain his composure.[1] Pilots are clamoring to be told what is going on in New York.

"There's an incident over Manhattan," he explains, feigning calmness. "I can't give you any more than that. If you want to leave, we can still have you depart. If you want, we can take you back to the gate."

He's not sure what he is supposed to tell them. He has never faced anything like this.

Limited relief is on its way. From across the road in her office in the airport terminal the airport manager has seen the flash out of her office window from United 175's impact, followed by the plume of more dark smoke.

"Was that a plane?" she demands. "Did we just see a plane, or is that more smoke coming out of the North Tower?"

The airport services manager has seen the impact and calls out, "That was a plane hitting Tower Two."

"Then this is no accident!" she responds. "Shut the airport down!"[2]

Within seconds, the stop order makes its way to the control tower, but that is only one issue solved for the overwhelmed controllers. They're working like crazy to maintain separation for inbound flights while also directing dozens of aircraft back to their gates. The departing runway is immediately converted into a taxiway to assist in getting planes moving.

Callahan is told to focus on inbound aircraft. He's got to get them safely on the ground. All planes heading toward New York's airspace have been put into holding patterns, but for the ones that have already started to descend toward the city, the controllers have no choice but to continue to guide them in. There will be no rest for him or any of the other controllers any time soon. Whatever they are feeling inside, they work to keep those feelings contained. There are no procedures for this situation, so they are inventing new rules on the fly.

"Everyone is coming back!" a tower controller breathlessly calls to ramp control, meaning that all the planes out on the taxiways and runways must be brought back to the gates. "How do you need us to give them to you?" he asks.

Since Newark is a hub for Continental Airlines, their jets make up a large percentage of the planes on the crowded taxiways. The controllers decide that Continental aircraft will back-taxi down the runway first and peel off at the various exits. Others will be routed off in the opposite direction. Landings will taxi to the end of the runway and down the west side, giving controllers room to "stack" them, or line them up in long lines, as they are guided back to the terminal. It is a massive operation.

In the back of the tower, a supervisor works to handle a nearly overwhelming flurry of frantic phone calls coming in from the FBI, New York Center, the FAA Command Center, and what seems like all of New York City: the police want information, nearby airports want to know what's going on, airline managers are calling in to make sure their planes don't go anywhere. It's madness.

One of the planes inbound for Newark is a Continental flight piloted by Capt. David Kozak. He decides to query ATC about the delays into the airport as his MD-80 rapidly approaches New York airspace. He has been watching a plume of smoke rise in the sky over New York for the past several minutes. Just yesterday, on an inbound flight from Florida, the plane was delayed due to a small fire at Newark Airport. Seeing all the smoke today, he is not surprised that ATC has informed him to expect a 15-minute hold.

"Maybe Newark is burning again," he remarks to his first officer, Mark Drent.

When the 15 minutes is revised to 30, though, Kozak figures it is time to query the controller for an explanation.

"Does this hold have something to do with that smoke?" he asks.

"Affirmative. A small aircraft has crashed into the World Trade Center," comes the shocking reply.

His first officer looks over at him incredulously. He doesn't buy that. Neither of them does.

"A small aircraft just doesn't hold enough fuel to make that kind of fire," his first officer comments. "This guy must have been carrying some extra 55-gallon fuel drums to make that kind of smoke."

Kozak agrees.

When they are 15 miles out of Newark, ATC issues them holding instructions with an "expect further clearance time" of one hour.

"No way," Kozak says, doing the fuel calculations in his head. "We can't accept a one-hour hold. We don't have enough fuel."

He hands off the flying duties to his first officer, who makes a right turn to enter the hold, and puts through a call to their dispatcher at Continental requesting an immediate diversion to Boston. His plan is approved, and he informs the flight attendant and then makes an announcement about the diversion to the passengers. He doesn't offer any further information for the simple reason that he doesn't have any.

After air traffic control issues flight instructions that will take them in a northerly direction before turning them east toward Boston, Kozak rolls out of his easterly turn. His first officer is staring intently at the city.

"It looks like both towers are burning," he comments.

"It's probably just blow-by smoke from the other tower," Kozak replies.

"No, both towers are burning," his first officer insists, turning to look Kozak squarely in the eyes.

Before Kozak has time to respond, a clearly shaken lead flight attendant comes into the cockpit to report that a first-class passenger speaking by Airfone to her husband has informed her that two airliners have been intentionally crashed into the World Trade Center. Kozak finds that news implausible—it just can't be for real—and he tries to offer her some reassurance.

"We'll find out the truth shortly, when we land in Boston," he tells her. "Please discreetly advise the passenger to say nothing of this to the other passengers."

Less than a minute later, the interphone in the cockpit rings and the same flight attendant worriedly reports that the passenger has now advised her that Boston was the starting point for both crashed flights.

"Why are we going to Boston?" she asks in a worried voice.

"If that is true, then Boston is now crawling with cops and it's a very safe place to go," Kozak assures her.

Like a good captain, he is trying to calm her down, but he is well aware that something very serious is going on. He looks solemnly at his first officer.

"Look at your watch," he says. "Note the time and remember the date, because life in America has just changed forever. This is the death of innocence."

"What do you mean by that?" his first officer responds with alarm.

"If what she says is true, then how many other aircraft out there are unidentified flying bombs? Where are they going? And are we one of them?"

Processing what Kozak has said, the first officer reaches for the cockpit's crash ax and looks nervously over his shoulder at the flimsy bifold cockpit door.

He won't let go of that ax until they are parked at the gate in Boston and every last passenger has deplaned.

Boston Center, Nashua, New Hampshire, 9:05 a.m.

After Boston Center managers received the clarification of the voice transmissions from American 11, they realized that other aircraft in the skies were at risk. In addition to immediately halting all departures from airports in the Boston control area, the operations manager instructs his controllers to advise all aircraft in Boston Center's airspace to heighten cockpit security.

How should they convey the urgency of the situation? No transmission of that kind has ever been made on air traffic control frequencies. What will the pilots think when they hear such a nonstandard and troubling warning? Controller Jim Ekins doesn't know, but he isn't willing to wait. Customary or not, an announcement must be made right away.

"All aircraft!" he announces over all radio frequencies in their sector. "Due to recent events that have unfolded in the Boston sector, you are advised to increase cockpit security. Allow no entry to your cockpit!"

Nearby controllers raise their eyebrows, shocked at the unprecedented move. But they know the pilots have to be warned and quickly realize, *Yes! That's exactly what we need to tell them!* Unfortunately, even this strong message will not be clear to pilots, who neither like nor expect unpredictability. Predictability is paramount in aviation—so much so that pilots train for all conceivable emergencies to the extent that emergencies, too, become predictable. Communications with controllers are as dry as they come, and to many pilots this announcement is so out of their realm of understanding, training, and experience that it simply doesn't make sense. It actually agitates some, who cannot help but view it as some new kind of "FAA bureaucratic bullshit."

The Center manager then relays a request to the FAA Command Center, suggesting a similar cockpit security alert be issued to all aircraft nationwide. The request never makes it to Ben Sliney, though. Tragically, it is lost in the confusion and never gets past the staff person monitoring Sliney's desk as events rapidly spiral out of control. No national cockpit security alert is sent out.

US Airways Flight 6805, Boston–LaGuardia, 9:05 a.m.

Approximately 15 miles out of New York City on their return trip to LaGuardia, Steve Miller and his captain, Ron Maxwell, were finally able to see that the smoke they had been watching over New York was coming from the World Trade Center. Then they watched in horror as United 175 flew into the South Tower.

Shortly thereafter, an ACARS message arrives in the cockpit from company headquarters asking if the crew is aware that airplanes have flown into the World Trade Center and if they will still be able to land at LaGuardia.

"Here's a piece of history for you," Miller says, tearing off a printed copy of the message and handing it to Maxwell.

Before they can respond, an odd air traffic directive comes over the radio: "All aircraft: New York's airspace is closed. Prepare to state your intentions."

Miller, who is an Air National Guard reservist, has seen and heard enough to know that America is at war. They need to get their plane and its passengers safely on the ground just as soon as possible, and he has to get himself to his F-16 at the 177th Fighter Wing of Atlantic City's Air National Guard Base.

"We need to get this plane down NOW!" he urges Maxwell.

Maxwell agrees, and when New York Approach radios to ask their intentions moments later, he replies without hesitation.

"US Air 6805 is VFR direct to LaGuardia for a visual approach."

Declaring themselves VFR, or visual flight rules, is a bold move. It takes their flight out of the air traffic control system, meaning they'll get no further operational guidance from air traffic control. Although they will still be visible on controller screens, the plane is no longer subject to their flight guidance or control.

Such a request is unheard of. Pilots of airlines do have the authority to override a flight plan and to go VFR, but they never do so. They always fly "in the system" by strict instrument flight rules, completely directed and managed by air traffic controllers. They don't call their own shots and they don't manage their own course, in the way that small private planes usually do.

But today is unprecedented in many ways.

The New York Approach controller pauses. The other aircraft he's radioed have simply responded with requests for flight instructions for diversions to alternative airports. Perhaps too overwhelmed by the surreality of the situation to object, and certainly with no time to debate, he simply responds, "Roger."

Maxwell dials in the tower frequency for LaGuardia and changes the transponder to the VFR squawk code 1200, and they're on their own.

Miller glances over at the captain, who simply shrugs his shoulders. Miller responds with a similar shrug and then switches off the autopilot with a flick of his thumb.

They are flying an Airbus, which is a nearly totally automated airplane—a flying computer. It has an electronic side stick and throttles, all of which are merely electrical switches wired into the flight control computers and engine controls. US Airways policy and training directs pilots to use the automation to its fullest capability. Pilots are taught to engage the auto throttles right at the beginning of the takeoff roll and then switch on the autopilot at 500 feet above ground level, and the automation is designed to remain on until 200 feet above the ground for landing. Miller and Maxwell are turning their flying computer back into an airplane.

Miller points the plane toward LaGuardia and rolls back the speed select button to bring the engines to idle, holding the plane at altitude to let the airspeed bleed off. He incrementally lowers the landing gear and then the flaps as the plane's decreasing airspeed allows, and then pushes the aircraft's nose down steeply. He's reminded of his previous life flying F/A-18 Hornets onto aircraft carriers. With finely honed skill, he gets the plane on the ground *fast*.

Not all aircraft will get down as fast. Miller, having witnessed the second crash into the World Trade Center, has the benefit of information that very few pilots in the air have. For these other pilots, their situations become increasingly complicated and confusing.

Midex 270, Milwaukee–Newark, 9:12 a.m.

Long since forgetting about the lovely sunrise he had watched on the climb out from Milwaukee, Midwest Airlines Capt. Chuck Savall cannot figure out how some pilot has flown himself into the World Trade Center. But he's beginning to realize that he's not going to make it to Newark today as a result. Feeling frustrated at his lack of information, he begins to coordinate a diversion with company dispatchers. His first officer, who lives in Upstate New York, tries to tune in a local radio station on one of his navigational radios to see if he can gather any additional information.

Savall is shocked when the dispatcher radios him, "The World Trade Center appears to be under attack and the FAA has requested all airlines to divert their flights as far away as possible from the East Coast." *What?* Savall feels blindsided. The dispatcher continues, "Do you have enough fuel to get back to Milwaukee?"

It takes several moments for the information—and the question—to sink in. *Can I return to Milwaukee?* Savall thinks, flabbergasted. He is already in New York and the dispatcher is asking him if he has enough fuel to return to Milwaukee. No, of course he doesn't have enough fuel. What's more, he knows that his dispatcher *knows* this. His MD-80 has just burned about 8,000 pounds getting to New York and will need even more to get back to Milwaukee due to headwinds.

Savall looks at his gauges. He has 6,000 pounds of fuel left on board. He tells the dispatcher what must certainly be apparent.

"No way!" he responds.

"Can you at least try?" the dispatcher shoots back.

Savall is completely floored by this exchange. The dispatcher must clearly be in panic mode. He isn't being logical. Savall looks over at his first officer.

"What in the world?" he complains. "Why doesn't this guy understand that running out of fuel over Lake Michigan is just *not* an option?"

The anguished dispatcher wants desperately to get his planes back home and out of harm's way, and he's not going to give up easily. He radios back with a new idea.

"I've done the fuel calculations and you can make it to Grand Rapids."

But Savall doesn't think he can make it that far and still have sufficient fuel for a safe landing. No way.

"I can get to Cleveland," he offers.

The dispatcher reluctantly agrees, so with a plan in place, Savall notifies air traffic control of the routing change and receives new course and climb instructions for the diversion. The crew exits the holding pattern and begins a climb back to the west. In the cockpit, both pilots silently process what has just transpired.

United Airlines Flight 23, JFK–Los Angeles

United Capt. Tom Mannello and his first officer, Carol Timmons, have been parked on a taxiway behind a long line of planes at JFK since shortly before 9:00, when they heard a startling report from a pilot on their frequency that an airliner had flown into the World Trade Center. Mannello knew it was going to take some time for the controllers to sort out the situation and deal with the backup of flights, so he shut down their engines to conserve fuel. Then they received an alarming ACARS message in the cockpit, from their United dispatcher, Ed Ballinger: "We have gone to heightened security. Do not open cockpit doors. Secure the cockpit."

He had never seen such a cockpit warning and he was shocked, instinctively reaching down to grab the crash ax while handing the heavy fire extinguisher to Timmons.

Timmons jumped out of her seat and started barricading the cockpit door with their suitcases, cramming them between the bulkhead and a metal storage compartment in the cockpit. Shortly after Mannello called the lead flight attendant to inform her of the security threat and that she should under no circumstances open the cockpit door, she chimes the cockpit, indicating that she would like to speak to him. She and the other flight attendants want to bring his attention to something they've noticed.

"We just think you should know this," she begins, "because we think it is unusual. We have four young Arab men sitting in first class this morning."

He and Timmons exchange glances, not sure what to make of the information. Is it relevant? They haven't received any clarification about what the nature of the threat is, or if it's in any way related to Arabs. He thanks her for letting them know and stores the information in his mind.

Minutes later, the ground controller comes over the radio with an unexpected announcement: "All aircraft, be advised that the airport is now closed."

"How can it be *closed*?" Mannello asks Timmons, looking around him at the dozens of aircraft moving around the ramp and coming in for landing. His disbelief turns to shock when the controller comes back with words that Mannello will never forget: "Ladies and Gentlemen, the airport is officially closed. We have been ordered to evacuate this facility. You're on your own."

Stunned, Mannello considers his next move. *Well, we're not flying*, he figures, *but we can't just stay here. Something very bad is happening and somehow I've got to get this aircraft back to the terminal.*

He reaches over to switch the radio frequency to his company Operations at the airport and lets them know of this odd development.

"What gate do you want me to return to?" he asks.

After making another announcement to the passengers, he fires up the engines to return to the terminal. Now he's got to find a way to make that happen. He joins in the fray on the radio as the crews of the 12 to 14 aircraft now lined up for takeoff begin to play "ground controllers" in a complicated effort to coordinate their movement back to the ramp.

When he taxies around the corner on taxiway Alpha, he nearly comes nose-to-nose with a wide-body Lufthansa. That's very bad, since neither plane can simply "put it in reverse" and back up. Luckily the Lufthansa pilot makes a last-minute turn onto another taxiway.

Surprisingly, none of the aircraft go nose-to-nose while taxiing back to their gates. The atmosphere in the cockpit takes on an eerie quality, and Mannello is keenly aware that he feels "completely weird." He looks toward the city and sees the smoke coming from the World Trade Center. *Both* towers now appear to be burning.

Approaching their gate, the pilots are grossly distracted. They force themselves to work slowly and precisely while they shut down the aircraft and allow the passengers to deplane. They know only that an airliner has flown into the World Trade Center, United has gone to heightened security, and the control tower has been evacuated. The Arab men they had been alerted about, along with the other passengers, are quickly hustled through the terminal and out onto the streets as the concourse is evacuated.

Mannello looks through the peephole in the cockpit door to make sure there is no movement in the cabin before he exits the flight deck. He is greeted by a mechanic and a gate agent at the jetway.

"What's going on?" he asks.

"I've been ordered to lock the airplane," the mechanic responds.

Looking for answers, Mannello and his crew enter the terminal, expecting to be greeted by a hubbub of activity. Instead, the place is completely vacant.

What the heck is going on? Mannello thinks. *Where is everybody?*

They spot another equally confused crew and make their way down to United's Operations. Joining the huddle in front of a TV, events soon come into sickening focus: coordinated attacks, hijackings, terrorists.

Mannello comes to a shocking realization and time seems to slow down.

"Wait a minute. All these airplanes are wide-body transcontinental flights loaded with fuel. I had four Arab men sitting in first class . . ."

The thought is quickly followed by another.

"Oh shit, this is me! I would have been next!"

Shell-shocked, he numbly walks into one of the flight manager's offices to share his story. The ashen-faced manager immediately escorts him to the chief pilot's office, where they call company headquarters, then the FBI. Although news reports reveal that Al Qaeda documents and box cutters are found in the Arab passengers' unclaimed baggage, and although the FBI will interview the crew nearly half a dozen times in follow-up, no information about the passengers—who seem to have simply vanished into the crowd evacuating the busy airport—is ever revealed to the public.

Indianapolis Center, 9:08 a.m. (EST)

While all hell is breaking loose in New York, Indianapolis Center is completely unaware of the events unfolding there. Indy controllers are focused on their own problem. Still unable to communicate with or locate American 77, the Center notifies Air Force Search and Rescue at Langley Air Force Base in Virginia of the loss of a plane, requesting that they search for signs of a crash. Next they contact the West Virginia State Police to ask if they have received any reports of a crash.

When an Indy controller puts through another call to American's Dispatch, dispatcher Jim McDonnell is on another call but picks up the phone anyway, and the controller overhears the other conversation.

". . . and it was a Boston–L.A. flight and 77 is a Dulles–L.A. flight and uh we've had an unconfirmed report a second airplane just flew into the World Trade Center."

The controller is shocked.

When McDonnell comes on the line with him a moment later the controller keeps his cool and asks, "Did you get a hold of American 77 by chance?"

McDonnell responds, "No sir, but we have an unconfirmed report the second airplane hit the World Trade Center and exploded."

"Say again," the controller replies, thinking he must not have heard correctly.

"You know, we lost American 11 to a hijacking," the dispatcher continues. "American 11 was a Boston to Los Angeles flight."

"I can't really . . . I can't hear what you're saying there. You said American 11," the flustered controller responds.

"Yes, we were hijacked . . . and it was a Boston–L.A. flight and 77 is a Dulles–L.A. flight and, uh, we've had an unconfirmed report a second airplane just flew into the World Trade Center."

"Thank you very much. Good-bye," the controller abruptly signs off. He immediately calls another radar associate to repeat what he has just heard, and they look through their flight plans but can't find any record of American 11 in their system.

Indy Center's Host computer, which performs critical radar and flight management functions, holds on to only active flight plans. Several minutes after the system stopped tracking the transponder data tag for American 11, the flight plan dropped out of the system.

The best the controllers can figure is that the flight was hijacked on the ground in New York and proceeded to take off for Los Angeles without a clearance. They're not sure just how this is relevant to the disappearance of American 77, if at all, and they've done all they can do for now. They've asked for assistance from both police and search and rescue, and they're still hoping that the flight will show up somewhere, having landed after a serious electrical malfunction. Confused, they return to their jobs.[3]

American Airlines Headquarters, Fort Worth

Driving to his office, American CEO Don Carty is still talking on his cell phone to his vice president of operations, Gerard Arpey, when Arpey informs him that Flight 77 has also vanished. There is no doubt in anyone's mind at headquarters that American has a full-blown crisis on its hands. With American 77 out of contact, most of the managers, specialists, and dispatchers assume that it's American 77 that has struck the South Tower. The managers have been in close contact with United Airlines officials since one of their flights was also declared missing, and they quickly notify United on the hotline that they have a second crash.

Arpey extends the ground stop, which was previously limited to the Northeast, to the entire American fleet. No more American or American Eagle flights will take off from any airport in the country until the airline can make sense of exactly what is happening.

"No takeoffs! No takeoffs!" thunders an announcement over the center's loudspeakers.

It is an unprecedented move, but Arpey is gambling that he's doing the right thing. His gut tells him that this decision will save lives.

Carty arrives in the Crisis Command Center to see repeating footage of the impact into the South Tower. When, minutes later, he first gets the word that United Airlines has also lost communication with one of its aircraft, he realizes the crisis is even more large scale than he'd imagined. In another unprecedented move, he orders that all American planes in the air land as quickly as possible. Such a grounding order has never been attempted, and he knows it will be a logistical nightmare, but it is the only option.

At 9:15 the order goes out to divert every airborne American and American Eagle flight to the nearest suitable airport. With two planes down, another manager calls for the activation of the crash teams, who are trained to deal with accidents and the families of crash victims. Such teams have been required by law since 1996, when Congress passed the Family Assistance Act after the explosion of TWA 800 off Long Island. American had a program in place several years before that. The teams accompany families and victims to crash sites, make hotel and flight arrangements, buy food and clothing, and even make funeral arrangements. The work is extremely emotionally charged.

United Airlines Headquarters, Chicago

Dispatchers at the United Operations Center in Chicago have been trying to establish contact with United 175 via ACARS messages ever since they got the word at 8:50 a.m. from the San Francisco maintenance center of the call made from the plane, reporting that it had been hijacked. When they watched the coverage of a second plane hitting the South Tower, they feared it must be their lost flight. But on the hotline with American Airlines, they've just been told it was an American flight.

For Capt. Hank Krakowski, United's vice president of safety, security and quality, there is little doubt. As he watches a close-up replay of the aircraft hitting the South Tower, he recognizes the United markings on the underside of the plane and knows for sure: the second aircraft to hit the World Trade Center belonged to United.[4]

The airline's attention quickly shifts to the security status of all United aircraft. Managers and dispatchers must now assume that every one of their flights is at risk. Dispatchers send out an alert to all of their pilots: "There may be terrorist acts in progress. Do not open cockpit doors. Secure the cockpit." Joe Vickers, the head of Dispatch, institutes a procedure for "positive contact," whereby every 10 to 15 minutes dispatchers must confirm by direct contact with each aircraft that every cockpit is still secure.

Executives from both American and United Airlines are quickly on the phone to FAA headquarters and the FAA Command Center. They're brought into a conference call that has now been set up with Secretary of Transportation Norman Mineta and Vice President Dick Cheney at the White House. The airline executives inform the secretary that they are each dealing with additional aircraft that they are unable to contact. They seek guidance, but there is none. The president is still reading to children in a Florida school room, and the highest echelons of government are still struggling to gain their own understanding of the situation. Phone calls are flying. The nation is under attack, but there is no plan in place, and no guidance is forthcoming from the top as the crisis escalates.

CHAPTER 8

NORAD Responds

NEADS, Rome, New York, 9:10 a.m.

While civilian aircraft and controllers struggle to comprehend what sort of drama is unfolding, the military begins to tighten its grip on the skies. NEADS Commander Bob Marr has a telephone to each ear: one to Nasypany, his mission crew commander on the NEADS Operations floor just below the battle cab, and one to his boss, Maj. Gen. Larry Arnold, NORAD commander for the United States. Marr has still not received authorization for the NORAD fighters to intercept any hijacked airliners. Even more frustrating, however, is that local FAA controllers are busy shutting down New York's airspace and are less than eager to grant the fighters access to the civilian airspace. They're afraid of fast-moving fighters colliding with the hundreds of airliners that are still in the area. Many of those flights are doing unpredictable things just now, such as canceling their flight plans and changing course, and controllers are not convinced that they can provide adequate separation if fast-moving fighters are added to the mix. They just need a few more minutes, they keep saying. But the Otis fighters are pushing to know what they can do.

"Can we give them a mission?" Weapons controller Maj. Steve Hedrick asks Foxy, the Weapons team leader.

"Right now their mission is to *hold*," Foxy replies curtly. Nasypany has been trying to get ahold of the military liaison at New

York Center, but no one is answering the phone. He wants the Otis fighters over New York, not in military airspace 100 miles off the coast, but he has little choice. Without permission from the FAA to penetrate the civil airspace over New York, NEADS must advise the Otis F-15 pilots Duff and Nasty to continue to remain clear of the city.

Now Duff and Nasty confront another problem. By flying supersonic to get to New York they used up a lot of fuel. They have been holding in Whiskey 105 military airspace off the coast for 5 minutes when they get a further order from NEADS to remain at their current position. Duff acknowledges the call and reports that they have only 30 minutes of fuel left on board. This is another vexing problem for NEADS. What good are fighters if they haven't got the fuel to fly? The only other aircraft available to them are on alert over 300 miles to the south, at Langley Air Force Base in Virginia.

"Find me a tanker!" Mission Crew Commander Nasypany thunders. He needs a plane that can deliver fuel to these fighters in the air, and he needs it now. Weapons controller Hedrick quickly gets on the line to McGuire Air Force Base in New Jersey to see if any of their KC-10 tankers are airborne. They aren't.

Next Nasypany gets on the shout line to the battle cab and requests that Marr scramble the alert F-16s at Langley. On the phone with General Arnold, Marr discusses the possibility, but neither thinks it prudent at this time to send additional fighters to New York. If the battle expands, they don't want to have all their assets in one place. Nor can they have them running out of fuel at the same time. After conferring, the commanders agree that they will try to find fuel for the Otis jets and make sure the Langley fighters are ready to go if necessary. Marr relays to his mission crew commander that the fighters will not be scrambled to New York; Nasypany will need to find fuel for the Otis F-15s.

As techs search for a tanker to refuel the Otis fighters, Marr orders the alert F-16s at Langley to battle stations. If a fuel tanker can't be found for the Otis F-15s, then he will launch the Langley fighters to relieve them.

Marr also decides that he is done waiting for FAA approval for his fighters to enter New York airspace. If there is heat to take later, then he'll take it, but now he is going to defend. He will play his ace card. There is one method for the military to override the FAA's authority over the airspace, and it is called AFIO, Agreement for Fighter Interceptor Operations. The declaration of AFIO gives the military emergency authority to enter FAA-controlled airspace without permission, taking over the responsibility for aircraft separation. Marr doesn't feel he has any choice. He's not waiting any longer for the FAA controllers to get airliners out of the way. He's going to make it clear that he means business, and *now*. On his direct line to the Operations floor below, Marr directs Nasypany to declare AFIO for New York airspace and to immediately move the fighters over the city.

"Okay, we're declaring AFIO at this time," Nasypany's voice booms across the Operations floor to the Weapons staff.

The directive is immediately relayed to Duff and Nasty.

"Proceed direct to Manhattan and set up Combat Air Patrol," Weapons controller Hedrick instructs. "NORAD has taken over control of the airspace." A combat air patrol, or CAP, is a tactical maneuver that allows fighters to detect threats and quickly intercept, identify, and destroy any hostile attackers before they reach their target.

"Okay, got that," Duff replies, instantly calling up New York Center on his other frequency, identifying himself with his military call sign. "Panta 4-5 needs to go direct to New York City and I need lower . . . *right now*," he demands. He can't defend the city from 20,000 feet up. The controller gives him a heading and clears him to descend to 18,000 feet.

He and Nasty are ready for anything as they exit Whiskey 105 at 9:13, heading directly for Lower Manhattan. When he reaches an altitude of 18,000 feet, Duff asks air traffic control for "lower" again. The controller grants him a descent to 16,000 feet. *That's still not enough*, Duff thinks. He asks again and receives another modest step down. Then he asks again. Finally, at 11,000 feet, he has had enough.

"Guys, I need all the way to the surface!" he insists.

"Roger. Panta 4-5 is cleared all altitudes," the controller replies, finally giving the pilots free rein.

Duff's mind is racing a million miles a minute now, trying to figure out just how he is going to set up combat air patrol over New York City. *Who's attacking us? How many planes are there? From what direction are they coming? How are we going to do this with just two jets?* Never in history have American fighters been faced with having to fly a combat air patrol over an American city, in skies filled with hundreds of airliners.

119th Fighter Wing Alert Detachment, Langley Air Force Base, Virginia, 9:09 a.m.

The 2,900-acre Langley Air Force base houses 8,800 military and 2,800 civilian employees. It is the headquarters for Air Combat Command, which trains active Air Force pilots to deploy for overseas combat missions, and the 1st Fighter Wing, one of the largest fighter wings in Air Combat Command. But Langley's forces, well-trained and equipped to fight foreign wars, are not tasked with protecting America. That duty belongs to NORAD, and on the opposite side of the runway from the central facilities of this large military base is a small, modest detachment from Fargo, North Dakota's 119th Fighter Wing. This Air National Guard detachment has only four aircraft and serves as one of NORAD's seven U.S. alert sites responsible for defending the United States against attack.

The Alert Unit is nothing to write home about. It's housed in two cramped '70s-era buildings, located off to itself, away from the central facilities of the base, and boasts a full-time staff of only 18. The staff is a great bunch, and they manage to keep their spirits up despite the continuous uncertainty about whether the unit might be shut down, as some in Congress have been agitating for. The mounting talk on Capitol Hill to disseminate 1st Air Force to the four corners of the country would signal a quick end to the detachment.

This morning, F-16 pilot Craig "Borgy" Borgstrom sits in his office in the small Administration Building at the detachment. Borgy arrived at Langley only three weeks ago. He'd been stationed at the 119th Fighter Wing in North Dakota—just pinned to the rank of captain—when his wing commander told him about an opening at Langley. For two years he'd been separated most of the time from his fiancée, Jen, who lived in Arizona, and they'd been talking about settling soon in Minnesota. But when he asked her if she'd like to head instead to Virginia, she had loved the idea. He's expecting to head home at 4:30 today to help Jen tackle their stacks of boxes; he can't wait until they've got everything unpacked and he knows where all of his things are again.

While Borgy does work in his office, Maj. Brad "Lou" Derrig sleeps and Capt. Dean Eckmann mulls about in his shorts and T-shirt in the center section of the alert hangar just next door. They're the only other pilots at the detachment today, having flown in to sit alert duty this week. Eckmann's full-time job is as a pilot for Northwest and he's a Guardsman part time. He hadn't been scheduled to work this week's alert shift, but it had been listed as an open shift, and he had asked the alert scheduler to let him have it. With a wife and infant son, he appreciated the extra income. Working 24/7 during just one week of alert duty counted as 21 military pay days, and that was no small boost of cash flow. Lou, unlike Eckmann, works full time for the Air National Guard as a flight training instructor. He's a family man, loves the outdoors, and would just as soon not spend one week each quarter out of town on alert duty. This quarter he managed to split his week and find someone else to cover the first half of his alert duty, so he just arrived last night and will work only four days. Both flew into Virginia from the detachment's home base in Fargo.

Alert duty can be monotonous. They're on 24-hour call, and the cramped center section is home for the whole week. It's about the size of a double-wide trailer, and about as fancy, with a small kitchen, a common area, a bathroom, two bedrooms, and a closet-size battle cab overlooking the runway on the upper level, and two bedrooms, a small TV room, and another bathroom on the ground floor, all done up in orange shag carpet. This morning, thankfully, there is a training mission scheduled, which will liven things up.

Earlier, Eckmann had called NEADS to request "download," or removal from alert status, at 11 a.m. so he and Borgy can fly the training mission, which has them joining some of the F-15 Eagles from Langley. They can't just come down off alert to go fly without first asking for permission.

Such requests for download are customary since the detachment typically flies two training missions each week, and as long as the other NORAD alert sites on the East Coast—at Otis on Cape Cod and Homestead in Florida—are up on alert, the requests are generally approved.

Unlike the alert pilots who cannot leave the center section, Borgy is the full-time Ops manager at the detachment and is trying to get some work done in his office next door before the briefing for today's flight. Customarily, and in the event of a scramble order, his job would be to man the battle cab and serve as the supervisor of flying, or SOF, to get necessary information to the alert pilots about their mission.

When his phone rang several minutes ago he saw on his caller ID that it was Jen and looked forward to the nice break, but she wasted no time on niceties. "Did you hear that some airplane just ran into the World Trade Center?" she asked.

"Probably some idiot out sightseeing or someone trying to commit suicide in a Cessna 172," he responded, not thinking much of it.

"It's a pretty big fire for a small airplane," she had countered, just as Borgy looked up to see the chief enlisted manager coming into his office.

"Hey . . . Darrin Anderson is on the phone and needs to talk to you right away," he said, referring to the unit's intelligence officer.

Borgy was up fast and trotted over to the main reception desk to take the call.

"Did you hear what happened?" the intelligence officer asked when Borgy picked up the line.

"Yeah, some airplane hit the World Trade Center," Borgy responded unenthusiastically.

"Yeah, well we think there might be more to this, so you guys get ready."

"Uh . . . okay," Borgy answered, almost flippantly. As an alert site, the pilots are always just 5 minutes away from rolling out of the hangars in their armed fighters. They live, eat, and sleep just steps from jets. They really can't be more ready than they already are.

Borgy told the chief enlisted manager about the call, then turned to walk out to the alert hangars, where, perched in front of a white board in his T-shirt and shorts, Eckmann was still thinking tactics and countertactics as he prepared to brief the morning's training mission.

Now Eckmann's crew chief has come upstairs with some information.

"Hey, have you seen the news?"

"No," Eckmann responds. "Why?"

"Well, I just heard that an airplane hit the World Trade Center."

"Poor, dumb sucker," Eckmann responds. "I hope no one in the building got hurt."

No sooner does he get up to look for the remote for the television to check out the news than the battle stations claxon blares and the light indicator on the ceiling turns from red to yellow. Eckmann is immediately out the door and down the stairs to his waiting F-16, where his flight gear hangs on the ladder. Borgy is halfway to the alert barn when the alarm sounds, and his walk turns into a run.

"Do you think this has anything to do with New York?" Eckmann asks his crew chief while he zips up the legs of his G suit.

"I can't imagine how," the chief answers. "The Otis guys could handle that."

Borgy arrives at the hangar and fills in Lou Derrig about what he knows.

"There's some wacky stuff happening. Some airplane just hit the World Trade Center. I don't have any more information, but I'm sure this is just precautionary."

He then starts jogging over to Barn One, at the opposite end of the hangar, to give Eckmann the same brief. But when he passes through Barn Two on his way, the crew chief holds out a phone to him and says, "Hey, Borgy, come here. Somebody from the Sector [NEADS] needs to talk to you."

The NEADS officer wastes no time on formalities. "How many airplanes can you get airborne?" he barks.

"I have two F-16s at battle stations right now," Borgy explains.

"That's *not* what I asked!" the officer responds with an urgency bordering on anger. "How many total aircraft can you *launch*?"

Borgy pauses for a moment. He's not on alert, but he *is* an F-16 pilot. "Well, the only other pilot here is me—I can fly," he replies. "I can give you three!"

"Suit up and go fly! We need all of you at battle stations!"

This is almost unthinkable. If he goes up, there will be no supervisor of flying. During a scramble, it is the SOF's responsibility to monitor the jets—to work with local controllers to ensure priority handling and to make sure that the pilots are receiving lawful launch orders. The SOF stays in close communication with NEADS to get any and all information about the mission to pass on to his pilots and assesses weather, airfield status, and spare alert aircraft status in case of an abort by one of the primary fighters. If Borgy flies, there not only will be no SOF, there will be no officer left at the detachment!

While Eckmann and Lou climb into their F-16s, Borgy hangs up the phone and runs back down the stairs to tell the others about this new development.

"They want us to launch all planes and all pilots if we get scrambled!" Borgy pants, out of breath, yelling up to Eckmann in his F-16.

"*What?*" Eckmann counters, taken aback by such a peculiar request. "Why?"

"Sector asked how many planes we could get airborne."

It doesn't make any sense to Eckmann, but he's a military officer and he'll follow orders. "Well, if they want you to go, then you'll just go as our number 3! Go suit up and take the spare," he says, referring to the third F-16 at the detachment, which is not on alert and so is not loaded with weapons.

Borgy is on his heels and flying back toward the stairs.

"Arm my gun! I've got to get my shit!" he yells to the crew chief behind him, directing him to at least put bullets in the fighter's six-barrel 20 mm gun. It's the only ammo he'll have. He takes the stairs two-by-two to retrieve his harness and helmet.

When he returns to Barn Two moments later with his gear, he can't shake the sense that this is all *wrong*. The whole situation is unprecedented and he's uncomfortable. He feels compelled to advise his immediate higher-ups, and reaches for the phone on the wall, punching in the direct number for the wing commander of the 119th, their home fighter wing in Fargo. The commander answers immediately.

"Sir, they're launching all three of us. I don't know what's going on, but there's no Ops supervision here at all!" Borgy blurts out.

The commander has seen the news and understands what's happening. But there is no time to explain to his young officer, so he says the only things that are important when sending an airman to battle: "Go! Our thoughts are with you. Godspeed."

Those aren't the reassuring words that Borgy was hoping for, but he hangs up the phone and runs to his jet. He realizes now that he is being sent to war.

177th Fighter Wing, Atlantic City, New Jersey, 9:10 a.m.

By this time, Air National Guard commanders across the region are snapping into gear, realizing without needing word from their higher-ups that the country is under attack. They're already preparing for whatever may come next.

In Somers Point, New Jersey, Lt. Col. Brian Webster, who is the acting wing commander for the 177th Fighter Wing in Atlantic City because his higher-ups are out of town, was enjoying a lazy morning at home on his day off. Then his wife called to him while he was in the shower to let him know that a plane had just flown into the World Trade Center.

He got out of the shower immediately and made a quick check of the television coverage. His full-time job is as a Boeing 767 captain for American Airlines, and he knew right away that only a big plane could cause such a large explosion. Then he saw United 175 make impact.

He grabbed his flight suit and dressed in a rush, and when his wife asked him why he had to go to the base, he called out simply, "That was a 767! That's why I have to go to work!"

Now screeching out of his driveway, he grabs his cell phone and calls the base to instruct the SOF to hold the launch of a scheduled training mission, a routine practice bombing run over Fort Drum in Central New York.

"Done that, sir!" Lt. Col. James Haye, the SOF, answers. The F-16s, which had been taxiing out for takeoff, have already been brought back to the hangar. Haye had seen the coverage too, and had ordered the planes back right away.

"Shut down the practice mission altogether and I'll be at the base within five minutes," Webster barks before hanging up. Next he calls the Command Post and orders, "Raise the base's threat protection level to Charlie!"

Military threat conditions range from "A" (peacetime) to "D" (base lockdown and under attack). Threat condition "C," or Char-

lie, is a wartime posture. It activates a whole slew of security measures to prepare for a possible attack. Webster knows that these
"accidents" have terrorism written all over them, and if America is
at war he's determined that Atlantic City is going to be ready to
respond.

In the years since the base was pulled off the Air Sovereignty
Alert Mission, the base's highly secured Command Post had gradually reverted to a highly secured storage closet, used just once a
month for duty weekends, when the troops would train. Personnel
are now quickly bringing the Command Post to life, turning on all
the lights and bringing the various computers and monitors online.
When the loudspeakers announce the transition to Threat Con
Charlie, their pace becomes frenzied.

Arriving at Operations a short time later, Webster finds one of his
master sergeants busy calling up staff and ordering them to report
to base. Nobody has told him to do so; nobody had to. The base is
rapidly transitioning from a nonalert peacetime setting to full war
status.

Webster instructs the Operations Support Flight commander to
offload the practice missiles and munitions from the fighter jets and
replace them with live ones. This will take some time, as the missiles
are not stored near the aircraft. A convoy will have to transport
them to the flight line, where the fighters are parked, with security
escort as a safeguard.

"Get me authenticators," he orders next, turning to Haye. He
knows that if he is uploading missiles, he is going to need these.
Each pilot is given an authenticator—a piece of paper with a code
in a series of letters—which is valid for only one 24-hour period.
When a pilot receives an order to fire, he must follow a strict protocol. He asks for an authentication code, and the code he is given
must match the one on his authenticator. If they don't match, he
cannot legally comply. The highly classified authenticators are
issued to all alert sites, as well as each controlling authority, in this
case NEADS, by courier each month. Unfortunately, Atlantic City
is no longer an alert site, so they don't have any authenticators.

They're going to have to get some—fast! Today Webster wants live missiles and he wants authenticators.

These orders at a nonalert fighter wing of the Air National Guard are unprecedented. Air National Guard jets don't simply fly around the United States with live missiles. Guardsmen train to fight wars overseas, not to fly armed combat over the United States. There aren't rules of engagement for war at home, and certainly not for fighters that aren't even part of the Air Defense Mission. Live missiles? Authenticators? The weapons chief is less than enthusiastic about these orders and he asks to have a word with the colonel.

"Just *do it!*" Webster responds, and turns abruptly to walk away. The matter is not up for discussion.

**121st Fighter Squadron, D.C. Air National Guard,
Andrews Air Force Base, Maryland, 9:15 a.m.**

The fighter squadron at Andrews Air Force Base has also snapped into action.

Just outside of Washington, the D.C. Air National Guard (DCANG), known as the "Capital Guardians," is set up differently from other Air National Guard units, not only because the unit protects the nation's capital, but because the District of Columbia is not a state and there is no governor to report to, as all other guard units do. This unique unit reports directly to the president, who, in turn, has delegated that authority to the Department of Defense.

DCANG officers were in their regular Tuesday staff meeting this morning when an intel officer interrupted and told them that a plane had just flown into the World Trade Center. They all agreed that it must have been a small aircraft.

But only minutes later, the intel officer burst into the room yelling, "It's happened again! The second tower has been hit! And it's on purpose!"

The officers flew out of the conference room and converged at the television in the break room down the hall. "Well, holy shit, if this is a terrorist attack, we need to get something in the air!" one officer blurted out.

Maj. Daniel "Razin" Caine, acting as the SOF, felt certain that airspace restrictions were going to be put into effect around Washington. He had three jets out on a training flight over Dare County, North Carolina, and he realized that he had to get them back right away. If the Washington airspace closed before they could get back, they'd be out of luck.

Another officer called the military liaison at Washington Center, the air traffic control facility responsible for high-altitude air traffic around Washington, to see if he could get any more information about what was happening. But they didn't have any news to pass on.

Given that the Secret Service provides protection to the president—and that the president, and the vice president when the president is not available, is the ultimate commander in chief of the military—the Secret Service also has certain authority over the military and, in this case, the D.C. Guard.

In the past, the relationship between the Secret Service and the Guard had been strained because of one too many close calls with Air Force One. When the president showed up at Andrews, any inbound fighters were forced to divert. Any fighters on the ramp were instructed to shut down their engines and turn their aircraft in the opposite direction of Air Force One; there was not going to be *any* possibility of a weapon accidentally being fired. The Guard felt there wasn't a whole lot of trust happening.

Under President Bush, who was a National Guard pilot himself, relations had improved. The wing extended an olive branch of sorts and the Secret Service responded. Eventually, several of the Secret Service agents went flying in the unit's F-16s. A synergy developed that made business much easier for DCANG, and a good working relationship was forged.

Razin had flown with one of the Secret Service agents just a few months earlier, and the two had kept in touch. He now decides to give the guy a call.

"Do you have any additional information? Are you guys going to need some help?" he asks.

"No," the agent responds, "but I'll call you back if that changes." Right now, the Secret Service is more concerned about finding a more secure location than a Florida school for the president and persuading the vice president to move to the Presidential Emergency Operations Center (PEOC) in a bunker beneath the East Wing of the White House. Counterterrorism Chief Richard Clarke has just left the vice president's office, where he spoke with both Cheney and National Security Adviser Condoleezza Rice about the videoconference he has ordered to be set up between department heads. That call has not yet finished being organized. On his way out of the vice president's office, Clarke counted at least eight agents outside the office, rather than the customary two.[1]

The Secret Service might not need the help of the 121st Fighter Squadron right now, but Razin is betting that that's most certainly going to change, and soon. Meanwhile, he needs to get word to the squadron's three fighters currently over North Carolina to get them heading back. Since they're out of radio range, he calls up the tanker refueling plane that they're scheduled to meet up with shortly and asks that their pilot deliver an urgent "RTB" (return to base) message.

CHAPTER 9

No More Takeoffs!

FAA Command Center, Herndon, Virginia, 9:10 a.m.

At the FAA Command Center, Ben Sliney is filled with an over-whelming sense that he is losing control of the situation. He needs information. "We have some planes" was the transmission from American 11. *How many planes?* He must find out. He puts the word out that he wants all air traffic control facilities around the country to keep him apprised of anything unusual: loss of commu-nications, an unauthorized change of course, or any radar target disappearing from radar scopes. Basically, anything at all out of the ordinary.

But that's not enough. He also wants to know about things that have *not* been suspicious in the past—things that are, in fact, com-mon occurrences on any normal day. If a flight overlooks a radio call, deviates from its course, misses a frequency change, or gets a transponder code wrong, he wants to know about it instantly. These glitches happen fairly regularly with commercial flights and are usually corrected right away. Sliney figures he can't afford to miss anything this morning, though; he needs all the information he can get if he's going to piece together the bigger picture. The special-ists at the Command Center start calling all of the regional centers to give them the word.

In response to the call for information, news of unusual activity quickly begins to pour in from air traffic control facilities: bomb threats, loss of communication, and loss of radar contact. Supervisors work furiously gathering the reports.

"Give me a list of the 'abnormal' flights on one of the screens!" Sliney directs, referring to the 11-foot screens that cover the walls at the front and side of the Command Center.

A specialist tries to comply, but there doesn't seem to be any easy way to set up the technology for that. Another staff member quickly shows up with a dry-erase board, placing it in the center of the room. On it, a manager begins to write a list of suspect aircraft: where they were last seen, who was working the flight, where they originated, where they are going.

Every few minutes, supervisors and other operational personnel congregate back in the middle of the Operations floor to share the information and discuss their options. One after another, flights are added to the list. Soon a dozen flights have been designated "high risk." Sliney watches as a specialist adds a US Airways flight. Destination: Chicago. Reason: NORDO, not communicating with air traffic control.

As he grapples with the flood of information, Sliney repeatedly asks himself, *How do I fix this?* He is desperate to get control of the situation. He sends a message via the teleconference to FAA headquarters indicating that he would like to stop all flights, an unprecedented order, and he hopes authorization will come fast. He still has no idea what military operations are under way. His only direct contact with the military is via the Command Center's military liaison, but he has no information from the military to offer. His job description, unfortunately, does not require him to be in the communication loop of the highest level military leaders at NORAD or the Pentagon, where Defense Secretary Donald Rumsfeld is currently receiving his daily intelligence briefing and Deputy Director of Operations Charles Leidig, of the National Military Command Center, is just realizing that the two crashes are most certainly a terrorist attack.[1] It's Leidig's job to put the president and the secretary of defense in communication with NORAD command, and Sliney has no direct link to their deliberations. He must trust that his higher-ups in headquarters are liaising with the military. For his part, the best he feels he can do is to get flights out of the air. Every airliner flying has now become a potential missile, and he wants all planes down, *now*.

Delta Flight 1989, Boston–Los Angeles, 9:15 a.m.

The FAA has advised all air traffic control centers to pay close attention to their wide-body transcontinental flights because the two planes that hit the Twin Towers were both in this category. Controllers at Cleveland Center have their eye on Delta Flight 1989, which is a wide-body Boeing aircraft. Not only that, but it departed from Boston and is heading for Los Angeles.

One unequivocal way to determine whether pilots are still in charge of an aircraft is to see how well the crew complies with controller instructions, so that's what Cleveland does. A controller radios pilot Dave Dunlap instructions for a course deviation, to the south. Dunlap radios back right away to acknowledge and complies. Then they tell him to head north, and then call for yet a third deviation to the west.

At the last instruction, Captain Werner has had enough. "I think we ought to bitch at them!" he says to Dunlap.

For the past 30 minutes they've been hearing controllers issuing course diversions and holding instructions to one flight after another. Any other day, they might really give the controllers some flack, as on such a clear morning these turns off course seem like nothing less than sloppy air traffic control work. But they can tell there must be something significant going on, so they're clearly *not* going to complain. They just laugh and figure soon enough they'll get an explanation.

Dunlap has no idea that air traffic controllers are trying to confirm that he's still in command of his aircraft. Not in a million years would that thought have occurred to him. His mind is happily elsewhere. While the captain reaches over to tune in the ADF

(Automatic Direction Finder) radio to see if he can pick up an AM radio station, the lead flight attendant arrives with two omelets from first class and Dunlap can't wait to dig in; he's starving. He is savoring the first bite when the captain finally tunes in a clear station and the first thing they hear is ". . . the two aircraft that crashed into the World Trade Center appear to be airliners out of Boston."

Dunlap drops his fork. Airliners have hit the World Trade Center? Airliners out of Boston?

The same thought hits both of them simultaneously. "What?" Dunlap exclaims. "What about *our* flight? *We* originated out of Boston!"

FAA Command Center, Herndon, Virginia, 9:20 a.m.

The supervisors at the Command Center are gathering information from the specialists and forwarding reports to Sliney with recommendations or inquiries for action. One air traffic facility wants to evacuate, but Sliney insists that they stay at their posts. As aircraft are deemed suspicious, follow-up inquiries are made as to course, speed, and any other manifested anomalies. Queries are also made to headquarters as to military operations and where the president is going. How will military operations interface with civilian operations? Sliney wants word about that.

He cannot get the words "We have some planes" out of his head. Air traffic controllers are trained to control, and he is desperate to do so. He's sought permission from headquarters to stop all takeoffs nationwide, but he still hasn't received the clearance to do so, and he's growing increasingly impatient.

At FAA headquarters, the hijacking net—which includes the Defense Department and the Department of Transportation—is underway, but it doesn't include NORAD or the National Military Command Center (NMCC). Past situations have always allowed for customary coordination between NORAD and the FAA, where information has time to flow up and down the normal chains of command. Even when Bob Marr took the initiative during the 1993 hijacking to push the process along, the authorizations took hours.

At the White House the videoconference that counterterrorism czar Richard Clarke called for with the department heads, Jane Garvey, the CIA, the FBI, and the Joint Chiefs goes live at 9:25, though it will not be fully attended for another 10 minutes. Garvey briefs first. Although American Airlines has still not confirmed the fate of American 11, she announces that the two aircraft were American 11 and United 175, both hijacked, and that all takeoffs out of New York have been stopped. When asked if it is possible to get every plane on the ground, she says that it's never been done before. She also relays that it's Ben Sliney's first day on the job.

Neither Sliney nor the NMCC director—who is in direct contact with NORAD and, therefore, the fighters—will benefit from these conferences. None of the information on the White House teleconference will be forwarded to those on the NMCC teleconference for more than an hour, and none of the conferences include all of the key players necessary for creating a complete picture and formulating an appropriate response.[2] Simply put, Sliney is getting no direction from above. Urgent communication back and forth is needed, yet he has no way to directly tell the military what he's learning, and the military can't tell Sliney what they can do about it.

With no information flowing through customary channels, it's a good thing that Boston controller Colin Scoggins, listening in on the FAA headquarter's hijacking net, has taken the initiative to feed information directly to NEADS. It's the only pertinent information that Bob Marr is receiving this morning, and even so it's somewhat delayed.

As for Sliney, like other operational-level commanders and managers, he must improvise his response as the morning unfolds. He has no choice but to take matters into his own hands. With the list of suspect aircraft growing longer, he tries desperately to keep a handle on things. "Where'd these flights originate from and where were they going?" he calls out to the floor.

"Boston . . . both flights were out of Boston! And both were going to Los Angeles," a supervisor reports.

Sliney has already stopped all takeoffs from New York Center's airports, but now he realizes he must go farther. The national operations manager does not usually make such unilateral decisions, and Sliney knows that these ground stops will wreak havoc on the airlines. But what choice does he have?

"Give me a ground stop for Boston as well as all flights bound for Los Angeles!" Sliney directs. He's unaware that Boston Center took the initiative themselves and stopped all departures after the second impact. This last order will keep all Los Angeles–bound flights nationwide on the ground. If there is a connection, he can't afford to miss it.

Next, he stops all departures out of Detroit.

Shortly thereafter, Sliney receives a report from Indianapolis Center. When controllers there heard about the events on the East Coast, they began to doubt their initial assumption that American 77 had crashed, so they've called the Command Center to recount the details of the missing flight. For Sliney, the news of lost radio contact, and then of no transponder communication, sounds ominously familiar. American 77 is added to the list of at-risk flights on the dry-erase board.

If the plane hasn't crashed, where is it? Sliney stares up at the Traffic Situation Display being projected onto one of the 11-foot screens and contemplates the tracks of thousands of aircraft over the United States. Where's American 77? Where is it going? Planes cannot just disappear. American 77 is somewhere and they've got to find it! Sliney orders that a notification go out to all the FAA field offices that American 77 is lost and feared hijacked, and that they should all begin an immediate search for primary targets on their radars. There is no time to spare.

Sliney has no idea that the plane has been flying directly

for Washington, D.C., at nearly 600 miles per hour for the past 30 minutes.

"We need interceptors!" he shouts, frustrated that he's had no word at all about whether military jets have been launched. "Find out where the interceptors are!"

What does the military know? What are they doing? Are fighters even in the air? If so, where are they? He feels as though he's operating in a vacuum, as if the Command Center and air traffic control facilities are in this alone. *Where is everybody?* he wonders.

He can't order jets into the air, but he's going to do more of what he *can* do. He's been waiting to hear back from headquarters about ordering a national ground stop, and he won't wait any longer. There are more than 4,000 flights still over the United States, and Sliney won't allow there to be any more. At 9:29, the FAA's Command Center sends out FAA Advisory 031 with an unprecedented order: no flights are to take off anywhere in the United States, regardless of destination. For those flights already in the air, however, there is no way of knowing which might be hijacked next.

United Flight 93, Newark–San Francisco, 9:23 a.m.

While Sliney is receiving the disturbing news about American 77 being out of contact, yet another flight falls under siege.

Forty-five minutes into his flight from Newark to San Francisco, just outside of Cleveland in northern Ohio, United 93 pilot Jason Dahl is thinking about a smoother ride for his passengers. Since arriving at his cruising altitude of 35,000 feet, the flight has been experiencing the turbulence that pilots call "light chop." If it's worse up ahead, he'll want to try another altitude. He's just been handed off to Cleveland Center.

"Morning, Cleveland," he calls. "It's United 93 with you at 3-5-0. There's some light chop here at 35, any ride reports?" It would be helpful to know if other pilots along his route have called in similar conditions.

"Just a little light chop," the controller responds. "Nothing worse than that, United 93."[3]

Dahl's attention shifts to an ACARS message that has just arrived in the cockpit from his dispatcher at United headquarters: "Beware any cockpit intrusion . . . two aircraft in NY, hit trade cnter builds." He reads it several times.

This is a most strange ACARS message. Was it meant for him? Has there been a threat to his aircraft? He and his first officer likely discuss the message until they hear their flight number on the frequency.

"United 93, Cleveland, 133.37," the controller announces, switching them to a new frequency.

"1-3-3-3-7. Good day. United 93," he responds, saying his farewell and signing off.

He calls up the new sector controller. "Good morning, Cleveland. United 93 is with you at 3-5-0, intermittent light chop." He waits for a response but doesn't get one. This can happen if another flight has transmitted at the same time, thereby blocking his transmission. He calls again.

"United 93, checking in 3-5-0."

The controller is quick to acknowledge this time. "United 93, 3-5-0. Roger."

Dahl returns his attention to the unusual ACARS. Looking for clarification, he types his response to his dispatcher, Ed Ballinger: "Ed, confirm last messg plz—Jason."[4]

"United 93," comes a call from Cleveland Center, "traffic for you is 1 o'clock, 12 miles, eastbound, 3-7-0." The controller is warning him of a plane nearby, just to their right.

"Negative contact," Dahl responds. "We're looking. United 93."

Seconds later, the Cleveland Center controller hears screams and what appears to be a struggle on the frequency. "Mayday! Hey! Get out of here! Get out of here!" He has no idea what plane the transmission is coming from—he's handling over a dozen.

"Somebody call Cleveland?" he calls.

"Get out of here! Get out of here!" the transmission continues.[5] On board United 93, two of the hijackers are forcing their way into the cockpit, while another knifes a passenger. Dahl has the presence of mind to key his microphone during the takeover so that the controller can hear what's happening.

The controller gets his first hint of where the transmission has come from when he notices on his radar screen that United 93 is making erratic changes in altitude.

"Oh, my God!" he gasps. "Oh, my God! What's this plane doing?"[6]

"United 93, verify 3-5-0," the controller calls. There's no response.

"United 93," he repeats, "verify you're at flight level, ah, 3-5-0."

"United 93, verify 3-5-0."

"United 93, verify you're flight level 3-5-0. United 93, Cleveland. United 93, Cleveland. United 93, do you read Cleveland Center please?"[7]

The pilot of another United flight, 797, now calls another company aircraft on the frequency.

"United 1523, did you hear the company, er, did you hear some other aircraft on a frequency a couple of minutes ago, screaming?" asks the pilot of United 797.

"Yes I did, 797, and, ah, we couldn't tell what it was either," the other United flight responds.

"OK."[8]

Acknowledging but not responding to the pilot-to-pilot communication on the frequency, the Cleveland controller follows the protocol for loss of contact. The crew can't talk, but maybe they can do something else, such as press the Ident button on their transponder to let Center know that they hear him. If they press it, the data tag on the radar console will light up, and at least he will know they are listening and able to comply.

"United 93, Cleveland. If you can hear Center, ident."

There's no response. So the pilots *cannot* comply.

"American 1060," says an American flight, identifying himself as he joins the conversation. "Ditto also on the other transmission."

"American 1060, you heard that also?" the Cleveland Center controller asks.

"Yes sir, twice."

"Roger, we heard that also. Thanks. I just wanted to confirm it wasn't interference."

It was not interference. Every aircraft on the controller's frequency has heard it. "We could hear that, er, yelling, too," the pilot of a corporate jet offers.

At 9:31, an unintentional transmission is made on the frequency. It's meant for the passengers, but transmitted on the air traffic control frequency.

"This is captain," the heavily accented voice announces. "Please sit down. Keep remain seating. We have a bomb on board." Of all the training the hijackers received, none was how to work the cockpit radios, and this hijacker too believes that by picking up the handheld microphone he is addressing the passengers.

"Uh, calling Cleveland Center," the controller calls, "you're unreadable, say again slowly."

There is silence until another flight calls in. "Center, did you hear the transmission where that plane said he had a bomb on board?"

"Uh, say again," the controller responds. "Was that United 93?"

"Yeah, the transmission was unreadable," the pilot continues. "Sounded like they said someone had a bomb on board." [9]

"That's what we thought," the controller responds. "We just didn't get it clear." He immediately notifies the traffic management supervisor, who passes the information to the FAA Command Center that United 93 has a bomb on board.

The manager next notifies United Airlines' System Operations Center that controllers are unable to make contact with the flight. Dispatcher Ed Ballinger is already shell-shocked after losing United 175, and this news sends a wave of panic coursing through his body. This can't be! He'd just communicated with the flight crew a few minutes ago and they seemed fine!

He immediately fires off a message to the flight: "ATC looking for you on 133.37." Then he types in another: "Beware of any cockpit intrusion—two a/c [aircraft] hit World Trade Center." [10]

CHAPTER 10

The Pentagon Is Hit!

NEADS, Rome, New York, 9:20 a.m.

While United 93 is being hijacked and American 77 is being identified as another possible hijack, the team at NEADS is struggling to make sense of the extremely limited information they're receiving. Shortly after the news goes out that American 77 is lost, Boston Center controller Colin Scoggins, who has been listening to the FAA headquarter's hijack teleconference, hears Washington Center announce that American 11 is still airborne and is headed for Washington. Perhaps he heard wrong, or perhaps Washington Center misspoke, but Scoggins immediately picks up his phone to notify NEADS of the startling information that American 11 is apparently still in the air. NEAD's ID tech Stacia Rountree picks up the line.

"Scoggins, Military, Boston Center," Scoggins says, hastily identifying himself. "I just got a report that American 11 is still in the air, and it's on its way towards—heading towards Washington."

"Okay. American 11 is still in the air?" Rountree responds.

"Yes."

"On its way towards Washington?" she asks incredulously.

"It was evidently another aircraft that hit the tower," Scoggins clarifies. "That's the latest report we have."

"Okay."

"I'm going to try to confirm an ID for you, but I would assume he's somewhere over, uh, either New Jersey or somewhere further south," Scoggins adds.

"Okay," Rountree answers, somewhat confused. "So American 11 isn't the hijack at all then, right?"

"No, he is a hijack," Scoggins urges.

"He—American 11 is a hijack?"

"Yes."

"And he's heading into Washington?"

"Yes. This could be a third aircraft."

Hearing her technician repeat back this new information, MSgt. Maureen "Moe" Dooley wastes no time calling out the news to Mission Crew Commander Maj. Kevin Nasypany.

"Another hijack! It's heading towards Washington!"

"Shit!" Nasypany shouts. "Give me a location!"

He immediately reports to Marr. "Okay, American Airlines is still airborne. Eleven, the first guy, he's heading towards Washington. Okay? I think we need to scramble Langley right now, and I'm going to take the fighters from Otis and chase this guy down."

Marr advises him not to move the Otis fighters from New York—he does not want the city left unprotected—but he concurs about scrambling Langley. At 9:23 Nasypany directs Tech Sgt. Jeremy Powell, "Okay, scramble Langley. Head them towards Washington area. If they're there, we'll run on them. . . . These guys are smart."

"Roger that!" Powell responds. The order is processed and transmitted to Langley one minute later, at 9:24. The jets' heading will take them almost due north toward Baltimore, northeast of the capital, with the plan being that there they will provide a barrier to American 11, stopping it from entering Washington airspace.

Nasypany is prepared to chase the aircraft down and turn it away, or, if necessary, to take more aggressive measures to keep it from Washington. His focus now shifts to finding the flight: he needs his technicians to locate the plane so that his weapons team can pass on the coordinates to the Langley fighters. "I need more trackers!" he bellows.

But his trackers cannot find the transponder code for the flight anywhere on their radar screens. "These guys are in the cockpit," responds Maj. Steve Ovens, a Canadian MCC in training under Nasypany. "They're not going to squawk anything," he adds, using the military lingo for broadcasting a transponder signal. He knows they're making themselves invisible on purpose. The techs begin individually calling up each track on their screens in the airspace between New York and Washington, and attaching a tag to each after it's been identified.

Redoubling his efforts, one technician draws a line on a map, connecting New York to D.C., to see which areas he must include in his new search: Philadelphia, Atlantic City, and Baltimore. *Now I've got to deal with all that?* he thinks. Staring at his console and the hundreds of radar tracks in that area, the task seems almost impossible. He can't shake the thought that he is living through another Pearl Harbor.

A call now comes into MCC tech Joe McCain from CONR headquarters in Florida, where General Arnold and his staff are trying to gather as much information as possible. They need to know the transponder codes for the Otis jets so that they can monitor their position. "Send it out on chat," the CONR officer requests.

The NORAD chat system is similar to the chat rooms on most Internet servers, but classified. Anyone with proper access can enter one of three chat rooms: NEADS, which connects ID, Surveillance, and Weapons to its alert squadrons and where NEADS gets status reports on fighter units and their aircraft; CONR, where all the CONR sectors—NEADS, SEADS, and WADS—communicate, and where the sectors write messages to "upchannel" information to CONR command; and the Air Warfare Center—or AWC— where the senior NORAD commanders from the three NORAD regions—CONR, Canada, and Alaska—communicate. NEADS is not allowed to type on that one, only to monitor it. When an exercise such as the one that had been scheduled for this morning is going on, there are also one or two additional chat windows open for exercise information to be passed around, helping to keep it from being confused with real-world information.

It is McCain's responsibility as the MCC tech to coordinate people, agencies, and Operational floor sections, and also to monitor the chats and keep paper logs of everything that is happening. He is also supposed to be taking care of the ever-dreaded upchanneling of operational reports to higher headquarters. The fact that CONR has had to call McCain to get information that by now he would normally have posted alerts him that he is falling behind despite his best efforts. These chat logs help to keep everyone on the same page, but in a situation like the one unfolding they have to be updated almost instantaneously to achieve that end.

Nearby, Nasypany is focused on what to do about American 11. As the mission crew commander, he cannot afford to simply deal in the present. He has to be concerned with what is coming *next*. That, he now realizes, may well be the need to order his fighters to fire on a commercial airliner. He needs to know if his troops are prepared to follow that order, so he makes his way across the Ops floor, directing the same pointed question to each Weapons tech and their team leader.

"Are you prepared to follow an order to shoot down a civilian airliner?" he demands. He needs to know *right now*.

Each of them affirms that he will give the order, and satisfied that he has the right men in place to do the job, Nasypany gets on the shout line with Marr.

"Have we already asked the questions?" Nasypany asks, referring to possible authorizations to take out an airliner. Those authorizations, he knows, are going to have to come from the president himself, passed down from senior NORAD command in Colorado Springs. Marr assures Nasypany that General Arnold is seeking those authorizations and is prepared to take any necessary action. He inquires about the armament on board the fighters.

Nasypany responds with the weapons configurations, then goes further: "My recommendation, if we have to take anybody out—

large aircraft—we use AIM-9s in the face. If need be." Marr notes the recommendation but does not respond.

Just a few feet away stands the NEADS chaplain, lovingly nick-named "Reverend Rambo." On any other day, he can be found handing out lollipops. He's discovered that they're the perfect ice-breaker: offer people a sucker and they instantly feel comfortable unloading their troubles.

This morning he is loitering with intent. He's aware that in the midst of this storm, he can bring at least a modicum of calm and peace. For hours, he will stand silently in meditation and prayer, looking around him at the troops. Every now and then, when he senses the need from one of his airmen, he moves from the center of the floor to offer a gentle pat on the shoulder.

In the battle cab, on a secured line with General Arnold, Marr asks about shoot-down authority.

119th Fighter Wing Alert Detachment, Langley AFB, Virginia, 9:24 a.m.

In the alert hangar at Langley Air Force Base, two of the three F-16s are at battle stations. Capt. Craig "Borgy" Borgstrom, having gone to call his commander in Fargo about his being called to fly, is just climbing the ladder of his fighter when the alert claxon blares and his heart jumps. He looks over to the status light on the wall of the hangar, and sure enough, it has turned from yellow to green. NEADS has issued a scramble order.

He rushes to fasten himself into his ejection seat and connect his oxygen. On the opposite end of the alert hangar, Maj. Lou Derrig starts his engine, wholly unaware that Borgy—even though he was slated to act as SOF today—has also been ordered to fly. The pilots know only that a plane has hit the World Trade Center, and they're mentally prepared to launch toward New York, not at all expecting to be sent to protect Washington.

"Quit check," Eckmann calls, indicating a radio check for his wingmen as he pulls out of the barn.

"Two," Lou responds.

"Three," Borgy interjects. "I'm going with you!"

Lou is stunned. *What am I missing?* He's a full-time instructor pilot for the Air National Guard and not much surprises him, but this does.

As they taxi toward the runway, the thought occurs to Eckmann that he is not actually authorized to lead more than one fighter. He has not yet qualified as a "four-ship" or mission commander. *Shit!*

"Hey, I'm only a two-ship!" he radios to the others.

Lou is not sure just what is going on, but whatever it is, it's clear to him that NEADS wants—needs—all three of them airborne. He's not going to deal in technicalities just now.

"Press! I'm an instructor," he responds, directing Eckmann to continue and not to worry about it. Authorized or not, he's giving his okay for the flight to operate as a three-ship under Eckmann's lead.

The crew chiefs and mechanics watch, bewildered, as all three pilots taxi out. They've just been left with no commanding officer in the midst of a situation completely foreign to them.

Taxiing out to the runway, the two alert F-16s are carrying live-loaded missiles, while Borgy's spare has guns only. His six-barrel 20 mm gun is capable of firing 6,000 rounds per minute, but it requires close range and it's no air-to-air infrared-homing missile. The Command Post forwards the scramble instructions from NEADS: 010 to 20,000, max subsonic (heading just east of North, altitude 20,000, speed assignment just below supersonic). That heading will take the fighters just north of Washington, D.C., where they can intercept the incoming plane. The pilots, and NEADS, have no idea that the aircraft they are looking for is not American 11 but American 77, and it's closing in on Washington airspace *fast*.

As with any alert facility, any time the jets are scrambled, orders are sent out over a scramble hotline to nearby facilities as well as to the command post at the alert site itself. In this case, those other facilities include area FAA (Langley tower, Oceana Approach, and Washington Center) and Giant Killer, the Navy air traffic control agency that handles all over-water military operations. This way, they can all participate in clearing their airspace to make way for the fighters. Ultimately, however, the FAA owns the civilian airspace and directs the jets. Although Marr made the decision to declare AFIO in New York and take over the handling of the Otis jets, the Langley fighters are still being handled by the FAA as a standard military scramble.

Eckmann and his wingmen don't need the entire length of the runway to take off, so as he approaches Runway 26 at taxiway India for a quick intersection departure, he calls to the tower for takeoff clearances.

"Hold for an air traffic delay," the tower controller responds. The Washington Center controllers have not had time to clear airliners out of the way for the northerly heading. Dozens of aircraft at various altitudes fill the jets' route.

"We're an active air scramble," Eckmann impatiently objects after a two-minute wait. "We need to go *now!*"

"Roger, Quit flight is cleared for takeoff, 090 for 60," the tower controller responds at 9:30, directing the fighters to fly due east for 60 miles.

Eckmann knows that the scramble calls for a northerly heading, but he assumes they are being vectored eastward in order to fly around the traffic in their way. He doesn't second-guess the instructions; he assumes that the controllers have more information than he does. The jets' targets are customarily out over the ocean, and this is the customary routing for active air scrambles from the base. He has no way of knowing just how different this scramble order is.

The three-ship launches in rolling takeoffs, 15 seconds apart, with Eckmann out in front and the others following in a half-mile trail. Leaving his F-16 in afterburner, Eckmann is quickly approaching Mach 1, when his jet will go supersonic and break the sound barrier. Lou calls out to him.

"Hey, they said max subsonic!"

Eckmann had heard "max speed," but now he brings the thrust back to "mil" (reduced) power to avoid going supersonic. The three-ship flies eastward just under that speed, out over the ocean. Neither Eckmann nor NEADS has any idea that the coordination has broken down and that air traffic controllers have given the fighters the standard scramble routing rather than the direction handed down from NEADS.

While the Weapons controllers anxiously wait to see the radar tracks of the fighters appear on their screens, in the NEADS battle cab Lt. Col. Dawne Deskins has been searching for the plane they think is American 11. She's just spotted a suspicious track on her radarscope. Watching for a few seconds, she realizes that the track is a fast-moving primary target, and that it's circling Washington.

Air Traffic Control, Reagan National Airport,
Washington, D.C., 9:30 a.m.

It's been a hectic morning, to say the least, in the control tower at Reagan National Airport. The weather is perfect and controllers are using all three intersecting runways to depart and land aircraft. It's quite the juggling act. For much of the morning, tower controller Eric Cole had battled with a private pilot with an Arab accent in a banner-tow airplane.

"Go further south!" Cole had instructed repeatedly.

"Okay, I'm going further south."

"No, you're *not* going further south! I can *see* that you're not going further south!" Cole finally yelled at him. But the guy just wouldn't give up. He kept busting into the airspace and asking to get closer to the city. Banner-tow airplanes in this area were almost unheard of, and Cole couldn't figure out why the guy was so persistent, almost argumentative.

Just before 9 a.m. they learned that a plane had flown into the World Trade Center. Like so many others, they had thought "small plane" until they heard the shocking news that the other tower had been hit. Then a ground-stop order came in for all flights to and through New York. Shortly after, they got the word to start securing the airspace around the capital and to turn away all nonairliner aircraft, such as private planes, which were considered high risk. They were happy to kick the annoying banner-tow pilot out of the airspace for good. Then came the exceptionally unusual ground-stop order one minute ago, which calmed things. There would be no more takeoffs, regardless of destination.

Moments later, the phone rings and it's American Airlines calling to say that they don't want any of their planes going anywhere.

"Don't worry," the tower controller says. "No one's going anywhere!"

Several stories below the tower, in a secured portion of the lower level of the National Airport terminal, the last half hour has truly been hell for the controllers in the Terminal Radar Approach Control, or TRACON. They guide aircraft within a 30-mile range into and out of the Washington airports. Departure controller Dan Creedon is relieved at the news of the ground stop. Cloistered in the darkened, windowless TRACON facility, without a television, he feels as if the whole world must know more than he does about what's going on this morning. He has no details; he knows only that two planes have crashed into the World Trade Center. He has a sinking feeling in his gut and is working hard to focus.

At 9:32, the TRACON phone rings and it's the Dulles Airport control tower, 22 miles to the west-northwest of them. In response to Ben Sliney's request that facilities search for the primary target for American 77, they have been scouring their screens and they've just found an unidentified blip, heading right toward the White House.

While one controller notifies the Command Center, another gets on the line to Washington's TRACON. "Hey!" the Dulles controller bellows over the phone line, "untracked target 15 west of you. Primary target eastbound! Heading toward P-56!"

P-56 is the restricted airspace around the White House. Creedon is shocked when he checks his console and sees the target just southwest of the city. It's at the intersection of Interstate 66 and the Capital Beltway, just about 10 miles west of the White House. The radar return is untagged, so he quickly attaches a data box with the word "LOOK" in it, allowing controllers to spot it right away. As soon as he attaches it, the aircraft's ground speed appears: 250 knots (290 miles per hour). At that speed, the plane will reach the White House in approximately 2 minutes.

"Hey, Vic!" he yells to his supervisor. "Look at this guy! He's coming right toward us!"

The supervisor takes one look and immediately picks up the direct line to the Secret Service. There's no time to communicate with anyone else. This plane poses an immediate threat, and the Secret Service has the authority to evacuate key officials and buildings. At this point, the target begins to turn south. "We have a target 5 west," he reports. "He's turning south but he's still on our scope. We're not talking to him. It's definitely a suspicious aircraft." They had thought the plane was headed toward the White House, but with its turn south, they're not so sure what its target is. How are people going to evacuate from so many possible targets in time?

While his supervisor reports to the Secret Service, Creedon, intently monitoring his scope, notices that a Minnesota Air National Guard C-130 cargo plane is climbing westbound through 3,000 feet just east of the airport. It's just taken off from Andrews Air Force Base, and it's heading right toward the unidentified incoming plane. This is a very real collision threat. "You'd better call that guy!" he says to the controller next to him.

"Gofer 0-6," the controller transmits to the C-130 pilot, using the aircraft's assigned call sign, "traffic at your 11 o'clock, 4 miles, eastbound. Do you have it in sight?"

Well, that's an understatement! C-130 pilot Steve O'Brien thinks. All he knows of the day's events is that some small plane had crashed into the World Trade Center; he learned that while he was doing his flight planning. Until this radio call, and his subsequent glance up to see an aircraft coming toward him, he was enjoying a great view of the Mall, pointing out the sights to his copilot.

"Affirmative, Gofer 0-6 has him in sight," he responds. *And he's filling up my cockpit window!* he'd like to add for emphasis. The aircraft has now begun making a very aggressive, descending turn.

"Can you tell us what kind of airplane he is?" the controller asks.

"Yes sir," O'Brien responds. "It looks like a 757 with a silver fuselage . . . probably American Airlines."

"Can you tell us what he's doing?"

"Yes sir, he's descending," O'Brien reports, startled by the increasing oddity of the conversation. Controllers are supposed to know such things. "He's in a turn to the southeast."

The controllers watch the suspicious plane for a few moments as it continues its turn, south and away from the city and the airport.

"Do you still have that airplane in sight?" the controller then asks O'Brien. But by now it's moved off to the C-130's right side, and O'Brien can't see him.

"Yeah," his copilot responds, looking out his window, "I still got him in sight."

"That's affirmative," O'Brien reports.

"Gofer 0-6, we need you to follow that airplane!"

What? In his twenty-something years of flying, O'Brien has never been asked to do anything like this. His is a transport plane, not a fighter. His copilot, Lt. Col. Bob Schumacher, obediently rolls the C-130 into a descending right turn to follow the airliner.

Creedon's mind is reeling. *How did terrorists get a hold of a 757?* Up to this moment that thought would have been inconceivable to him.

NEADS, Rome, New York, 9:30 a.m.

At NEADS Tech Sgt. Jeremy Powell calls the Langley SOF to give him additional information about what his fighters should do. The jets will need to know that their mission is to set up a combat air patrol over Washington and intercept a hijacked civilian airliner headed toward the city. But the phone just rings and rings. Borgy isn't there to answer.

When a sergeant finally picks up and Powell asks to speak to his SOF, the sergeant responds, almost nonchalantly, "Oh, he's not here."

"Yeah, right," Powell says. "I need to speak to the SOF."

"He's not here!" the sergeant snaps back.

This is an active air scramble, and Powell knows that the alert detachment has ground crews, pilots, *and* a SOF on duty 24/7. He's just scrambled them! *What does this guy mean "He's not here!"?* "This is Huntress and I need to talk to your SOF *now*!" he shouts.

"He's one of the three that got airborne!" the flustered sergeant explains. But this makes no sense to Powell.

"Three? I only scrambled two!"

"No, he took off in a spare jet."

Powell leans back in his chair to absorb what he's just heard and what it means. The order to send all three jets hadn't gone through him. He's speechless. "Wow . . . okay," he finally answers, hanging up the phone. There is no direct communication between the battle cab and the Weapons controllers. Marr and the other senior officers in the battle cab do as they see fit, and communicate as necessary with Nasypany, the mission crew commander in charge of the Ops floor. Powell simply follows the orders passed from Nasypany to the senior director and then to the Weapons crew. The officers in the battle cab certainly don't owe him any explanations, but Powell sees the implications in what they have done. *The battle cab has taken serious measures to increase our air power.*

"Hey, Langley's got three of them airborne now, not two!" he says to the controller next to him.

A few feet away, NEADS Staff Sgt. William Huckabone now picks up the radar returns of the Langley F-16s and notices that rather than heading north as directed, they're heading straight out over the water. They appear to be flying to military training area Whiskey 386. He points this out to fellow Weapons Director MSgt. Steve Citino, then immediately gets on the phone with Giant Killer, the controlling authority for offshore military airspace. He can't get word to the jets through their SOF—he's flying! And NEADS has no direct method of contacting the jets, as they are out of radio range over the ocean in Giant Killer's airspace. Protocol dictates that Giant Killer direct the jets until they reach Washington Center's airspace, where the FAA controllers take over. NEADS is not an air traffic control facility. They own the jets but not the airspace. It is the controlling agency's responsibility to get the fighters where NEADS wants them without colliding with civilian aircraft on the way.

"Those fighters need to go north toward Baltimore, and now!" Huckabone tells the Giant Killer controller.

Unfortunately, the Navy controller doesn't seem to grasp the urgency of the circumstances.

"You've got Quit flight [the Langley F-16s] moving east in airspace. Now you want 'em to go to Baltimore?" he asks.

"Yes, sir," Huckabone responds. "We're not going to take 'em to Whiskey 386."

"Okay, once he goes to Baltimore, what are we supposed to do?"

"Have him contact us on auxiliary frequency 234.6. . . . Tell Center they've got to go to Baltimore."

"All right, man. Stand by. We'll get back to you," the controller responds.

There doesn't seem to be an appropriate degree of hurriedness in the controller's voice, and Huckabone can't contain his frustration. He has no desire to provide route clearance and aircraft separation for the fighters—that's not his job—but he *does* need them heading in the right direction, and he needs to be able to get them their mission details.

"I'm going to choke that guy!" he snarls after hanging up the phone. He watches on his screen, furious, as the fighters continue their trek out over the ocean.

Moments later, Boston Center controller Colin Scoggins calls NEADS to report that he has just heard on the FAA teleconference that an aircraft is closing in on Washington.

"Latest report," he begins, "aircraft VFR [visual flight rules: not in contact with air traffic control], 6 miles southeast of the White House, deviating away."

Nasypany doesn't yet know that the Langley F-16s he has scrambled are heading out to sea. He orders his senior director, Major James "Foxy" Fox, to direct the jets to the White House.

"Okay, Foxy. I got an aircraft 6 miles east of the White House! Get your fighters there as soon as possible!" he orders.

"Do you want us to declare AFIO?" Foxy inquires, aware of the difficulties with airspace controlling authorities this morning.

"Take 'em and run 'em to the White House," Nasypany directs. As for AFIO, he's done it in New York and he'll do it in Washington— he'll assume the responsibility for keeping his fighters away from other aircraft. "I want AFIO *right now*!"

"We're going direct D.C. with my guys," Foxy reports to his team. "Tell Giant Killer that we're going AFIO!" Weapons Director Citino attempts to contact the fighters directly.

"Quit 2–5, Huntress!" he calls urgently to Langley flight leader Dean Eckmann, using his call sign. "Squawk AFIO, 7777, direct 330!" But he gets no response; the fighters are not yet in radio range. While Citino keeps trying, Huckabone gets on the radio with Giant Killer and declares the AFIO. "Ma'am, we are going AFIO right now with Quit 2–5. They are going direct Washington."

"We're handing 'em off to [Washington] Center right now," she responds, offering only modest reassurance that the fighters will now be given the appropriate clearance.

"Ma'am, we need that expedited right now!" Huckabone urges. "We need to contact them on 234.6. . . . *Do you understand?*" he demands. Next to Huckabone, Citino finally reaches Borgy on the radio. The fighters are finally within radio range.

"Squawk quad-sevens and head 010!" he calls to Langley F-16 pilot Borgy, directing him to dial 7777—the code for AFIO—into his transponder. Instantaneously, Borgy is on the radio to Eckmann.

"Huntress wants you to squawk quad-sevens and head 010!"

The declaration of AFIO startles Eckmann. He has never, in all his years of flying, received such an order. He's only heard about it and, to him, it means no less than the start of World War III.

The planes have by now flown nearly 60 miles out over the ocean and they are 150 miles from Washington. Even flying supersonic, it will take them nearly 9 minutes to get over Washington airspace.

Meanwhile at NEADS, one of the techs spots the track for American 77 and sees that it's now just a handful of miles south of the White House, heading north.

"Right here, right here, right here!" he calls out. "I got him. I got him!"

"Get me coordinates!" Nasypany barks. He picks up the phone to quickly brief Marr in the battle cab, then turns back to his senior director, Foxy.

"Where's Langley at?" he demands. "Where are the fighters?"

"They're in [Whiskey] 386 and going up north," Foxy responds.

"Why'd they go there?"

"Giant Killer sent them out there."

Nasypany is dismayed to learn that they are out over the Atlantic and authorizes Foxy to order them supersonic. "I don't care how many windows you break," he yells. "Goddammit! Okay. Push them back!"

**102nd Fighter Wing, Otis Air National Guard Base,
Cape Cod, 9:35 a.m.**

While NEADS command struggles to get fighters to Washington, the Otis alert jets sent to New York are keeping a tight clamp on the airspace over the city. When Otis pilots Duff and Nasty arrived over New York City at 9:25, Duff established a "point defense" that he thought would best protect the city. He decided that one F-15 would remain over the city at all times while the other flew intercepts, flying up close to any planes that entered the airspace and steering them away. They wouldn't commit "out"—leave the immediate area to investigate targets of interest farther away—because that would leave the city unprotected. They had decided to let the enemy come to them.

The process is keeping them extremely busy; dozens of airliners are still in the airspace, in addition to all kinds of helicopters and smaller aircraft that are not on filed flight plans. The interception process is standard: Duff or Nasty pulls up uncomfortably close alongside the unsuspecting aircraft that has flown into New York airspace and rocks his wings. Military pilots are accustomed to flying nice and close, but for a civilian or commercial pilot, such proximity is absolutely unnerving. On a rare occasion, Duff and Nasty are able to communicate by radio, on the "Guard" frequency, which is for emergencies but which many pilots monitor while en route. On most intercepts, though, to turn an aircraft away they fly right across its nose, an unmistakable way of saying "You need to go this way!" When instead they want a plane to follow, they fly up close and then turn off in the direction they want the aircraft to fly, as a way of saying "Follow me this way."

If the intercepted pilot is slow to understand, Duff or Nasty repeats the process, but approaches even closer, utilizing the more intimidating method of "nudging" the pilot in the direction he needs to turn. In such cases, the pilots get the point immediately.

By now their fuel gauges are sinking lower, and they need to find a tanker right away that can air refuel them. They've been waiting for word from NEADS, but now Nasty figures out a solution. Because he was acting as the scheduling officer before he was put on alert duty, he knows that the training exercise that the Otis jets had been scheduled to fly today called for refueling, and for that reason there's a KC-135 tanker from Bangor, Maine, that should be available. By now, Nasty knows, it should be en route to military area Whiskey 105, where it had been scheduled to rendezvous with the Otis fighters on their training mission about 20 minutes from now.

"Duff, we have a tanker scheduled for the training missions this morning off the coast in 105," he calls.

That's my tanker now, Duff thinks. He calls NEADS to request that the tanker orbit at 20,000 feet right over JFK Airport. Within minutes, NEADS has coordinated with Bangor to borrow their tanker and Duff and Nasty are taking turns refueling.

Back at NEADS, Nasypany has already ensured that his Weapons Team is prepared to give shoot-down orders; now he checks that the pilots are willing to execute those orders. He directs the Otis Weapons controller to radio Duff with a bone-chilling inquiry.

"If we get another hijack track, you're going to be ordered to shoot it down," he says. "Do you have a problem with that?"

"No—no problem with that," Duff responds, somewhat taken aback by the question. *If I have a problem with that order*, he thinks, *I am in the wrong seat*. He's doing what he's been trained to do. He's just never trained to do it over America, or against civilian aircraft. But if he gets a legal, lawful order to take out an airliner, then that's what he's going to do. He knows every other fighter pilot would do the same. It might be hard to live with afterward, but he'll follow orders nonetheless.

Duff and Nasty know this war routine. Compartmentalizing their emotions, they steadfastly continue to pursue their targets. They are confident no plane will get past them: they'll do what it takes, and follow any order, to protect New York.

Back at the Otis base on Cape Cod, commanders have been

taking decisive action. Shortly after the impact of United 175 into the South Tower, they reconvened in the Operations Building, where the Installation Operations Center (IOC) sprang to life as officers took their posts. At the core of the IOC is the glass-enclosed battle cab, where the senior commanders gathered around a large conference table, overlooking the two main operations centers: the Command Post, where the air war is coordinated, and the Survival Recovery Center, where the support functions for around-the-clock operations are handled (security, food, lodging, medical care, etc.).

Senior commanders conferred with intelligence officers in the battle cab to attempt to bring order to the chaotic circumstances. "We need to start doing some things preemptively," Logistics Group Commander Lt. Col. Paul Worcester declared.

As a part of 1st Air Force, Otis is highly responsive to direction from NEADS—they've got a pair of jets under NEADS command at all times—and NEADS would normally be down-channeling information to them to keep them apprised of the situation. But NEADS is accustomed to "symmetrical" threats: concrete, well understood, and definable. They have never confronted an enemy like this, and they are working furiously to grasp the nature and extent of the threat. They have not yet been able to determine what assets they will need, or where they may need them. Cities? Which ones? Military installations? Nuclear power plants? They have not had time to down-channel *any* information to Otis.

The Otis commanders decided to "lean forward" in anticipation of what they *might* be called upon to do. But there has never been an air attack on America, and there is no protocol in place to tell them how to respond. They knew intuitively that they could not wait on guidance from the higher echelons of NORAD. This attack could easily expand, and they needed to be prepared. Taking their places at the conference table, they quickly established their agenda: recall all training flights and begin loading fuel and weapons onto all available fighters. The officers smoothly undertook the task of transitioning to a wartime posture.

Ever since the Aircraft Maintenance Squadron officer watched the second crash into the World Trade Center, he had been waiting for orders. It's his job to get the aircraft ready for combat, and he'd been fully expecting that the remaining Otis jets would be called into action. Less than 15 minutes after the second impact into the World Trade Center, the order came.

"Listen," an officer from the battle cab directed, "I want you to generate as many airframes [fighters] as you can!"

Immediately he began directing all manpower to the flight line to prepare the base's 18 F-15s for combat. The six jets that were in the air on training missions also had to be brought back to base immediately.

When the jets arrive at the base 20 minutes later, the pilots receive harried radio instructions as they taxi in. "Cock your jets for alert!" Squadron Commander Lt. Col. Jon "Tracer" Treacy calls. "Cock your jets for alert!" Rather than park and shut down their fighters as they normally do, they are being instructed to prepare their jets to be scrambled from the flight line, with all of their instruments, controls, and switches set for immediate takeoff orders. The pilots have never been ordered to do such a thing.

After preparing their jets as ordered, they jog quickly into the Operations Building to find out what's up. There they gather around the television in the break room just inside the door. They stare at the screen in amazement.

121st Fighter Squadron, DCANG, Andrews AFB, Maryland, 9:30 a.m.

Meanwhile the military machinery of the D.C. Air National Guard at Andrews Air Force Base has also been ramping up into full gear. The intelligence officer has gone to his "intel vault" in search of message traffic on the SIPRNET, the Department of Defense's classified version of the civilian Internet. He's on the phone with anyone he can think of who might have more information: Air Combat Command Intelligence Squadron at Langley, the 9th Air Intelligence

Squadron at Shaw Air Force Base in South Carolina, Washington's FBI field office, the White House Joint Operation Center (JOC). *Someone must know more than me!* he thinks. He feels as though he is spinning his wheels, calling one agency after another. He can't seem to find out anything more than what he's seen on TV. As DCANG is a general purpose F-16 unit, no one is specifically tasked with keeping the squadron informed. Like other nonalert units, they train to deploy overseas.

Maj. Razin Caine, who had called his contact at the Secret Service earlier to see if they needed any fighter assistance, is at the SOF desk when, as he expected, he gets a call from the Secret Service at the White House JOC. They now need the squadron's help, urgently. They've just learned from the Washington TRACON at Reagan National Airport Center that a suspect aircraft is 5 miles east of the White House, turning south. "Can you guys do anything?" the agent wants to know. "Can you get some fighters in the air as soon as possible?"

At Operations with Razin, the 121st Fighter Squadron Commander Lt. Col. Marc "Sass" Sasseville knows his fighters are unarmed, equipped with training rather than live ordnance. Worse, most of their pilots are back at their airline jobs, having just returned three days before from two weeks of the large-scale training exercise "Red Flag" at Nellis Air Force Base in Las Vegas. They have only seven pilots available, and three are on a training mission in North Carolina.

Razin has already sent word to the refueling tanker to send the three-fighter training sortie home, but now the jets are needed immediately and they aren't back in radio range yet. He has 15 jets on base and four pilots, and he's going to get those planes armed and in the air immediately. Preparing, Sass calls over to the wing commander to get a sign-off on the loading up of war-reserve missiles. Such missiles are never touched, but are kept operational and in minimal numbers for nonalert wings like the D.C. Guard to allow for contingencies such as this. The wing commander gives the go-ahead, and Razin calls to the "bomb dump" across the base and barks out, "Get some live AIM-9s and bring them over!"

That will take some time, though. The missile-laden trailer will need a security escort and has a speed limit of 8 mph. It will take an excruciating 45 minutes for the missiles to arrive at the flight line.

"Speed!" Razin tells them.

At the same time Sass calls the maintenance officer to order that the jets on base be readied for launch. The capital's best defense for now lies with the three fully armed Langley alert F-16s that are in the air, but they are still miles out over the ocean.

**Air Traffic Control, Reagan National Airport,
Washington, D.C., 9:32 a.m.**

Oblivious to the discovery by TRACON controller Dan Creedon several stories below that an errant airliner has been spotted circling Washington, tower supervisor Chris Stephenson picks up a ringing phone in the control tower at Reagan National Airport. It's one of the maintenance guys calling to see if he can bring a small tour group up to the tower. They're FAA guys from headquarters, there to go over some maintenance issues, but they're curious about how things work up there in the tower. They apparently haven't heard about the morning's events. *Now?* Stephenson thinks. He's dealing with the chaos caused by the Command Center's ground stop, and the timing couldn't be worse.

"Yeah," he answers begrudgingly, "but I'm not going to have any time to talk to them. You're going to have to deal with them."

They arrive moments later, and Stephenson does his best to ignore them, even though they're standing right behind him. Meanwhile, 200 feet below in the TRACON, Creedon intently watches the flight path of American 77 and the C-130 that is now following it. The C-130 pilot, Steve O'Brien, is trying to maintain visual contact with the plane, but it's not easy in the sunny haze. He catches only sporadic glimpses of the aircraft's metallic frame as it continues its descending turn. Given its flight path, O'Brien figures the airliner has experienced an in-flight emergency and is returning to the airport.

Creedon watches as the airliner travels almost 10 miles south of the airport and then, ominously, begins a turn back toward the city. Once again, it appears to be directly lined up with the White House. He hears his supervisor on the phone again to the Secret Service.

"What I'm telling you, buddy," the supervisor barks, "if you've got people, you'd better get them out of there! *And I mean right goddamned now!*"

The controller next to him grabs the phone to call up to Stephenson in the tower. "See in the sky, 5 miles west of you?" he says when Stephenson answers. Glancing down at his radarscope, Stephenson identifies the target that he believes the TRACON controller is referring to. But it's the wrong one.

"No! The 'LOOK' tag! See the 'LOOK' tag? It's a 757!" he demands. "Do you see anything out there?"

Stephenson turns his 6-foot-2-inch frame around to look behind him out the southwestern side of the control tower. There it is! The plane is less than a mile from the control tower, coming in fast.

"Out! Get out!" Stephenson yells to the tour group.

They instantly turn to go down the stairs, but the last in line looks up points at the descending plane, and asks, "What's that guy doing?"

"GET OUT!" Stephenson roars at him, pushing him into the stairwell. The plane is clearly going to hit something, he just doesn't know what. The horrified controllers watch the airliner disappear behind the buildings of Crystal City to the west, and then they see an enormous fireball burst into the sky.

For several seconds, they just watch, astonished. Massive amounts of paper debris begin filling the air. The local controller assigned to the landing aircraft has the presence of mind to reach back to grab the crash phone, which instantly connects the tower to airport operations as well as the police and fire departments. "Aircraft down at the Pentagon! Aircraft down at the Pentagon!" he yells.

Stephenson calls down to the TRACON. "It was an American 757! It hit the Pentagon. It was a 757 and it hit the Pentagon. American!"

C-130 pilot O'Brien has witnessed the fireball close up, and when he is able to detect an outline of the Pentagon through all the smoke, he gasps. He still has no idea, though, that the crash was the third of this unprecedented morning, and that the country is under attack.

FAA Command Center, Herndon, Virginia, 9:36 a.m.

At 9:36, the Cleveland Center manager makes another call to the FAA Command Center to let them know that his controllers are still tracking United 93 and to ask if someone has requested military interception. He volunteers, if not, to contact the nearby military base in Toledo to make a request. The Command Center advises him that FAA personnel well above them in the chain of command are working the issue.

Ben Sliney's mind is reeling. Only a few minutes ago he received a call from Washington Approach Control that a plane with its transponder turned off had been spotted just miles to the west of Washington. He still has no idea if military jets are intercepting. Nothing is fitting into the scenario for hijackings up to this day; before this morning, hijackers had always commandeered aircraft to make political statements. They made demands for what they wanted: ransom, escape from the law, political asylum. Pilots and controllers were trained to deal with hijackers. The system seemed to work. *But today*, he thinks, *the hijackers don't want to go anywhere! They are bent on mass murder and suicide. Today they are on missions, and they are only looking for targets.* He's already ordered an unprecedented national ground stop; but he knows he must do more.

He sees Linda Schuessler, the manager of tactical operations, come onto the operations floor. She has been on the phone with headquarters and is holding a clipboard in her hand that outlines how she is reassigning everyone in order to help out. Sliney hasn't had a chance to speak with her since her confusion began.

"I am thinking about shutting everything down," he says. He is contemplating ordering all planes out of the sky.

"Do what you want," she says, waving him off with her hand. "*You* have the operation." Sliney is desperate for guidance from above, but he's still not getting it. Whatever decision he makes, he's going to have to do it on his own.

On the NMCC's "significant threat" conference call, operators have still been unable to bring the FAA into the call due to equipment problems. The systems run on two different secured networks, and they are incompatible. NORAD commanders on the teleconference have asked three times to confirm the presence of the FAA, but have received no reply.[1]

The FAA Command Center's teleconference is being monitored at FAA headquarters by a staff member who is forwarding information to Jane Garvey—still on the White House video conference lead by Richard Clarke—but this is not yet going to the NMCC or NORAD. While these higher-ups continue to struggle to comprehend the situation they are dealing with and to coordinate a response, those on the front lines are furiously taking action.

The Cleveland controller notices that United 93 is beginning to turn off course and begins to move nearby aircraft out of the way. "Executive 956," he instructs, "Turn left heading two-two-five. I'll get you away from him."

"He's climbing," he adds, "so I want to keep everybody away from him."

"Okay," the pilot responds, "I think we got him in sight."

Word arrives at United's Operations Center that a call has come in to the San Francisco maintenance office from a flight attendant on board United 93. The flight attendant reported that one hijacker has a bomb strapped to himself and another is holding a knife on the crew. The others are in the cockpit. Unlike the other hijacked flights, where few phone calls were made, following the takeover of United 93, ten passengers and two flight attendants are able to make phone calls on the seatback Airfones. As a result, vital information is relayed to those on the ground, and passengers learn about the other hijacked flights.

Ballinger sends out a final message to United 93 asking if dispatch can be of any assistance. In the United crisis center, supervisors isolate United 93 on the large Aircraft Situation Display screen 300 miles to the east of Washington. They watch as it makes a 180-degree turn placing it on a direct trajectory toward the city.

CHAPTER 11

Every Plane Out of the Skies!

Across the country, airports begin to close down as managers take steps to protect their airports and aircraft from terrorist threat. They don't know how hijackers are taking over planes and crashing them into buildings. Are pilots being apprehended in terminals and forced to fly? Have the pilot ranks been infiltrated by terrorists? And if airliners are being attacked, are airports also a target? They can't take any chances—none can risk being targeted. Across the United States, managers take steps to secure their facilities. Waves of evacuation orders begin, and thousands of passengers are rushed out of the terminals.

Midex 7, Milwaukee–LaGuardia, 9:35 a.m.

After a near-miss with United 175 and then an extended wait on the ramp at LaGuardia, staring at the inferno of the World Trade Center towers, Midex 7 is finally cleared to taxi to a gate. Capt. Gerald Earwood parks at the gate and notices a fellow pilot and some mechanics standing in the jetway. When his passengers have deplaned, Earwood walks over to talk to the group, eager to tell them about his experience and the fire at the World Trade Center. But the group is unaware of the happenings outside of the isolated jetway, and the pilot immediately begins telling Earwood about some troubles with his aircraft.

The more the group acts as though everything is normal, the

more Earwood feels as though he is stuck in a *Twilight Zone* episode. While they continue their benign conversation, Earwood takes out his cell phone and notices that he has three messages from his wife. They're all frantic—not at all customary for her—begging him to call her as soon as possible.

He steps aside from the other pilots and dials her number. "Thank God! Where *are* you?" she cries when she hears his voice on the line.

"I'm in New York," comes his bewildered response.

She proceeds to rattle off all that's happened. Earwood interrupts her to call out the information to the others on the jetway. Their shocked expressions say it all.

"Oh my God!" his wife wails. "Another aircraft has just hit the Pentagon!"

"Another just hit the Pentagon!" Earwood calls to the others. His colleague runs up toward the terminal while the mechanics quickly disappear out of the jetway's stair-door.

"I love you. I have to go!" Earwood calls to his wife, running back to his plane. His crew is busy getting the cabin ready for the next flight.

"Get your stuff and get off now!" he yells. He has a habit of joking and they all look up at him, smiling, figuring he's at it again.

"We are under attack by terrorists," he yells at them, "we have to get out of here!" Just then a Port Authority police officer comes onto the plane.

"Captain, we need you and your crew to evacuate the airport immediately."

Midex 270, Milwaukee–Newark, 9:40 a.m.

Having long since realized that his Milwaukee–Newark flight is not going to end up anywhere near New York today, Midwest Airlines Capt. Chuck Savall has finally convinced his flustered dispatcher that Grand Rapids is not an option and that he will divert to

Cleveland. He is quickly on the radio advising air traffic control of his intentions, and the controller promptly issues a new route as well as climb instructions. Savall initiates the climb and turns west, away from New York.

His first officer, listening simultaneously to the main radio frequency as well as a local radio station he tuned in trying to get more information, hears that a second aircraft has impacted the World Trade Center and there has been some kind of explosion at the Pentagon.

"And there's something about smoke at the White House," the announcer adds. The first officer calls out the news to Savall, who attempts to process the rapid influx of information. *One airplane hitting the World Trade Center would be freaky*, he thinks, *but two on the same morning and a third at the Pentagon can only mean one thing: an aggressive attack!*

His mind sifts through scenarios a million miles a minute: *What the hell am I involved in here? A country under attack by its own airliners . . . what does this mean? How large scale is it? Crap, are we possibly part of it? Is it bigger than just airplanes? Could this be an attack by another country's military, or possibly terrorists?* Savall arrives at a realization: *he* has become the enemy and every airliner in the sky is being treated as a potential threat.

It's time to say something to the passengers, he decides. On this idyllic day, it will take a mighty tall tale to justify why they cannot go to Newark, so he opts instead to tell them the truth.

"Well, folks," he begins, "you're no doubt wondering why we've turned around and started climbing again."

Disgruntled passengers grumble and fidget with annoyance as he continues.

"We've learned there has been an attack on our country . . . possibly two aircraft hitting the World Trade Center, and another attack at the Pentagon and the White House."

Gasps of shock and confusion echo through the cabin.

"We've been instructed to fly our aircraft as far from the East Coast as possible," he continues, "and are currently heading for

Cleveland. I'm not sure what awaits when we land there, but rest assured I'll keep you informed."

He releases his microphone, his heart pounding, and turns to his first officer. "Aviation as we know it," he says in a hoarse whisper, "has changed forever."

Up ahead in Cleveland Center's airspace, that same thought is occurring to Dave Dunlap.

Delta Airlines Flight 1989, Boston–Los Angeles, 9:40

Radio communications have been silent in the cockpit of Delta 1989 since the flurry of activity when United 93 was hijacked. Dunlap had heard it all on the radio. He stares out the cockpit window of the Boeing 767, his mind racing with thoughts about the hell those pilots are going through.

Pilots are taught that, in the event of a hijacking, the safety of the aircraft and its occupants is the primary consideration. If the plane is on the ground, a pilot is taught to attempt to disable the aircraft so that it cannot fly—or even use the emergency rope to escape the cockpit. The common thinking has been that a plane cannot go anywhere without the pilot. If airborne, the tactic is to keep things calm and under control and to take the hijackers where they want to go. If necessary, the pilots can permit a hijacker into the cockpit to keep a volatile or escalating situation under control. But the hijackings today are breaking all the rules.

He's jolted from his thoughts when he hears his flight's call sign on the frequency.

"Delta 1989, I have traffic for you at your 11 o'clock," the controller says, "15 miles southbound, 41 [41,000 feet] climbing, looks like he's turning east."[1] United 93 has turned around, and it's coming their way.

Dunlap and Captain Werner scour the skies for the aircraft, but they can't spot it. Then, out of nowhere, it flashes past, just above their left wing.

Just then, the hijackers get back on the plane's radio. "Ah, this is the Captain," a foreign voice says. "I would like you all to remain seated. There is a bomb on board and we are going back to the air-port, to have our demands met. Please remain quiet." [2]

"United 93 calling," the controller fires back. "United 93, under-stand you have a bomb on board. Go ahead." He gets no response.

"Executive 56, did you understand that transmission?" the con-troller calls to another flight on the frequency.

"Affirmative," the pilot replies. "He said there was a bomb on board."

"And that was all you got out of it also?"

"Affirmative," the pilot answers.

"93, go ahead," the controller tries again.

He begins to hand off his flights to other controllers so that he can invest his full attention in the hijacked flight. In the distraction of the emergency, the crew of Delta 1989 misses the hand-off to the new frequency. The new sector controller for Delta 1989 calls out to the plane several times and gets no response.

News travels fast. Soon, word on the FAA's open teleconference call is that a fifth aircraft is out of radio contact: Delta 1989, a Boe-ing 767 en route from Boston to Los Angeles, and the flight is added to the list of suspect aircraft.

Now an ACARS message arrives in the cockpit from Delta's Dispatch: "Land immediately in Cleveland." They've already passed Cleveland, but Captain Werner types in a quick "ok." He won't put up a fight, he just wants to get the plane on the ground.

After a couple minutes, another message arrives in the cockpit from Delta's Dispatch: "Confirm landing in Cleveland. Use correct phraseology."

Dunlap and Werner look at each other quizzically. *What the hell is that about?* There's such a thing as correct phraseology on the *radio*, but there is no such thing when typing back and forth with Dispatch on ACARS. Those messages are usually casual.

Flustered, the captain does his best to figure out what "correct phraseology" Dispatch is looking for. He carefully types a response: "Roger. Affirmative. Delta 1989 is diverting to Cleveland."

Dunlap is starting to really worry now. *They think something is going to happen to this plane,* he thinks to himself. *They're trying to figure out if we're still in control!*

Meanwhile, the captain calls up the Center controller to request an immediate diversion to Cleveland, and then starts inputting the new destination into the flight computer. Dunlap rolls the 767 into a 30-degree bank back toward the airport and pulls out his approach charts.

The Cleveland Center controllers are not happy that Delta 1989, which was out of radio contact for several minutes, has now made a turn toward the large city. They didn't initiate the diversion and they don't know that Delta Dispatch has done so. An abrupt change of course for a transcontinental B767 out of Boston raises further suspicion, and a supervisor announces the new development on the FAA teleconference.

In the cockpit of Delta 1989, Dunlap and Werner both heard the word that there was a bomb on United 93, and they are acutely aware that many bombs are designed to detonate with changes of altitude, so they are extremely tense about descending into Cleveland. What if *they* have a bomb on board? Maybe that's why everyone is treating them so strangely.

In training, pilots spend a lot of time imagining themselves in dire situations, having to figure out how to save the day. Dunlap, like most other pilots, has always put on that "Aw shucks, it's easy" routine, but the fact of the matter is that he takes the safety of his aircraft and the people in it very, very seriously. His worst fear as a pilot is that he will make a mistake and hurt people, or fail to think of the appropriate solution to a crisis.

As he starts the descent into Cleveland, he cannot shake the feeling that today is going to be *his* opportunity to save the day. *But how?* He focuses hard on flying and scanning his display screens while the captain does the busy work: talking on the radio, making sure the flight attendants are briefed, and ensuring that they haven't overlooked anything.

Dunlap is going over in his mind every detail he has ever learned about any system or procedure on this 767. If something catastrophic happens—if a bomb goes off or if someone tries to come through that cockpit door—he is damned if he is not going to make every effort to get the plane down. The one thing he refuses to be is fodder for some pilot training class for years to come, an example of "what not to do." He may not live to tell about it, but no one will be reading the transcripts of this cockpit flight recording and discussing his doomed flight to figure out what he should have done differently. He thinks of the captain of TWA 800, whose airplane broke in half after an explosion in the center fuel tank. The front portion of the 747, including the cockpit, had remained intact until impact, and the captain was found to have broken wrists and ankles when they recovered his body. Investigators determined that he was still trying to fly the plane when it hit the water. He never gave up, and neither would Dunlap. Nor would any pilot.

As hydraulic schematics and emergency procedures fill his head, he hears Cleveland Center on the radio.

"Delta 1989, I hear you're 'late' * today."

The controller has used the code word for hijack, the code that pilots use to signal to controllers when they are not able to communicate openly because hijackers are in the cockpit.

"Fuck!" Dunlap says out loud as he tightens his grip on the controls.

"Negative," the captain responds emphatically. "Delta 1989 is *not* a 'late.' "

"Let's just get this thing on the ground," he then says to Dunlap.

---

* The codeword has been changed to protect airline security procedures.

FAA Command Center, Herndon, Virginia, 9:42 a.m.

As reports of hijacked and missing planes continue to pour in, Ben Sliney seeks input from managers on the floor as well as the teleconference, which is now connecting all air traffic control facilities around the country. He stands in the main aisle of the command center, with tiered rows of western U.S. flight controllers on his left and eastern flight controllers to his right. The airline desks, military, and various technicians rise up on tiered rows behind him as he looks toward the 11-foot screens on the center's front wall. His instincts are telling him to get every plane out of the sky. *The skies are filled with guided missiles*, he thinks. *Filled with them!*

When the news arrives at 9:42 a.m. that a third aircraft has crashed into the Pentagon, he knows only one thing for sure: this must stop!

"That's it!" he yells, turning away from the screens. An FAA veteran and one of Sliney's dear friends is standing next to him, talking on the phone. The friend knows what Sliney is contemplating and fears the ramifications for Sliney's career. When Sliney turns to head up the center aisle, his colleague reaches out and grabs his shoulder.

"Ben, wait a minute," he says. "Do you want to think about this?"

"John, I've thought about it already," Sliney responds. "It's NOW."

He's not waiting anymore for approval from headquarters. On his first day on the job as the national operations manager he heads up the center aisle of the command center calling out a historical order.

"Clear the skies!" he commands, "Order everyone to land! Get everything on the ground—NOW!"

Within seconds, the specialists head to their consoles to send out the order to every air traffic facility in the country. For the first time in history, the government is ordering every aircraft out of the sky.

American Eagle 713, Dallas–Memphis, 9:50 a.m.

After 16 years with American Eagle Airlines, Capt. Kenneth Marczak has moved up the pilot ranks and now serves as a simulator instructor and check airman at the airline's training center. He's responsible for training new hires in the simulator and upgrading pilots from first officer to captain.

He regularly gets out of the simulator to keep his own flying skills sharp, and today he had chosen to fly a nice Dallas–Memphis–Dallas round trip since the Dallas airport was operating without delays.

Just after takeoff, he received a highly unusual communication from air traffic control.

"Everyone listen up," the controller said. "This is Fort Worth Center. The national airspace system is now closed. I need everyone to determine the closest airport at which your aircraft is capable of landing and begin making plans to divert there. I am going to call your numbers and I want you to tell me where you intend to land."

"What the hell is that all about?" Marczak had hissed. He scanned the horizon in search of a mushroom cloud or rocket contrails from a nuclear attack.

Another aircraft on the frequency asked the controller, "What's going on?" and got the curt reply, "I don't have time to talk about it. Contact your companies for more information."

Marczak typed a quick ACARS message to his company Dispatch, and they responded the same. "No time to talk about it," their ACARS message back read. "Let me know where you intend to go."

Marczak chose to divert to Memphis—after all, the folks in the back had paid to go there—and though several other flights were also diverting there, he seemed to be the first in line. He was glad. For the first time in his life, he was feeling truly afraid in an airplane.

When faced with trouble in the past Marczak had always managed to channel any apprehension into the process of problem solving. He might let himself feel a little fear later, after the situation had been resolved and he had time to reflect on its severity, but not at the moment. This time, as he approaches the Memphis airport, he is simply and utterly afraid.

His flight is indeed first in a long line to land and is quickly cleared to taxi to the terminal. When Marczak is guided into his gate, he notices the American Eagle gate agent preparing to drive the jet bridge over to the plane. She's crying, looking as if she is on the verge of hysteria, and mascara is running down her face. Marczak's fear mounts.

"We're at war!" he hears the bridge operator tell the flight attendant when she opens the main cabin door. "They are bombing New York!" Marczak's worst fears seem to be materializing.

The passengers are all attached to their cell phones as they deplane, spouting off bits of information and misinformation. "Some planes were shot down." "The White House was bombed." The parking checklist, required each time the aircraft is shut down, seems trivial and an almost impossible task with that kind of chatter in the background. Before he can complete the checklist, the ramp agent asks that he be ready to release the parking brake as soon as the passengers have deplaned. They need to move the aircraft off the gate to accommodate other inbound flights.

When Marczak releases the parking brake, he expects them to push the aircraft to a parking spot on the tarmac. Instead, the tug driver wedges it between the jet bridge and the terminal building. Marczak is dumbfounded to watch a B757 immediately pull into the same gate, blocking in his aircraft.

"What is happening here?" he demands of the ramp controller.

"We're going to be parking all the airplanes this way so that as many as possible are blocked by other aircraft and equipment," the controller responds. His fear rises yet again.

Just as he is completing the checklists, a police officer steps into the cockpit. "Take off your uniforms and come with me," he says to Marczak and his copilot.

"I have no intention of walking around the airport in my underwear!" Marczak retorts.

"No, not everything," the officer explains. "Just your shoulder board, ties, hats, wings . . . anything that makes you look like pilots."

Utterly confused, the pilots quickly comply. The police officer escorts them through the terminal, stopping at the nearest exit and telling them, "You need to leave the airport."

"What!" Marczak demands. "Leave? Where should we go?"

"All flight crews have to leave the airport immediately!" the officer responds.

"Can I at least go rent a car?" Marczak begs.

"No!" the officer barks. "You may not reenter the terminal." Marczak can tell by his body language that he will use force, if necessary, to get them out that door.

Shocked, but somehow managing to think clearly, he hails a cab. He doesn't know where he is going, but he figures that he might as well get there. He climbs into the taxi van with his first officer.

"Do you know where the American Airline crews stay in Memphis?" he asks the driver. The driver nods affirmatively and takes off. There is a television in the taxi and the crew is finally able to discover what's really been happening. The cab driver is silent while the crew soaks up the news.

From what they can tell, at least one plane has struck the World Trade Center and one has crashed in D.C. There is uncertainty about how many planes still in the air are hijacked. Then a video clip comes on confirming that two planes have hit the Trade Center towers. Marczak watches as they show the footage of the second impact over and over, and he begins to feel ill.

United 829, Boston–Chicago, 9:50 a.m.

The day has been going steadily downhill since United Capt. Rick Johnson first crossed the ramp at Boston Logan and felt goose bumps as he nodded to the first officer of the United 767 Flight 175 getting ready to push back from the gate. He had gotten over it and had enjoyed breakfast and an uneventful flight until he began hearing the nonstandard warnings from Boston Center.

He hasn't gotten any answers since he sent off an ACARS message to Dispatch asking "What's going on?" All he knows for sure is that he has heard two very unusual radio transmissions on his Boston Center frequency—FAA alerts—advising all aircraft to increase cockpit security. In his many years of flying he has never heard of an "FAA alert." Nor has he ever heard such a transmission. He would like some answers, but they don't seem to be forthcoming.

His routing to Chicago has him flying through Canadian airspace, and he's just been handed off to Toronto Center. Waiting for a break in the radio chatter so that he can check in, he hears the controller say something very odd. "You can't go to Detroit," he tells a Northwest flight, "Cleveland Center won't take you."

Johnson is thinking, *How strange*, when he hears the controller add, "New York Center won't take you either."

Johnson's first officer Tony Stella has tried to keep his cool as things have gone from bad to worse this morning, but these transmissions push him over the top.

"This is *really* fucked up!" he exclaims, "Something *bad* has happened!"

"It's probably just an overreaction to some minor bullshit," Johnson replies, trying to downplay things. But inside, he too is having his own worries.

Finally, an ACARS message arrives from Dispatch, a response to his inquiry. He looks down to read the same words he has already heard on the radio: "This is an FAA alert. Increase cockpit security."

"Well, this is just *not* very helpful," he says wryly. His agitation is increasing as his efforts to come to some understanding of these unusual events are met with a complete lack of information. Still, he's convinced that things will soon return to normal.

The frequency is much busier than usual and, when he finally gets a chance to check in with the new controller, they acknowledge him in the customary fashion.

"They seem fine here," he says to Stella.

But then another ACARS message arrives from Dispatch: "Land as soon as possible. Deplane the passengers normally."

With that, there is simply no room for denial. Johnson knows that something is very wrong. But what? His mind races: *Is this a threat specifically against our airplane? No, that can't be it, because we've heard other aircraft being told that they can't continue to their destinations. What, then? War? A nuclear attack? What?*

He can't formulate any likely scenarios, and he's becoming angry—angry at feeling so helpless, angry at not being in control, and angry that something major is under way and he isn't able to get answers. It's like flying blind and he doesn't like it, not one bit.

In another ACARS message, his dispatcher suggests Buffalo as a landing alternate. Why would he want to turn around and go back to New York? It's the wrong direction!

"Am I correct in assuming that we will not be able to proceed to Chicago?" Johnson asks Toronto Center.

"That is correct, sir," the controller replies.

"Can we turn around and go to Buffalo?" he asks.

"No sir, I have to keep you in my airspace. U.S. airspace is closed."

HOLY SHIT.

A controller has just informed him that he cannot reenter U.S. airspace. He can hardly believe what he's heard.

He's getting more irritated by the moment. The company is telling him to go to Buffalo, and Toronto Center is saying he can't go there. Now he can't even reenter the United States. Thankfully, he's carrying a lot of extra fuel this morning, "ferry fuel" they call it. Due to his irritation, he now makes a tactical error.

"Well," he responds to the controller, "just put us into holding, wherever you can. I have enough fuel to hold until *tomorrow* if I need to! I'm going to get a straight answer from somebody before I do anything!"

He had thought that perhaps this bold move might shift the information stalemate in his favor, but unfortunately Toronto is busier than they have ever been and they are more than happy to comply with this request. That makes one less aircraft for them to worry about.

"United 829, you are clear to hold at your present position," the controller instructs. Johnson's head drops to his chest. *Shit!* he thinks. *That was not what I was looking for!*

CHAPTER 12

Generate! Generate! Generate!

NEADS, Rome, New York, 9:45 a.m.

When news that American 77 has crashed into the Pentagon spreads on the NEADS Operations floor, the shock and fury are palpable.

"Goddammit! I can't even protect my NCA!" Maj. Kevin Nasypany yells, referring to the area around the White House, known to the military as the "National Capital Area."

Technicians and team leaders encourage each other to stay focused and keep their eyes off the televised coverage at the front of the room. There are three airplanes down already, and who knows how many more are out there.

Now another call arrives from Boston Controller Colin Scoggins. "Delta 1989, a Boeing 767 out of Boston, is also missing," he reports. The flight is out of communication with controllers.

"Delta 1989, that's a hijack," the ID tech taking the call announces. "They think it's a possible hijack! We have a squawk code on him now."

"Good! Pick it up! Find it!" her team leader orders. Then, in utter dismay, the team leader turns and bangs her fists on the counter.

Efforts to separate fact from fiction become increasingly difficult as reports of still more suspected hijackings pour in. The U.S. mainland has never been targeted, and, with only four dedicated fighters armed and prepared to defend at two alert sites on the East Coast, the challenge is both obvious and ominous. Inadequate resources combined with outdated equipment and communication systems have left the military little to work with. But failure is not an option.

At the NORAD headquarters for the continental U.S. region, CONR Commander General Arnold has been trying to piece together the nature and scope of the attack. It is his job to see the bigger picture and to anticipate scenarios that *could* materialize. Immediately after learning that the attack is no longer isolated to New York, he mobilizes all the nation's alert sites, contacting all of his sectors with unequivocal instructions: "Generate, generate, generate!" His meaning: Get as many fighters as you can into the sky now!

In response to the report about Delta 1989, a NEADS Weapons technician makes a call to the 127th Wing of the Selfridge Air National Guard Base in Michigan, which he knows has two F-16s in the air on a training mission. The fighters are unarmed and do not have large amounts of fuel, but the commander agrees to turn them over to NEADS, keeping them airborne so they can head south to intercept Delta 1989, which commanders believe to be heading for Chicago, possibly to the Sears Tower.

While the Weapons tech talks on the phone, MSgt. Joe McCain calls across the Ops floor with an update: "Delta [19]89! Hard right turn!" The technician knows that the Selfridge fighters may not be able to get to the plane in time, the 180th Fighter Wing in Toledo is much better positioned. He makes a call to the wing, where pilots have just returned from a training mission and are unaware of anything but a simple plane crash in New York, which they had heard about prior to their departure.

"We need you to scramble two airplanes right now," he says when F-16 pilot Ed "Gus" Rinke picks up the phone. But to Rinke, the order makes no sense. Toledo is not an alert squadron and does not report to NEADS.

"Hey, we've got a phone call at the duty desk," Rinke yells

down the hall. He's only a part-time pilot and he figures he needs someone better equipped to field this odd call. "Some guy wants us to launch alert fighters!"

"What? We don't do that!" pilot Scott "Scooter" Reed responds.

Gus pushes the phone toward him. "You take it! It's somebody on drugs."

"Major Reed here," Scooter answers.

"Major Reed, we need you to scramble two airplanes," the Weapons tech repeats.

"You're calling Toledo, Ohio," Scooter objects, completely floored by the odd request. "Do you not understand who you're calling here? Who are you trying to call, because you are obviously calling the wrong people. This is *Toledo*. We don't have any alert birds. This is Toledo. Do you understand that?" Thankfully, the wing commander then picks up the line. Within minutes, he instructs Gus and Scooter to grab their stuff and get airborne in two jets. *Things must be really bad*, Gus thinks, *if NEADS is launching Toledo on an active air scramble!*

At this point, Weapons controller Trey "Smurf" Murphy comes sprinting onto the Ops floor. A Weapons School graduate, the 6-foot-2, muscular officer was the "little guy" as a Marine, although in his street clothes he could easily pass for an IRA hit man. But now, serving at NEADS, he is the "big guy."

He had been at home drinking a cup of coffee from his most treasured Marine mug when he first heard the news of an airplane crash into the World Trade Center. The news brought to mind one of his briefings: What if a terrorist flies an airplane with a weapon of mass destruction into the World Trade Center? It had always been one of the military's big fears. As a Weapons director, Smurf didn't think that anything like that had happened, but the image on the screen certainly reminded him of his briefing. When he watched another airliner come onto the screen and explode into the second tower, his hand involuntarily opened and his cherished Marine mug fell to the floor, instantly shattering.

"You gotta be shitting me!" he howled. "This is a fucking coordinated attack!" Soon he was dressed and racing across town, busting all speed limits between his home and NEADS.

As he arrives on the Ops floor, he's greeted by Foxy, the senior director, who fills him in that fighters are coming up from Selfridge and they need instructions. Toledo will be coming up too. Both have been advised to contact Huntress on frequency 328.0.

"Roger that," Smurf responds, sitting down and plugging in at his station. "I need authenticators!" He can't just start giving orders. The pilots will need to validate his orders—however extreme—and they can't do that without authenticators.

In the battle cab, Bob Marr realizes that having put all of his alert fighters in the air is not enough. He now directs his troops to contact every Air National Guard unit in the northeast sector to get their jets airborne.

"The nation is under attack," he exclaims. "Get 'em in the air!"

In the battle cab and on the Ops floor, officers begin to call one unit after another, and they're astounded by what they're finding: wing commanders have anticipated the call for help and are already busy uploading fighters with all available armament.

Although wing commanders do not necessarily have the authority to arm their planes with live missiles, nor Marr the authority to call them into action, these are not ordinary times. Marr can't help but think that the incredible response is due to the fact that the Guard units are Title 32, or state-owned. They report to the governors of their respective states, and the wing commanders have every confidence that their governors will support them. Likewise, governors trust the commanders, who cannot and will not sit by and let their cities be attacked. It is simply not going to happen as long as they have the ability to do anything about it.

Meanwhile Weapons Director Steve Citino has been having trouble communicating with the Langley fighters heading toward Washington. NEADS radio coverage east of Washington is poor, and the noise level on the Operations floor has only been exacerbating the problem. At 9:40 Citino forwarded coordinates to the jets, telling them to establish a combat air patrol (CAP) over the city.

The coordinates he gave them were incorrect, though. He inadvertently transposed two of the coordinates, and the F-16s turned onto a flight path that would take them 60 miles southwest of Washington. Compounding problems, no sooner had they turned to their new heading than the bearing pointer on Eckmann's HSI, the instrument showing his jet's position relative to his intended destination, froze. As the flight lead, that was really not good. He had to get the heading from Borgy, all the while banging on his HSI, hoping to unstick the needle, and before long his knuckles were bloodied.

Within moments of giving the pilots the wrong coordinates, Citino notices that the jets are heading in the wrong direction again. Not realizing that he had mistakenly transposed the coordinates, he surmises that although NEADS has declared AFIO, a Washington Center controller has turned them to avoid traffic. He radios Borgy with the proper course heading, then emphatically adds, "Just to reiterate. You are under AFIO control! Take *all* direction from Huntress!"

Borgy acknowledges, but advises the Weapons controller that the new heading does not match the coordinates he was given several minutes earlier. "We're showing a CAP point of 250 [heading], 20 miles."

"Negative!" Citino roars. "That's incorrect! The CAP is 312, 20 miles!"

Borgy immediately relays the correction to Eckmann, and the three-ship instantly turns toward the new coordinates. It is now 9:51. Eckmann looks to the spot on his radar where he has been asked to set up a combat air patrol and sees that it's filled with air traffic. *What's our de-confliction?* he thinks. How is he supposed to set up a CAP and stay clear of all those planes?

"I need 3,000 feet of altitude in a 20-mile ring around D.C.," he tells Washington Center.

"Uh . . . say reason," the controller replies.

Eckmann wants to say, "Goddamnit, because I said so!" but instead quickly counters with "Higher headquarters' request!"

The controller comes back with an altitude range of 25,000 to 27,000 feet and Eckmann is glad for the small miracle. In his efforts to figure out how he is going to put together a CAP over this congested area, at least remembering the altitudes he's been cleared for will be easy: it just so happens that he is Quit 2-5, Lou is Quit 2-6, and Borgy is Quit 2-7.

"Okay, counterrotating CAP!" he directs his wingmen. He hands out the altitude assignments: he'll fly 25,000 feet; Lou, 26,000 feet; and Borgy, 27,000 feet. Although the NEADS MCC, Nasypany, had directed that the fighters go supersonic, in the confusion on the ops floor, they are never ordered to do so. They race toward Washington just under the speed of sound, at 700 miles per hour. In retrospect, neither their airspeed nor their routing would have made a difference in their getting to Washington before American 77.

When, a few minutes later, Langley F-16 pilot Lou Derrig looks up to see smoke on the horizon in front of him, he assumes that he is looking at New York. He had heard about an aircraft hitting the World Trade Center just before they were scrambled, and with all the changes in coordinates they've been given, he has no idea that he's looking at Washington.

"Look at that," he calls to Eckmann, referring to the smoke. "That's why we're here."

The Russians snuck one in! Eckmann thinks when he looks up. As the flight lead in direct touch with air traffic control, he knows he's looking at Washington. He recalls that the Russians were conducting an "exercise" today, which was the reason their alert jets were uploaded with additional fuel and weapons, at Bob Marr's orders. He figures that the fire has been caused by a cruise missile. He would never have dreamed that the Russians would have done this.

In fact, the Russians have already called NORAD headquarters to express concern about the unfolding events and notify commanders that they are canceling their exercises.

Generate! Generate! Generate!

121st Fighter Squadron, DCANG, Andrews AFB, Maryland

As the Langley jets contend with the snafu about their heading, 200 miles south the D.C. Guard three-aircraft training sortie over Dare County, North Carolina, has continued its training run, not yet having received the word that they should return to base.

The leader of the three-ship, Maj. Billy Hutchison, has had to send one of his wingmen back early, though, due to a fuel problem. He hated to send a pilot out on his own, especially a new one, and especially since he knows the young lieutenant is not yet familiar with the airspace around the D.C. area.

Several minutes after the young wingman headed back, he radios to say that he's having trouble getting clearance to reenter the Washington airspace. Gaining entry into the crowded airspace over the capital can be overwhelming for a newer pilot, so Hutchison isn't all that surprised, and he gives him the radio frequency to contact Razin Caine, the supervisor of flying back at Ground Ops, for assistance.

"Keep me posted," he calls in closing.

Hutchison then continues to the refueling rendezvous point where he and his wingman are scheduled to take on minimum fuel. As soon as he hooks up with the tanker, the boom operator informs him that an airplane has hit the World Trade Center. That seems very odd, but Hutchison assumes it was a small airplane with an inexperienced pilot. *Stranger things have happened*, he thinks. When his wingman finishes refueling, though, the tanker pilot announces that the tanker has been instructed to land and that the F-16s have been requested to return to base. Hutchison gets a sinking feeling in his gut. Something is wrong.

He switches to the air traffic control frequency to pick up his clearance to return home. It's a simple one: "Bully Flight is cleared direct Andrews." Hutchison is startled. The fighters *never* get direct clearances. Getting into D.C. usually requires a complicated series of directions to merge into the crowded skies above the city. The best he can figure is that there is some ground stop in D.C. But why?

Back at Andrews Air Force Base, when DCANG 113th Wing Commander Col. David Wherley hears that the Pentagon has been hit, he runs from his office on Perimeter Drive to the fighter squadron building down the street.

He arrives at the SOF desk to find Razin with a phone to each ear. "Boss . . . here, you take this one!" his SOF says.

Razin then hands the other phone to Lt. Col. Phil "Dog" Thompson, who will have to take over the SOF duties because Razin is going to fly. He has trained all his career for this, and he is not going to be left holding the phone. He quickly joins the other pilots, already suiting up and busy with mission planning.

Wherley finds that it is the Secret Service Razin has been talking to. They want the DCANG to put up a combat air patrol over the capital. Wherley knows that there has never been a CAP anywhere over this country, much less over Washington. Such a request—coming from someone not even in the military—is unheard of. He understands the power of the Secret Service, though. They have a responsibility to protect the president and clearly have some authority and precedence over everyone else, including the military. But still, such an order from a Secret Service agent seems rather far-reaching.

"I would feel more comfortable," he responds, "receiving such an order from someone higher in the chain of command, preferably in the military."

The agent gives him a phone number and tells him to call over to the White House Operations Center, where Vice President Cheney has been ushered. *Well*, Wherley thinks, *that's high enough for me!*

While Wherley dials the number and waits for someone to pick up, he looks over at the television coverage. The phone rings and rings, and just when it occurs to Wherley that he may have to make this decision on his own, a Secret Service agent finally answers.

"We want you to put a CAP up over the city. We need some fighters *now*," the agent implores.

"Is there anybody else there from the military available to talk?" Wherley asks. He's simply not very comfortable taking orders from a Secret Service agent. That's just not how things are done.

"No," the agent responds.

"Is the vice president available?" he tries.

"No, he is on the phone with the president."

Wherley's mind flashes back to when Secretary of State Alexander Haig famously rushed to say "I am in control here!" after John Hinckley shot President Reagan. He was ruthlessly criticized and made the butt of numerous jokes for his dramatic leap into the pilot's seat that day. Wherley doesn't want that to be him.

What about the military chain of command here? he asks himself. Still, he feels like a doctor arriving on the scene of an accident. He has the skills and ability to defend the capital. How can he *not* act?

"Okay, then," he says, deciding he is going to take this order on faith. "What *exactly* do they want me to do?"

FAA Command Center, Herndon, Virginia, 9:50 a.m.

Ben Sliney is expecting pushback from his order to land everything, but he doesn't seem to be getting any. Requests are quickly coming in, though, from aircraft wanting to land at airports other than the "nearest suitable."

"No!" Sliney says. "Just land them at the nearest airport. I need everybody down." At this point, he's looking at them all as potential missiles. He wonders if he has overstepped his authority, but then thinks back to a conversation he had when Jack Kies offered him the position of national operations manager.

"What is the limit of my authority over the NAS [national airspace]?" Sliney had asked him. "Unlimited," Kies had responded. "You own the NAS." He sure hopes so, but there is no more time to think about it. His staff is working furiously to determine the status of the flights listed on the dry-erase board. Are they safe or not? Each time they're able to erase one after confirming it's not in jeopardy, they say a silent prayer, then move right on to the next one, hoping there will be no others. Unfortunately, it seems that as soon as they clear one flight, another is added.

Sliney struggles to determine which information is reliable and which isn't as he works to manage the crisis. CNN, which is being projected onto two of the large screens at the front of the room, continues to replay the footage of United 175 hitting the South Tower. Sliney can tell that his people are becoming increasingly distressed watching the horrible sight over and over. One of his assistants has even called his wife to say I love you and good-bye.

"Take CNN down!" he orders.

Meanwhile, at FAA headquarters in downtown Washington, Jane Garvey is furiously pulling information from the various FAA facilities and forwarding it to Transportation Secretary Norman Mineta. On a phone call with Mineta, American Airlines CEO Don Carty asks for confirmation that the plane that crashed into the Pentagon is one of his. He cannot contain his frustration when he gets no definitive answer.

"For God's sake!" he exclaims. "It's in the Pentagon. Can't somebody go look at it and see whose plane it is!"

"They have," Mineta explains. "The problem is that they just can't tell." [1] They will not learn until later that it is indeed American 77 that has impacted the Pentagon.

Having been updated by Cleveland Center about United 93, Sliney notifies Garvey that the plane is "about 29 minutes out of Washington." [2] Soon Garvey gets a call from Delta CEO Leo Mullin.

"We can't find four of our planes," he tells her. "Four of our transponders are off."

A distraught Garvey returns to the White House videoconference hosted by Richard Clarke, where leaders are weighing significant military decisions: the use of force against hostile aircraft, the physical safety of the president, and the implementation of the

Continuity of Government (COG) plan, among other things. The COG plan, which coordinates the evacuation of key government officials to secret, secure locations, was developed during the cold war to ensure that vital government departments could continue operations following a catastrophic attack, but it has never been implemented.

After Garvey announces that United 93 is closing in on the capital, the decision is made to evacuate the White House and institute COG for the first time in history. Mineta and other senior government officials are quickly relocated to more secure locations, remaining in contact via their cell phones in the interim.

At the Pentagon, the National Military Command Center is responsible for coordinating communications between the National Command Authority—the president and the secretary of defense—and who can act on their orders, in this instance, NORAD. But this morning, not only is the NMCC getting late and limited information, they have not heard from the president and cannot locate Rumsfeld,[3] who is currently assisting with evacuations from the burning Pentagon, or Joint Chiefs Vice Chairman Dick Myers, who is part of the White House videoconference. NORAD commanders are not part of the White House videoconference and have no means of securing the shoot-down authority they seek.

On the NMCC's Significant Threat conference call, NORAD briefs on the hijacking of Delta 1989 and tries again to confirm the presence of the FAA on the call. But despite best efforts, compatibility issues between the two secure phone networks have not yet been resolved. Consequently, most of the information going from the FAA to the military is being relayed through the FAA headquarter's hijack teleconference to Colin Scoggins listening in at Boston Center, who is in turn reporting to NEADS. The information coming into NEADS is then being passed by Marr up the chain of command to General Arnold and NORAD headquarters, then finally back to the NMCC. They've improvised a solution, but the process is costing precious response time.

NEADS, Rome, New York, 9:50 a.m.

While calls for assistance are going out to bases all over the country calls are also coming back in. Minutes after Smurf Murphy checks in the Selfridge F-16 pilots and gives them orders to intercept Delta 1989, his cell phone rings. It's one of his Marine buddies from the 321 Marine Fighter Attack Squadron at Andrews Air Force Base.

"Dude, get us in the war," he says. "I've got wrench-turners on our planes uploading weapons. What can we do?"

On any other day, there would be no question of Smurf issuing them orders. Active duty forces are not part of NORAD or under any state's control. They train to deploy overseas and they respond only to the U.S. Joint Forces Command, commonly known as JiffyCom, and based in Norfolk, Virginia. Smurf doesn't miss a beat, though.

"Convince your higher-ups at JiffyCom to get you transferred over to us!"

Minutes later, Smurf's phone rings again. It's a general from the 321. Unfortunately, though, Delta 1989 has Smurf's full attention. "General! Can't talk! But we could use your airplanes," he blurts out before hanging up the phone. *I just hung up on a general!* he suddenly realizes. Just then, there's a tap on his shoulder.

"Your wife just called," the master sergeant says. "Your dad's in the building."

"Huh?" Smurf responds, confused.

"In the World Trade Center."

"Thanks," he growls. "I need *that* like a kick in the Jimmy!" He clenches his jaw and looks back down at his scope to focus on the job at hand. *There's nothing I can do for him now*, he thinks, pushing the thought from his mind.

In moments, the senior director is over at the Weapons station with a message.

"The boss wants you two," Foxy says, pointing to Smurf and

Weapons controller Michael "Animal" Julian next to him. Both are graduates of the Air Force's Fighter Weapons School, and Marr needs their help.

When the two Weapons controllers head up the stairs and into the glass-enclosed battle cab, they encounter Marr with a phone to each ear, going back and forth between two conversations. He stops to look at them.

"You Weapons guys . . ." he begins, before interrupting himself to continue one of the phone conversations. They patiently wait.

After more conversing, Marr looks up at Smurf.

"What do you need me to do?" Smurf asks.

"Un-fuck this!" Marr responds.

Smurf knows what the commander is saying: "Right now, I have chaos. Bring me order. Make me a battle plan."

"C'mon!" Smurf says to Animal, turning to leave the battle cab. They grab their notebooks and pens and leave the Ops floor to find a quiet place to work. They have spent years training for this and they're ready. As they head down the hallway, they decide that what they need are point defense caps over the major population centers in the Northeast.

"They're not going after wheat fields in Kansas or lakefront property in Minnesota," Smurf notes. "They are looking to go downtown to our most populous cities and landmarks. We'll go point defense and let those bastards come to us."

"Rock on, brother," Animal agrees.

They find an empty conference room and get to work building a defense plan for the United States, beginning at the East Coast and working their way inland, laying down the defense framework.

"Okay . . . Boston," Animal begins. "Red Sox!" he suggests for the name of the CAP.

"Fuck no!" Smurf objects. "I am a Yankees fan and I can't stand those bastards. I won't name anything Red Sox!"

Animal begins to laugh hysterically, dropping his pen. "Leave it to you to make me laugh at a time like this!" he scolds.

"I just needed to break the ice, bro," Smurf says calmly. "Let's go with Patriots." They move on from there.

"Okay . . . New York!" he continues. "CAP over New York."

"Yankees!" Animal says.

"Washington," Smurf calls next.

"Redskins!"

"Chicago!"

"Cubbies!"

With the major cities covered, they move on to altitudes, deciding to keep at midlevel altitudes. They will keep the fighters low— between 10,000 and 14,000 feet—because the terrorists seem to be coming in low and fast. The fighters will need to be in a position to not only locate any targets, but also have minimal time between engagement and destruction. They'll keep the tankers higher, between 20,000 and 24,000 feet. The radio frequencies are more difficult. The UHF radio frequencies that the military uses are stretched thin, and NEADS has been assigned only a small number. They decide to alternate the frequencies between CAPs to prevent any "bleedover."

Within minutes, they have pieced together an extensive plan: the fighters, the altitudes, the tankers, the frequencies—everything that needs to be in place to defend American cities. They quickly return to the battle cab with their plan, and are soon hard at work making it a reality.

CHAPTER 13

Chaos in the Skies

Delta Flight 1989, Boston–Los Angeles, 9:50 a.m.

Dave Dunlap and his captain realize that their flight has become suspect, but they have no idea how concerned Cleveland Center is about them. The descent into Cleveland seems to be taking a small eternity. Dunlap would like to keep their 767 close to the airport. "Ask them for a tight, high pattern right to the numbers," he asks Capt. Werner. But Cleveland Center has its own ideas for the flight.

On approaches that are not straight in, a pilot flies a U-shaped pattern that usually takes the aircraft parallel to the landing runway, about a mile or so from the airport. Depending on how many other aircraft are in line to land, a pilot can expect to fly past the airport on a downwind leg for a couple of miles before being turned back toward the airport. On a bad day, the downwind can end up being 30 or even 40 miles.

But today is worse than even the very worst of days. Air traffic control is keeping Delta 1989 so wide and taking them so far past the airport that Dunlap can no longer even see it. And he can't see any other aircraft in sight to justify such a trajectory.

He doesn't know that controllers are giving themselves time to evacuate the airport since his flight has been confirmed hijacked and since they believe it contains a bomb intended to detonate when the aircraft crashes into the terminal.

Even FAA staff leave, following an evacuation plan, exiting the building via the stairs and making their way to the huge NASA hangar next door. "If they are coming in with a bomb," one employee muses, "are they going to bomb a little brick building," referring to the FAA building, "or an enormous hangar that says 'NASA' across the front in 20-foot letters?" The thought doesn't give anyone much comfort.

Meanwhile, oblivious to the evacuation or the F-16 fighters that Smurf has just ordered to shadow his 767, Dunlap flies what he believes to be the widest approach pattern ever flown. His ignorance is most likely a good thing, since the knowledge might have sent him over the edge.

Midex 270, Milwaukee–Newark, 9:50 a.m.

Having convinced his dispatcher that returning to Milwaukee is not an option, Midwest pilot Chuck Savall notifies his passengers that they will be diverting to Cleveland. The pilots discuss their options while they start their descent.

"Do we really want to land at a major airport?" Savall asks. "Maybe terrorists have taken over some airports and are waiting to get their hands on more aircraft."

Could there be terrorists on their own plane? Should they land at the closest airport to prevent any chance of being hijacked? They discuss diverting to Cleveland's general aviation airport, Cleveland Burke Lakefront.

"We can simply disappear for a while until we can figure out the situation," his first officer proposes.

All Savall knows for sure is that he needs to protect his plane, get it on the ground, and keep any terrorists away from the cockpit. He's distracted by a discussion on the radio.

"How many feet do you require to land?" the controller asks a corporate jet.

"We can land with less than 5,000 feet of runway," the captain responds with bravado not uncommon to any proud Learjet crew.

"Learjet, can you see that small airport at your 2 o'clock and 30 miles?" the controller queries.

"Affirmative."

"Make an emergency descent and land there!" he commands.

"Ah, do you have the name of that airport?" the surprised pilot asks. "I don't think we have the charts on board for that particular field!"

Savall isn't surprised that they seem to have no idea what's going on. Unlike airliners, corporate aircraft don't generally have dispatchers to keep them in the loop.

"It doesn't matter," the controller responds, losing patience. "I am exercising emergency authority and you are ordered to descend and land immediately at that airport using visual flight rules."

Well, that's the end of that discussion, Savall figures, correctly.

The controller radios Savall next. "Midex 270, make an immediate emergency descent and land at Pittsburgh."

So much for the Cleveland plan! Savall thinks, immediately initiating the emergency descent into the airport, which is less than 50 miles away: thrust levers to idle, flaps down, gear down, nose down. He and the first officer prepare for a short approach into an airport they never use in normal operations. They're soon handed off to Pittsburgh Approach Control and cleared for a visual approach to runway 28 Right.

"Midex 270, contact tower on one-one-niner-point-one," the controller says.

The first officer dials in the new frequency and checks in. "Pittsburgh tower, Midex 270 is with you for 28 Right." It's been a flight from hell, but nothing could prepare Savall for what he hears next.

"Midex 270, the airport is officially closed and the tower has been evacuated." The evacuation order had come in at 9:49, when Cleveland Center called Pittsburgh Flight Control to warn them that a plane, which was United 93, was heading toward Pittsburgh and refusing to communicate. This lone controller had refused to leave his post. Savall is so stunned at what he's just heard that he can't provide even a simple response.

"I am the only controller left here," the controller explains. "I can't issue you an official landing clearance, but you may land at your own risk."

Wonderful, Savall thinks, *what the hell are we flying ourselves into?*

"Roger," he says. "At least we haven't been greeted by some terrorist," he comments to his first officer.

When he touches down in Pittsburgh, he notices two military Boeing KC-135 air-refueling tanker aircraft taking off in loose formation on the parallel runway.

"That can only mean one thing," he says. "We are in full war mode, and the fighters have been in the air long enough to already be thinking of where their next batch of fuel will be coming from." He is correct on both counts.

United 829, Boston–Chicago, 9:52 a.m.

Thanks to Toronto Center's kind offer of an indefinite hold, Rick Johnson is now circling high above southern Ontario. He picks up the microphone and tries to think of something to say to his passengers. What he says comes out something like this: "Well . . . although we are going in circles, we aren't lost. Yet. But there is something very strange going on, and air traffic control will not let us proceed to Chicago. And . . . uhhh . . . there is something very strange going on. I don't know what's happening, but I will let you know as soon as I do."

Well, that takes care of that! He now has completely flustered passengers in the back!

Next he sends a message to Dispatch advising them that he is not able to proceed to Buffalo as they had requested. A minute or two later, the lead flight attendant calls on the interphone to request permission to come to the cockpit.

When his first officer lets her onto the flight deck, Johnson can see that she is shaken. "What's wrong?" he asks.

"After you made that announcement," she begins, "a business-man in first class called his secretary on one of the Airfones. She told him that there's been a terrorist attack, and a plane has hit the World Trade Center."

"Not one of *our* planes," he interrupts. "Not an *airliner*. It'll be all right."

"He said a plane has also crashed into the White House!"

That idea is so outlandish that Johnson quickly dismisses it. "Whatever he said, that is preliminary and unconfirmed," he tells her. "There's no way that could be accurate."

Just then a chime indicates the arrival of an ACARS message in the cockpit. He interrupts their conversation to read it. "Land in Toronto" is all it says. No other explanation. *Shit*, he thinks. First, he realizes, he must deal with his traumatized flight attendant.

"Listen, we're going to be making a normal landing in just a few minutes," he tries to reassure her. "I need you to go and prepare the cabin. Everything is going to be *fine*."

He looks back down at the ACARS message. Toronto? *Not happening*, he thinks. He's been to Toronto a hundred times and has found that he generally gets screwed when he goes there. United has no dedicated gates in Toronto. The ground handling crews work for Air Canada and the United flights always seem to be their last priority. And that's on a normal day. Johnson figures he'll be on the aircraft a good 24 hours if he has to divert there. But as much as he hates it, he'll try to comply with company wishes. He calls Toronto Center and requests a diversion there.

"Well, sir," the controller responds, "you said that you had a lot of holding fuel, and now aircraft are lining up from all four quad-rants for Toronto. From your quadrant . . . uh . . . you'll be about number six."

No, that's not going to happen, Johnson thinks. He's been hold-ing for about 15 minutes while things around him seem to be going from bad to worse. He wants to land, and the sooner the bet-ter. He takes out his flight operations manual and checks the airport pages for nearby Hamilton airport. It has a capital letter "A" next to its identifier that indicates it's a good alternate, as opposed to a marginal one that may not have the services they need. And it has to be better than waiting for Toronto.

Johnson sends an ACARS back to United: "How about YHM?" he types, using the airport identifier for Hamilton. Almost as soon as he presses "send" a response comes back: "YES . . . land in YHM!" He spirals down from 33,000 to the airport directly beneath him, and lands uneventfully. This is fortuitous, since as the day proceeds even small airports like Hamilton will be overrun with diverting aircraft, challenging their ability and capacity to park aircraft and process passengers through Customs and Immigration.

FAA Headquarters, Washington, D.C., 9:55 a.m.

With the number of plane crashes and suspected hijackings increasing, Jane Garvey determines it is time to evacuate the FAA headquarters and move key staff to a more secure location. She also turns her attention to the hundreds of international flights that are airborne and heading toward the United States. Over the North Atlantic alone there are currently over 400 such flights. There is no way she can allow them into U.S. airspace. They must be diverted.

Canada's air traffic control authority, NAV Canada, has already established both tactical and strategic command centers to respond to the crisis and its effects. Shortly after 9:45, when America shut down its airspace and ordered everything to land, Canada followed suit. But with American and Canadian airspace now shutting down, international flights—getting dangerously low on fuel—have few options. As flight crews near North America and reestablish radio contact, they are now told that American airspace is closed. Many concerned pilots are beginning to dial their transponders to the emergency code. One foreign crew dials in the 4-digit code for "hijack," just to let the authorities know they are aware of what is taking place. FAA radar displays begin to highlight a growing flurry of flights transmitting warning codes over the oceans.

Responding instantly to America's call for assistance, Canada agrees to open up its airspace to recover all diverted international flights. Operation Yellow Ribbon begins. It will be no easy task and will require enormous coordination between facilities. NAV Canada begins the huge mobilization. For security reasons, they instruct their air traffic control facilities to keep the diverted aircraft away from large urban areas. But this leaves only smaller airports, most of which are ill equipped to handle large aircraft and huge numbers of foreign passengers.

While Canada begins to relocate security and immigration specialists to remote airports along its coasts, huge volunteer efforts spring into action to prepare for the influx of stranded passengers. For the radio operators communicating with the transoceanic international flights, relaying messages between airlines, air traffic control, and flights over the ocean becomes a nearly impossible task. Many of these flights have no other means of communicating, and no other manner in which to receive rerouting instructions. In many cases, the language barrier becomes the most frustrating obstacle.

One radio controller futilely attempts to explain to an Asian pilot that he will not be permitted to land in San Francisco, or anywhere else in the United States for that matter. "No problem, we go to Oakland," the pilot kindly offers.

"Negative, sir," she attempts to explain again. "You are unable to land in United States airspace."

"Oh . . . roger! We go to Los Angeles then!" the pilot responds.

"No, sir. You cannot go to the United States. The United States is closed."[1]

Everyone understands the concept of a closed airport, but it's a huge cognitive leap to grasp the notion of a whole country being closed. After the long silence that comes in response, the radio operator recommends that the pilot divert to Vancouver. The radio controller has managed to maintain her composure. Then one of the foreign pilots signs off with a simple and unexpected expression of sympathy. "Our condolences," he says. With that, she excuses herself from her post and breaks down in sobs.

The hectic pace will continue for hours as the controllers attempt to forward the throngs of requests and messages. Some of the pilots get so frustrated at their inability to get through to their companies for any solid information or instructions that they turn off their assigned courses and head back toward Hawaii, acting as their own dispatcher and air traffic controller while they exit the system to go it alone.

Northwest Airlines Flight 22, Tokyo–Honolulu, 9:55 a.m. EST

Northwest B747 Capt. Ron Silverman has known good days and not-so-good days in his years of flying for the airlines, but today is a category all its own. Northwest 22 had taken off out of Tokyo at 8 o'clock (EST). The first indication Silverman had that something might be amiss was a transmission between two JAL pilots about an hour and a half into the flight, each wanting to know if the other was turning around. Silverman wonders why they would be doing so.

Some time later, Northwest 22, along with two other Northwest flights over the Pacific that had departed Osaka and Tokyo, receives a Selcal (Selective Calling) radio message from San Francisco Radio.

"We have a company message for you," the radio controller instructs each of the flights as they check in. "Stand by." Once all three flights have checked in, he relays the brief message from Northwest Dispatch: "All three of you will most likely have to declare an emergency to get into Honolulu today."

There is an extended silence on the frequency while the pilots wait for further information following this bizarre message.

"Because?" one of the pilots finally asks, breaking the silence.

"That's it. That's the message. Over," the controller announces before disconnecting.

In international transoceanic airspace there aren't traditional air-to-ground radio communications. Pilots are generally out of contact for hours. While out of radio range, they monitor a common air-to-air frequency—123.45—where they are able to communicate with other pilots. Almost immediately after receiving this bizarre Selcal, one of the pilots is broadcasting on the pilot-to-pilot frequency.

"Can anybody tell me what the fuck is going on?" he begs.

"Is this the Twilight Zone?" another asks.

"Why would we all have to declare an emergency to get into Honolulu?"

No one seems to know what is going on, nor does anyone seem to be able to get any additional information until about an hour and a half later, when a JAL pilot comes on to the frequency suggesting that crews tune in the Voice of America over an HF (High Frequency) radio.

Silverman gets quite an earful when he does. In fact, he has a hard time believing what he is hearing: multiple hijackings, aircraft targeted into buildings, World Trade Center South Tower has fallen. One thing he knows for sure: he is facing a serious problem and he needs to get busy!

With 14 flight attendants on board, many of them in crew rest, he calls downstairs with an order to wake them all—everyone's break is canceled. He wants them all on duty and available for a brief.

He goes downstairs to brief his inflight crew and approaches one of his male flight attendants with unequivocal instructions.

"You are no longer a flight attendant. I need you at the bottom of the stairway here, and I don't want anybody getting past you. Arm yourself with a fire extinguisher or anything else it takes, but don't let anyone up these stairs."

It occurs to him that he has two police officers on board today—or at least they presented themselves as armed police officers when they boarded the flight. If they are indeed who they say they are, then they'll be an invaluable resource. If they aren't, he's got another problem on his hands. He instructs one of the flight attendants to request multiple forms of identification from both men and then to deliver the IDs to the cockpit for his review.

When Silverman returns to the cockpit, his first officer informs him that every flight behind them seems to have been turned back toward Asia. Their flight is the last in line still heading for Honolulu. The best his first officer can determine, the hijackings are continuing in the United States: three already confirmed and more suspected. Silverman considers the information. He doesn't have much to work with, but he knows for sure that his flight is not going to be one of the hijackings.

After verifying the identities of the police officers, he asks that they be directed upstairs for a briefing. He leaves the cockpit to greet them. They are reassuringly burly and imposing.

"We have a problem," he begins. "Are you willing to help us?"

"Absolutely. We'll do whatever you need," one of the officers quickly responds.

Silverman gives them the limited information he has and asks if, for the duration of the flight, one officer can walk the plane looking for anything suspicious while the other takes a seat upstairs to keep an eye on the passengers and guard the cockpit.

"Thanks, but I think I'll pass on that seat. I'd prefer to stand right here in front of the cockpit," one officer says. Silverman agrees with him and returns to the cockpit.

The police officer is rather conspicuous loitering there in front of the cockpit door, facing the passengers with his arms crossed over his broad chest, his weapon in his hand underneath his jacket. One particularly alert passenger is watching him with raised eyebrows, he has flown enough to know that something must be wrong. After observing the officer for a few minutes, he cannot sit still any longer.

He approaches to ask what is going on, but the officer is not inclined to engage in conversation.

"Sir, don't worry about it. You need to back away and take your seat, *now*."

Some things just don't need repeating—the tone and the content of this message told the passenger all he needs to hear. He heads back to his seat and knows he won't be sleeping any more on this flight!

Nearly 130 miles out of Honolulu, the cockpit crew makes their first radio contact with Honolulu Center. They are greeted with an extraordinary announcement.

"Northwest 22 Heavy, all U.S. airspace is closed. State your intentions."

That's the first time Silverman has ever heard such a transmission from air traffic control. In spite of the earlier Selcal that had prepared him for difficulties getting into Honolulu, he's still surprised. But thanks to the message from Dispatch, he knows what he has to do.

"Honolulu Center, Northwest 22 Heavy is declaring an emergency," he announces.

He reaches down to change his transponder to the emergency squawk code. Northwest 22's data box instantly flashes and changes to a highlighted bold on the controller's screens in Honolulu.

"Roger, Northwest 22 Heavy," the controller responds. "We have your emergency. Proceed."

But a few minutes later, the controller announces that the Honolulu airport is closed and that all flights will be required to divert.

Now what? Silverman thinks. He grabs his chart to check his options. His first choice is Kalaeloa Airport, a former Naval Air Station on Barber's Point in Oahu. He makes the request.

"Negative, Northwest 22, you cannot go there," the controller responds.

Looking back down at his chart, Silverman requests another airport on his chart.

"Negative, Northwest 22, you can't go there either. It's Maui or Kona."

This is just not going to work. His mind is racing as he considers his options. He is confident he has sufficient fuel to divert to Kona, but there are not a lot of airports in Hawaii that have runways long and wide enough to accomodate a 747. He would certainly feel more comfortable landing in Honolulu. His perspective changes somewhat as he watches two F-15s move in to intercept his plane, their missiles hardly concealed. It is evident that the powers that be are quite serious about not wanting any airlines near the densely populated cities of Honolulu and Waikiki. He calls up Dispatch to tell them that he will be going to Kona.

Heading to Kona will cut into his fuel reserves, but at least they have a nice long runway there.

"No!" the dispatcher responds without hesitation. "You need to go to Honolulu!"

Noticing on his Traffic Collision Avoidance System (TCAS) that the fighter escort of F-15s has now moved in behind him, Silverman does not wish to belabor the point.

"Well" he explains, "right now we've got fighters on our tail with guns pointed at us, and they outrank you, so we're going to Kona. What I need from you is a radio frequency for whoever handles us there. And please call to let them know we're coming."

That's the end of that conversation. He calls Honolulu Center to let them know that they will divert to Kona.

"Northwest 22 Heavy is cleared direct Kona," the controller responds.

Then a third of the way to Kona, as they are initiating their descent, a call comes in from Honolulu Approach.

"Northwest 22 Heavy, your company called to say that you do not have the fuel necessary to get to Kona."

"Well," Silverman responds, "there is no other place for me to go." There is a whole lot of ocean and not a lot of land in the middle of the Pacific, and he doesn't have the fuel to make it to Maui. "We are not going to Maui," he continues. "What are you offering me? Are you offering me Honolulu?"

"Affirmative, Northwest 22. We will allow you to land in Honolulu," the controller responds. "You are cleared direct."

As Silverman banks into a wide turn back toward Honolulu, a

scary thought crosses his mind. "Damn, I sure hope they have told those F-15s that we're turning back."

He notices that the fighters are turning with him, still right on his tail, as he calls up Honolulu Approach.

"Honolulu, I would really like these F-15s to know that we are turning at your instruction."

"Roger, Northwest 22 Heavy," the controller responds. "They know . . . but they won't be leaving you anytime soon."

American Airlines Flight 60, out of Tokyo-Dallas

Typhoon Danas had just come inland on September 9 when American Airlines Capt. Ted Christensen, after holding over the Pacific, finally lowered the nose of his Boeing 777 onto the runway in the driving rain in Tokyo, 13 hours and 19 minutes after taking off from Dallas. Not a big deal for Christensen, an experienced captain and check airman, but perhaps a little more stressful for one of his three first officers, Arno Knapen, who was on his first flight on the airplane after weeks of training in the simulator.

The weather had not cooperated on the layover, but still, Tokyo was Tokyo, and there were a lot worse places you could debrief with your crew than over a beer in a nice Tokyo hotel watching news clips of a typhoon. Now, two days later, they're facing a more daunting threat.

They have a planned crew swap 5 hours into the flight, so two of the first officers went directly to the bunks after takeoff for the required crew rest. Halfway across the Pacific Ocean, Christensen hears from a United 747 on the pilot-to-pilot frequency.

"Uh, I'm listening to an AM radio station out of San Francisco and they just announced that an aircraft has struck the World Trade Center—reportedly a small plane."

"How the heck does that happen?" Christensen comments to his first officer. They can't come up with any reasonable explanations. Minutes later, the United captain is back on the frequency.

"They're saying now that it's an American Airlines flight that has hit the World Trade Center, and possibly a United Airlines flight as well."

"Holy shit, what's going on?" Christensen yells. "We need to get hold of Dispatch!"

He grabs the satellite phone to call his dispatcher but can't get through using regular priority. He tries again on the high-priority line.

"Dispatch, Flight 60, we're hearing some weird stuff," he says when he finally gets through. "Are the reports out of the East Coast accurate?

"That is affirmative," the somber dispatcher responds. "All aircraft are advised to secure the cockpit and land immediately."

Christensen is stunned.

"Uh . . ." he replies, "well that's easier said than done when you're 3 hours from the nearest piece of concrete!" There are hours of ocean between his 777 and either Honolulu or Seattle.

"Proceed to the West Coast with a planned landing in Seattle," the dispatcher advises. "And secure your cockpit!"

Christensen calls the purser and tells her to get all of the flight attendants out of the crew rest quarters, and he orders the relief first officers back up to the cockpit. There is no more time for sleeping. Next he disables the satellite telephone service to prevent passengers from making phone calls.

He briefs the newly awakened first officers and then leaves the flight deck to brief the inflight crew. His primary concern is that a hijacker may be lying in wait on his flight, preparing to take action when the aircraft is over the United States. He instructs flight attendants to make constant patrols of the cabin and to report any suspicious behavior, then posts two male flight attendants in the jump seats just outside the cockpit door with orders to stop anyone from approaching the cockpit.

The radio is now jammed with communications as news of the multiple hijackings makes its way over the pilot-to-pilot frequency high above the Pacific Ocean. A United captain just ahead of Christensen's B777 surpasses his frustration tolerance level.

"I cannot get hold of company so I am out of here," he announces as he exits the transoceanic track to head south. "Honolulu looks good at this point."

It's looking good to Christensen too, but he has already received instructions to continue to Seattle.

Several pilots on the frequency cannot get in touch with their dispatchers and begin to request information from other flight crews. Many request assistance in relaying messages to their companies. In an incredible rally of cooperation and crew resource management that spans all nationalities and airlines, Christensen forwards messages from other airlines through American Airlines dispatchers, who use landlines to contact the other airlines and then provide feedback for Christensen to pass on to the querying pilots.

It's a long flight over the Pacific from Tokyo. The entire crew remains on high alert and Christensen refrains from making any cabin announcements. He is hoping to be able to wait until just before landing to communicate with the passengers. He doesn't want to tip off any hijackers that might be on his flight.

When he is close enough, he contacts Seattle Center.

"Seattle Center, American 6-0 checking in flight level 3-9-0."

"American 6-0, Seattle Center," the controller responds. "United States airspace is closed."

"This is *not* good," Christensen laments to his first officers. He knows that if the Canadians do not open up their airspace and airports, things are quickly going to get interesting. They can stay airborne for only so long.

He makes a quick call to Dispatch and they confirm that they are working with the Canadians for permission to land there. Several minutes later, the dispatcher notifies Christensen that the Canadians have granted his flight permission to land in Vancouver.

He's incredibly relieved as he changes course to head north toward Vancouver. He watches with interest while some F-15s out of Portland escort a China Airlines flight in front of him. It all seems surreal. He thinks about his own days of flying Air Defense in the F-16 for the Fresno Air National Guard and he knows that his boys are doing their jobs today.

Thirty minutes from landing, it is time to update the aircraft computers, which will change the moving map displays in the back of the aircraft. Christensen thinks carefully about this, then goes ahead and inputs the change. He knows the time has come to talk to the passengers, so he delivers a very succinct message.

"Ladies and Gentlemen, the United States has been threatened and has therefore shut down its airspace. Consequently, we will be landing in Vancouver in 30 minutes. There is no threat directed at this flight. I will get back to you with more information upon landing."

The announcement breeds a stunned silence in the cabin, and for the first and only time in his career, Christensen knows he has the attention of 100 percent of his passengers.

United 856, Hong Kong–Los Angeles

Over the Pacific, en route from Hong Kong to Los Angeles, United 747 pilot Tom Welborn has been receiving a rather peculiar collection of ACARS messages from United's Dispatch. Finally he decides that it is time to wake up the captain from crew rest. He minces no words while attempting to rouse him.

"Captain! You need to wake up," he calls. "The world has gone to hell in a hand basket. They are crashing planes into the World Trade Center and we're probably going to be diverted."

Unfortunately, the captain is a very sound sleeper and doesn't seem to process this extraordinary information. "Wake me up if we get a diversion," he responds simply before dozing off again.

Not sure exactly what to make of this unanticipated reaction, Welborn steps back to reassess his situation. "Well . . . sure," he finally says, "Uh . . . I guess I can do that." The captain is already fast asleep again when Welborn turns to leave. He arrives back in the cockpit rather flustered.

A minute later, the relief first officer, who has been in crew rest, comes out to take a bathroom break, dressed only in his boxers and T-shirt. Welborn tells him what's happening and, unlike the captain, he responds instantly. Unfazed by his state of undress, he sits on the jump seat to pour through the ACARS messages.

The next message is short and simple: "Are you okay?"

"Yes," Welborn types in response. He is okay, but only until the next message comes in. It sends them all into high gear. "All U.S. airspace is closed. Prepare to divert. Look out for suspicious activity. Multiple hijackings in progress."

"Oh my God!" he exclaims. The relief first officer, still in his boxers, jumps up and begins to barricade the cockpit door. He grabs the cockpit crash ax and then his penknife, and perches himself on the suitcases, a weapon in each hand.

While they work to devise a plan of action, the pilots have never felt so vulnerable. They decide to disable the air phones and the moving map display that shows the aircraft's location and route on a screen at the front of each cabin. If they have hijackers on board, they could be using either to coordinate an attack.

Welborn calls the lead flight attendant. "There has been terrorist-related activity in New York," he tells her. "We need a flight attendant positioned at the stairs to monitor and report on activity in the upper cabin."

They consider emptying the upstairs, which another United flight will do by claiming "The oxygen-mask system is showing inoperable and we need to move you downstairs," but decide that might send up a red flag. They agree to keep operations as normal as possible.

Another message informs them that both of the World Trade Center towers have fallen. The pilots sit in silence. Welborn pictures the towers falling sideways. He can't even fathom such a catastrophe.

Instructions from Dispatch arrive advising them to divert to San

Francisco. The crew starts to make preparations until, minutes later, new instructions arrive: divert to Anchorage. They begin again. Next, they get instructions to divert to Honolulu . . . then Vancouver . . . then Honolulu again.

"That's it!" Welborn says finally, pushed past his breaking point. "It's time to wake up our sleeping captain! Dispatch is completely losing it, so it must be REALLY bad down there!"

When the captain arrives on the flight deck, he is quickly brought up to speed. The ACARS messages continue to come in, becoming increasingly shocking. The diversion instructions also continue to change, which they will do until the 747 is on final approach into Honolulu. They are being shadowed for the last 150 miles by two F-15s. Just two miles from the runway threshold, with the aircraft's flaps fully extended, the landing gear down and locked, and the landing checklist complete, the first officer reads the newest ACARS message to arrive on the flight deck.

"Divert to Kona," is all it says.

"Hell no, we're landing Honolulu," the captain responds. Enough is enough, he wants his plane on the ground.

United Flight 105, Auckland, New Zealand–Los Angeles

Captain Gerald Baker is flying his retirement flight and is asleep in the lower bunk of the crew rest quarters when he is startled awake by one of the relief pilots shaking him. He has slept right through their attempts to wake him with call chimes.

"You'd better get up," the first officer says, "it's really bad!" This being Baker's last flight, he wonders what mischief his pilots are up to in the cockpit.

But when he enters the flight deck, his relief first officer simply passes him a handful of ACARS messages.

UA842 AKL-LAX 13:03 (09:03 EST)
REALLY BAD NEWS . . . AN AMERICAN AIRLINES 737 WAS
HIJACKED AND FLOWN RIGHT INTO THE UPPER FLOORS

OF THE WORLD TRADE CNTR IN NEW YORK, APPROX 75
TO 85TH FLOORS . . . ITS BURNING AND THE BUILDING
LOOKS LIKE A CHIMNEY. HORRIBLE MESS . . . WE ARE
WATCHING LIVE HERE ON CNN NEWS. . . .

He moves onto the second slip.

2ND PLANE, PSBLY A CESSNA 172 HAS NOW CRASHED
INTO THE 2ND BUILDING OF THE WORLD TRADE CNTR
AND BOTH BUILDINGS ARE ON FIRE. . . . I THINK THEY
ARE UNDER SIEGE. . . .

You got me! Baker thinks, figuring this has to be a joke they're play-
ing on him. *Very sick humor, but you got me!* He continues reading.

NO JOKE . . . WE WILL KEEP YOU ADVISED.

His relief first officers obviously had the same thought.

. . . THERE MAY BE ADDITIONAL HIJACKINGS IN
PROGRESS . . . YOU MAY WANT TO ADVISE YOUR
FLIGHTS TO STAY ON ALERT AND SHUT DOWN ALL
COCKPIT ACCESS.

Baker finally understands that this is a true crisis. He starts to
read faster.

. . . . ALERT. . . . THIS IS NO DRILL. . . . .
2 COMMERCIAL FLTS HAVE CRASHED INTO THE WORLD
TRADE CNTRS . . . ONE AMERICAN . . . AND ONE UNITED
. . . (FLT 175)
OTHER HIJACKINGS IN PROGRESS . . .
THE PENTAGON HAS BEEN BOMBED . . .
WE ARE GROUNDING EVERYTHING AND U.S. AIRSPACE
WILL BE CLSD. THIS IS VERY BAD . . . BE VERY ALERT. . . .

By now, Baker's palms are getting sweaty. Not only is this a crisis, but it's unlike anything he could have ever imagined. He reads the last slip of paper.

WE NEED YOU TO DIVERT TO LAS [LAS VEGAS] . . . U.S.
AIRSPACE SHUT DOWN . . .

Baker hastily rereads each slip, making sure he hasn't missed or mis-understood anything, having just awoken from his deep sleep. He looks questioningly toward his relief first officer. "That's all we know," the officer shrugs.

Clearly, something horrible is happening, Baker thinks, *but why would they want to divert us to Las Vegas? And how could we even do that with the U.S. airspace shut down?*

"No way," he says finally. "Something's not right here. I may not be thinking clearly, but neither is he. Tell him we will divert to Honolulu."

The relief first officer sends the message back to Dispatch. A response is quickly forthcoming:

GOOD IDEA . . . WE ARE IN A MESS HERE . . . DVRT TO
HNL [HONOLULU] . . . THANKS . . .

Baker's wife has joined him for the send-off flight. As she watches the flight attendants scurry about the darkened cabin, whispering, her unease builds to the point where she can no longer sit silently, and she approaches one of them.

"Is there a problem with Gerry?" she asks. *Is that why they won't tell me what's happening?*

"No, it's not Gerry, but it is really bad," the flight attendant responds, offering no additional information.

Baker's wife knows that whatever is going on, she must return to her seat. She thinks perhaps there has been a very bad earthquake on the West Coast.

In the cockpit, one of the pilots wonders aloud, "Could it be a worldwide attack of some kind?" He's been growing more anxious and concerned about his family with the arrival of each message. "Why don't we raise the cabin altitude to 15,000 feet to anesthetize the passengers and protect the cockpit?" he asks.

It's hard for Baker to believe that this could be a worldwide attack, but the comment from his first officer tells him that the stress level is taking its toll on his crew. Although the comment might appear logical on the surface, it makes no sense. By raising the cabin altitude, the crew could indeed create a hypoxic condition, where there is too little oxygen in the cabin. Hypoxia usually causes fatigue and a general feeling of well-being. Certainly, hypoxic passengers would pose little threat to the aircraft since their brains would be working at the level of very happy—and calm—5-year-olds. But as soon as the cabin altitude reached 10,000 feet, the oxygen masks would automatically deploy—long before anyone had time to develop hypoxia. The plane would rapidly transition from a darkened cabin with sleeping passengers to a very animated and agitated melee of confused passengers grabbing for their oxygen masks.

Most of the passengers are asleep, and the crew decides to keep it that way for as long as possible.

Baker remembers that the husband of one of the flight attendants is on board and is a former Navy Seal, so he decides to recruit him, along with one of the male flight attendants who has a military background, to guard the cockpit door.

Three very tense hours later, United Flight 105 touches down in Honolulu.

CHAPTER 14

Weapons-Free

**102nd Fighter Wing, Otis Air National Guard Base,
Cape Cod, 9:55 a.m.**

Otis fighter pilots Duff and Nasty are now intensely engaged with intercepting and escorting dozens of aircraft away from New York City.

"We're having the same problem in D.C.," a controller tells Duff as he flies south of New York to intercept an aircraft approaching from the south.

The news arrives like a body blow. He's sickened at the thought that attacks are happening elsewhere around the country. *Knock it off*, he tells himself, quickly checking his thoughts. *That is not my city today. Today, this is my city and this is my mission.* He cannot allow himself to be distracted by things he cannot change.

Down below, watching the Otis fighters from the Newark control tower, air traffic controllers watch the last plane land and taxi to a gate. The airport is eerily quiet. They stare at the burning World Trade Center while helicopters collect like bees around the hive that is southern Manhattan. All airborne news crews have been ordered to land. The skies belong to the military now. In the tower, all nonessential staff—and anyone else wanting to leave—have long since departed. Others have stayed on to do their jobs as best they can.

As Nasty finishes chasing off an aircraft and turns back toward

Manhattan, his radar picks up a target transmitting a "foe" code—
a very uncommon enemy transmission. The target is low over the
Hudson River, and he locks onto it and dives. When he's close
enough to finally identify the foe at the center of his screen, he sees
that it's a large yacht moored in the river. *Shit!* he exclaims. It had
come close to being a very unlucky vessel this morning. He climbs
back up over the city, thinking that he could have done without that
close call.

A little while later, as Duff is escorting an airliner toward JFK
Airport, he notices motion out of the corner of his cockpit and
looks over just in time to see one of the Twin Towers disappear into
a plume of smoke.

He stares, momentarily mesmerized at the cloud of dust. "What's
happening?" he asks Nasty on the radio. Nasty looks toward the
skyline to see that the South Tower has disintegrated into a cloud of
debris.

"Damn!" he exclaims. "They just got another one past us!"

"No, I think the building just collapsed," Duff responds. He
radios NEADS.

"I'm not sure what happened," he reports. "I can still see the
North Tower, but there is this huge cloud of dust. I think one of the
towers just fell."

Tens of thousands of people have just been killed, Nasty thinks
in horror.

The controllers left in Newark tower have watched the collapse
from a front-row seat. Already shell-shocked before witnessing
the collapse, several controllers are pushed over the top by the
sickening spectacle. One throws in his hat. "That's it!" he
announces. "I'm out of here!" He can't take any more; he needs
the refuge of his home. He walks out of the control tower and into
the parking lot below, looking around at the surreal scene before
him: thousands of people wandering the streets and parking lots
with their suitcases in tow. Everyone appears stunned, not sure
where to go or how to get there.

While fear grips the nation as the scene of the South Tower collapsing is played again and again on TV screens, Duff and Nasty refocus on the job at hand. Any qualms they may have felt about shooting down a plane have now completely vanished.

Air Traffic Control, Reagan National Airport,
Washington, D.C., 9:55 a.m.

Tower supervisor Chris Stephenson has just taken a call from the FAA Command Center. "You have another one headed your way," the caller announced. "Confirmed bomb on board." *A bomb?* Dan Creedon thinks when word makes it to the TRACON. *They're already a missile!*

The FAA Command Center has changed the information it had for the flight plan for United 93 so that it shows a destination of Reagan National Airport. By doing so, controllers are now able to track the flight on their situation displays. But with the news that the plane has a bomb on board, the facility manager is thinking about employees, responsibility, and safety, and he decides it's time to evacuate the tower. Following his manager's instructions, Dan Creedon tries repeatedly to call up to get word to the tower, but he can't get through. He finally leaves his post to make his way up there.

For Creedon, coming from the windowless TRACON into the 216-foot control tower is like stepping into another world. He gets his first glimpse of the smoke and debris from the Pentagon when he exits the elevator and climbs the last few steps into the control tower cab. Pieces of paper are still swirling in the air, and several have plastered themselves against the tower windows. A huge plume of smoke is billowing into the sky, blowing almost directly toward the airport.

Creedon announces the order for "minimum bodies" in the control tower: skeletal staff only. One of the controllers had called his wife after the Pentagon was hit and tried to convince her to pick up their kids before the schools placed them in bomb shelters. "But it's employee appreciation day here and the VCR raffle is in two hours. I can't just leave!" she had argued. He hasn't been able to get his mind off his kids since then, and volunteers to leave with three other controllers.

Down in the terminal, the police yell "Everybody's got to go!" while the group from the tower works its way through the panicked crowd. "There are no more flights! Leave your stuff! Just go! It doesn't matter where you go, just get away from the airport."

The remaining tower controllers decide to abandon the tower to move operations to an emergency mobile unit. As they prepare to leave, they overhear a commotion on the radio. One of the D.C. police helicopters, Condor 1, has arrived and wants a park police helicopter—which had taken off with medical personnel just minutes after the crash—to stay away from the Pentagon.

"Everything's cool. It's fine," the park police pilot tries to reassure. "I'm coming up same thing as you."

"No, you need to stay away," the D.C. police pilot orders. "I forbid you to come near the Pentagon."

"No, dude. I'm fine. I'm fine. I'm fine," the park pilot pleads. But he loses the battle and finally leaves the area.[1]

The tower controllers temporarily turn over airspace command and control to the D.C. police helicopters before leaving for the mobile unit. With Secret Service escort, they make their way down from the tower and through the terminal to operations. They're quickly approached by police officers telling them that they need to leave.

"We're okay!" the Secret Service agent responds, flashing his badge.

121st Fighter Squadron, DCANG, Andrews AFB, Maryland, 9:50 a.m.

When D.C. Air National Guard F-16 pilot Billy Hutchison came off the refueling tanker with instructions to return to base, he was puzzled by the unusual interruption of his training mission, but he was more concerned about his young wingman who had been having difficulty getting into Washington's airspace. As soon as he was within radio range of Andrews, Hutchison called the SOF to confirm that his wingman had made it back to base. The response caught him off guard. Razin Caine had been assigned as SOF today, but Lt Col. Dog Thompson responded, and he was clearly uptight about something.

"Bully Flight, we need you here now! You need to return to base 'buster'!"

Hutchison was surprised to hear the code word, which means push the thrust lever into afterburner and fly the plane as fast as it would go, all the way to its limits. He'd never actually heard it used. He didn't know what was going on, but he knew it must be something very, very bad.

Now coming up over the southern end of the Potomac supersonic, he sees a column of smoke rising out of D.C. "Hey, you see that up there?" he calls to his wingman. *Is it a bomb?* he wonders.

Too much is just not adding up. Washington Center hasn't said a word, they've just handed him off to Washington Approach. Hutchison would like some answers, so he calls the Andrews SOF again.

"Do you all see that black smoke?" he asks.

"Yes," Thompson responds. "Just get back here!"

But the Washington Approach controllers have other ideas. Controller Vic Padgett hears F-16 pilot Hutchison check in on the frequency. He tries to get him to divert to go after United 93.

"I'm telling you, mister," Creedon hears Padgett say to Hutchison, "I need you to get up there and I need you to get up there *now* because these guys are coming!"

"We're bingo fuel," Hutchison calls back, indicating that he and his wingman don't have the fuel to legally extend their flight. They had not filled their tanks when refueling, and they've since flown supersonic much of the way to D.C. His wingman is especially low. "We'll turn around as soon as we can but we've got to get down." Hutchison feels awful denying the controller, who is clearly upset. *But what can I do?* he thinks. *We're low on fuel and I don't take orders from air traffic control.*

Back at the 121st Fighter Squadron's Operations Building at Andrews AFB, Wing Commander Col. David Wherley stands next to the SOF, Dog Thompson, waiting on the line for the Secret Service at the White House PEOC. He's been waiting for further instructions about setting up a CAP over Washington. He had asked for specifics, and clearly the agents were working hard to get him the information he needs.

A new agent finally comes on the line and tells him, "We want you to intercept and turn away any airplane that attempts to fly within 20 miles of the Washington area. If you are not able to turn them away, use whatever force is necessary to keep them from hitting any buildings downtown." The instructions have come directly from the vice president.

Wherley has already set the wheels in motion: missile trailers are slowly making their way across base and ground crews are working frantically to offload training armament and upload fuel. But until he can get armed fighters in the air, he knows that his best bet rests with Hutchison and his wingman, unarmed and just a mile away on their return from their shortened training mission.

"How much fuel do they have?" Wherley asks his SOF.

"Bully 1, how much fuel do you have?" Thompson calls to Hutchison.

"What's going on?" Hutchison begs.

"Just get here . . . and how much fuel do you have?"

Hutchison still has some fuel, but his wingman is out. "I've got 2,800 [pounds]," he calls as he lines up with the runway to land.

"Send him around!" Wherley orders.

"Go around!" Thompson calls. "We need you up!"

But it's too late. Hutchison's F-16 is about to touch down. He brakes hard and exits at the first taxiway. *Shit!* he thinks. *What the fuck is going on?*

"I'm already down but I'm coming back around to take off!" he radios while he high-speeds back on the parallel taxiway to take off again. The SOF is back on the radio with instructions from the wing commander.

"Go where ATC directs," Thompson relays. "Intercept that airliner and use whatever force is necessary to prevent it from getting to D.C. Do not let the wreckage fall within 20 miles! You are weapons-free. Do you understand?"

"Yes, sir!" Hutchison responds; he is keeping his cool, but he is shocked. "Weapons-free" means that the decision to engage a target now rests solely with him. He doesn't know what is going on, but he understands clearly that he is being sent to take out an airliner. He has no weapons on board, and the realization hits him like a body blow—he may have to take out the plane by flying his own plane into it.

Andrews tower frequency clears him for takeoff before he even gets to the runway.

"Bully 1, you are cleared for takeoff. Over to Approach." Quickly rounding the corner onto the runway and adding takeoff thrust, a fleeting thought passes through his mind of his young son, the most precious thing in his world. No time for that, though, and he pushes the thought out of his mind and calls Washington Approach.

"Bully 1 is looking for a contact."

"We have an intercept for you northwest of here and coming down the Potomac," Padgett calls from Washington Approach.

Hutchison swallows hard, then inhales deeply through his oxygen mask. His loud breath seems to echo in his helmet.

Rather than climbing steeply, he flies low over the White House and Georgetown to conserve fuel and gain airspeed, which he gradually converts to altitude. A Washington Center controller, busy scanning the airspace for other suspect aircraft, notices the fast flyer over the White House. He immediately radios the information to the Langley flight lead, Dean Eckmann, who is currently between Washington and Baltimore several miles up, at 25,000 feet.

Padgett quickly relays to Hutchison the location of United 93, but Hutchison cannot understand exactly where he is supposed to be looking for the target. It doesn't help him to know where the plane is relative to some city or navigational aid. He needs to know where it is in relation to his own aircraft.

It occurs to him that he and the controller are not speaking the same language. The military works to bring aircraft together—and hence has very specific methods for relaying target location information—while air traffic controllers work diligently to do the opposite: to keep planes apart. The controller is doing his best to give Hutchison the location of the hijacked airliner, but his directions are not in terms that Hutchison can understand. Seeking a solution, Hutchison tells the controller to give him a vector from his current location along with a distance to the target. This method works, and Hutchison quickly spots the aircraft on his radar. But just after locating the target, United 93 disappears from his screen. It has descended too low, blending in with the ground clutter—false radar returns resulting from the radar beam scattering off objects near the earth's surface. He struggles to spot the return again while he aims his F-16 up the Potomac. A minute later it reappears, as United 93 climbs back through 10,000 feet.

He's been in combat many times, with multiple tours in Iraq, but he's never been in a situation like this. He begins to think about any options he has for taking out the airliner, other than crashing into it. He has 105 training rounds on board and he quickly comes up with a plan: he will first try to take the plane down with practice rounds fired into one of the engines, and then across the cockpit. He'll have to get close to attempt either. If that does not sufficiently disable the aircraft, then he will use his own plane as a missile. He thinks again of his son and prays to God that his mission won't end that way.

United 93, 10:00 a.m.

One hundred and eighty miles to the west, about 20 miles northwest of Johnstown, Pennsylvania, a heroic struggle has just taken place aboard United 93. Brave passengers are taking their destiny into their own hands. In doing so, they will spare other Americans greater pain and suffering, and most likely Billy Hutchison his life.

Their plans began soon after the hijacking, when passengers and surviving crew members started to make calls on the GTE Airfones. They learned of the attacks on the World Trade Center and the Pentagon. "Don't worry," passenger Tom Burnett told his wife, "we're going to do something." [2]

Moments ago, as Billy Hutchison began his pursuit of the airliner, the group stormed the front of the plane, trying to break into the cockpit as the aircraft descended.

"Shall we finish it off?" a hijacker asked when it became apparent that the passengers were going to penetrate the cockpit.

"No. Not yet. When they all come, we finish it off," another replied as the aircraft climbed back steeply to 10,000 feet.

When a beverage cart smashed through the cockpit door, the hijacker asked again, "Is that it? I mean, shall we put it down?"

"Yes, put it in it, and pull it down," came the response. The hijackers then rolled the plane upside down, and one ordered, "Pull it down! Pull it down!"

The inverted plane turned down toward the ground at a 45-degree angle. "Allah is the greatest! Allah is the greatest!" were the last words on the cockpit voice recorder. [3]

Not long after Hutchison loses the target again, the Washington controller loses it also. Hutchison works his radar to scan all the airspace in front of him, high and low, but it's just not there anymore. He is perplexed. The airliner has simply disappeared. After another minute of searching, Hutchison knows that he must make a choice. If he keeps looking, he risks not having the fuel to get home. If he flames out, he will crash. He looks again at his fuel gauge and realizes that he must turn back toward the city. He doesn't have the fuel to continue flying outbound for a target that can't be located, and losing power and crashing his F-16 is not an option.

In yet another of the day's strange coincidences C-130 pilot Steve O'Brien, who less than 30 minutes earlier had witnessed the crash of American 77 into the Pentagon, is now flying over Pennsylvania. He gets a traffic call from air traffic control. "Gofer 0-6, Cleveland Center," the controller calls. "We've got traffic at your 12 o'clock, altitude unknown. Do you have any traffic in sight out there?" Unknown to the controller, the plane is in its final dive. Since the controller hasn't given the traffic's altitude, O'Brien scans up and down in the skies in front of his C-130.

"Negative, Cleveland Center," he tells them after looking. "We don't have traffic in sight."

"Gofer 0-6, roger. Fly heading 3-6-0," the controller directs, turning the aircraft to keep them away from United 93.

"Hey, we've got smoke off our left," the loadmaster behind O'Brien reports after they make their turn. O'Brien looks down at black smoke coming from an open field. He hopes it is a tire fire or something similarly benign, but he advises Cleveland Center just in case.

"Cleveland Center, Gofer 0-6. We've got smoke coming off the ground at our 9 o'clock, 15 miles."

"Roger, thanks," the controller says. "That traffic I was calling out isn't on our scope anymore. That's about where it disappeared."

O'Brien is stunned. He cannot believe the horror he is witnessing—first in Washington, and now over Pennsylvania.

119th Fighter Wing Alert Detachment, Langley AFB, Virginia, 10:00 a.m.

When the three Langley alert fighters arrive over the Baltimore-Washington area at 10 o'clock, Borgy is still speaking to NEADS on his UHF radio while Eckmann talks to Washington Center. They're communicating between themselves as needed on their auxiliary frequency.

Borgy has just heard a startling message broadcast on the emergency frequency. It is in response to Ben Sliney's order to land everything, and very specific instructions from the Secret Service.

"Attention all aircraft! Attention all aircraft! You are ordered to land at the nearest suitable airport. All aircraft must land immediately. Violators will be shot down."

We're under attack! Borgy realizes. He doesn't know who the enemy is, or that commercial airliners are the weapons, but he understands the seriousness of the situation. He is on the front lines of a war that he knows nothing about.

"The Secret Service has just entered the building," the Washington Center controller advises Eckmann. Controllers have been busily looking for any suspect aircraft in the vicinity, and now they find one: it's coming up fast, following the Potomac toward the White House. This is actually Billy Hutchison, heading off to United 93, but the Washington controller doesn't know that.

The controller explains that all airplanes in the United States have been ordered to land and that Eckmann is to "protect the House at all costs by order of the vice president." Unknown to NEADS, their lead F-16 pilot over Washington is being given shoot-down authority directly from the Secret Service, bypassing the military chain of command.

Eckmann immediately relays the information about the aircraft heading toward the White House to Borgy, who quickly gets on the radio to NEADS Weapons Director Citino, asking for specific instructions.

At NEADS, the Ops floor has been reeling from multiple reports of suspect aircraft. Bob Marr has Col. Dawne Deskins from the battle cab go to speak with Nasypany directly, to be sure that all the information they're getting from different sources is flowing back and forth between them. There is another hijacked flight coming down from Canada, Deskins advises Nasypany, and Marr has contacted Syracuse to go after it. (This report of a plane incoming from Canada, like many, is later found to be erroneous.) Meanwhile Toledo is getting airborne, at Marr's orders, to go after Delta 1989, she informs him.

"I've got two coming up on status at Fargo and two at Sioux City," Nasypany adds to her summary. "I went above," he continues, indicating that he gave those orders on his own accord rather than waiting for authorization.

At 10:05, controllers at Cleveland Center are still trying to locate United 93, which has just crashed. The military liaison there—still unaware of the flight's fate—puts in a call to NEADS to make sure they know the flight is heading directly for Washington. Communicating with NEADS is not one of his responsibilities, but he's calling nonetheless just to make sure they're in the loop. NEADS specialists now begin to search frantically to locate United 93's radar return on their scopes, working from the last known coordinates and the transponder code for the flight. Nasypany listens in on the phone line to the Cleveland Center controller and simultaneously reports to Marr. He knows one thing for sure: this plane is *not* going to be allowed to make it to Washington. He will push as hard as necessary to prevent that. It is while Nasypany is conferring with Marr about the report on United 93 that the radio call from Borgy comes in, asking for specific instructions on how to handle the aircraft the Secret Service has ordered them to shoot down if necessary.

"Any words?" Borgy says.

"Stand by," Citino tells him. He turns to Foxy, the senior weapons director, and asks, "Do you copy that? Center said there's an aircraft over the White House. Any words?"

"We've got an aircraft coming up over the White House," Foxy calls to Nasypany, who is still on the phone to Marr.

"Intercept!" Nasypany shouts to his team. "Intercept and divert that aircraft away from there!"

"Okay, did you hear that?" Nasypany reports to Marr on the shout line. "Aircraft over the White House. What's the word? Intercept and what else?"

Marr has a phone to each ear and information is coming at him from multiple directions. He doesn't hear Nasypany's news of an aircraft over the White House. "Aircraft . . . *over* . . . *the White House*!" Nasypany repeats again, pausing this time on each word for emphasis.

The shocking news forces the issue of shoot-down authority. Marr and General Arnold must now immediately make a decision. They've been trying to sort out exactly what the rules of engagement are in respect to potential targets, but now there is no more time. Although Cheney has issued shoot-down orders to the DCANG through the Secret Service, CONR commander General Arnold has received no such orders from his higher-ups at NORAD. He talked to Maj. Gen. Rick Findlay at NORAD headquarters and asked him to get shoot-down authority from the vice president, but he's still heard nothing back. In light of the imminent attack on the White House he decides he will exercise the authority he has to protect the nation in an emergency.

"We will intercept and attempt to divert," he says to Marr. "If we can't, then we'll shoot it down."

At the weapons station, Citino relays orders to the Langley fighters: "Quit 2-5, mission is to intercept aircraft over White House!" he instructs. "Divert the aircraft from the House!"

"Divert the aircraft," Borgy orders. Instantly, Eckmann rolls inverted and pulls his aircraft down and toward the White House, quickly breaking the sound barrier. As the ear-splitting sonic boom thunders above the city, terrified Washington workers, spilling from government buildings, share one thought: D.C. is under attack. Among the sidewalks and streets filled with sobs and panicked footsteps, a woman seeks comfort by touching a stranger's shoulder; a man stares wide-eyed into the pulsing mob; a police officer urgently coaxes him onward. But Billy Hutchison's jet is long gone by now, farther up the Potomac.

In the battle cab, Marr immediately turns his attention to United 93. The commanders do not want to leave Washington vulnerable by pulling the Langley fighters away from the city too soon to intercept this flight. What if there is yet another aircraft coming in from a different sector? They'll let United 93 get closer, then they'll issue orders to take it out. "We will take lives in the air to save lives on the ground," Arnold proclaims.

The commanders face a critical decision: Do they pass on

weapons-free authorizations, or keep the authority to shoot down at NEADS? Marr does not want to pass on kill authority to the pilots until he can determine how they can safely implement the order. His fighters are accustomed to operating under highly specific rules of engagement. There is a strict challenge-response protocol in place for shooting down a hostile target, and all of the pilots train for that scenario. Before he tells them to make the call on their own, he wants to be sure they have a method of verifying that an airliner is a threat. He is *not* going to shoot down civilians without making sure the threat is real. He has experience with the fog of war and knows how readily tragic mistakes can be made.

The decision is not without merit. Across the nation, several flight crews who are anxious to get on the ground are canceling their flight clearances—pulling themselves entirely out of the air traffic control system. They're changing their assigned transponders to the codes normally used by small, private aircraft. They're landing at airports not intended for them and not on their filed flight plans. Some are turning around and aiming for large cities. They're doing whatever it takes to get their planes safely on the ground and may well give the impression of being hijacks.

The commanders decide to issue kill commands as required, using the standard rules of engagement and keeping shoot-down authority in their own hands. Orders will come from the battle cab, and pilots will follow their training and challenge the Weapons controller for authentication. The commanders know that if they must issue such an order, it will be a lose-lose situation. It will likely mean an end to their military careers and a future filled with endless legal battles. But they'll do it.

They have not confirmed that the flight over the White House that the Langley flight lead is intercepting is hostile, and they have just learned from the chat log that the White House also has fighter assets over the capital.[4] They cannot give Eckmann an order to attack unless they can positively identify the aircraft and confirm it as a threat. Marr forwards instructions to Nasypany on the Ops floor, where the order is quickly passed on to the Weapons Team.

"Negative clearance to shoot!" Nasypany instructs his weapons controllers. "ID/Type/Tail!" The orders mean that the fighters must identify the target over the White House by aircraft type and tail number, and do nothing more, waiting for further instructions.

Citino attempts to forward the additional instructions to Borgy, but cannot get through. The reception is weak over the Washington area, and NEADS loses the ability to communicate whenever Borgy flies below a certain altitude.

"They can do whatever they need to do to divert it, but they are *not* cleared to fire," Foxy reiterates. But Citino still cannot get through to them.

"I have no comms!" he exclaims. "They're very low!" He calls again, and finally gets through. Highly agitated, Citino tries to reassure himself. "We're doing good, Huck," he says to Sergeant Huckabone, his teammate. "We're doing good! We're doing good!"

"Quit 2-5, when able, say type of aircraft," he radios to Borgy. "What is your distance to target?"

Borgy explains to the Weapons controller that he is not Quit 2-5. He is Quit 2-6 and he is relaying orders to Quit 2-5, Eckmann. He also responds that Eckmann is 15 miles from the White House.

Eckmann is near the surface now, searching for the incoming plane, but he can't see anything other than a slow-moving sheriff's helicopter and a Huey UH-1. He figures they are evacuating wounded from the Pentagon. He passes the word back up to Borgy—who relays the information back to NEADS—then loops around and decides to fly low over the Mall to see if he can spot anything unusual. He looks up just in time to find that his F-16 is heading straight for the Washington Monument.

"Whoa!" he says out loud, quickly checking his aircraft to the left. *Yeah, that would be real great if I fly this F-16 into the damn monument!* That's not the distinguished place in history he'd prefer.

Delta Flight 1989, Boston–Los Angeles, 10:10 a.m.

Many miles away, military jets are closing in on another potential target. Dave Dunlap is not only unaware that the Cleveland Airport is being evacuated for his impending arrival, he also doesn't know that fighters from nearby Air National Guard bases have been scrambled to intercept his flight.

Fortunately, Delta 1989 is closely following all controller instructions. In what he believes to be the widest approach pattern ever flown, Dunlap quickly realizes that his 767 is being descended out over the water. This realization doesn't do much to comfort him as air traffic controllers call up three more times with the same query: "Delta 1989, are you 'late' today?"

"Negative. Delta 1989 is not 'late' today," the captain responds firmly to each query. Finally, the plane is turned to final approach and instructed to contact the tower. *Almost there*, Dunlap thinks, happy to hear other aircraft on the frequency. He hadn't heard any other radio communications in quite some time and had begun to feel he was alone in the sky. It hasn't occurred to him that air traffic control has directed his flight to a discrete frequency after determining it was hijacked so that no other flights were communicating on it. Now on the frequency with the tower, he's hearing other communications again.

Established on final approach and talking to the control tower, Dunlap notices that flights landing before his are being instructed to "taxi immediately" to their gates. He cannot help but dwell on the word "immediately" conspicuously added to each clearance. Almost without exception, pilot-controller communications are one of those highly standardized areas in aviation, and that simple extra word speaks volumes. Also, pilots don't generally clear the runway, then loiter before meandering to their gates. Dunlap tries hard to disregard the unsettling clearances while he maneuvers the 767 gently toward the touchdown zone.

An enormous sense of relief rushes over him when he eases the main landing gear gently onto the runway center line. Pulling up on the thrust levers, then pushing them back toward their rearmost détente, he deploys the thrust reversers. The barreling aircraft obediently decelerates.

He waits for the same "Left turn at the end of the runway and taxi immediately to your gate" clearance that the controller has issued to so many other flights. But as he rolls out the controller instead tells him to make a right turn off the runway. *Okay*, Dunlap figures, *the normal path to the gates is clogged and they're taking us around the other end.* He backtracks down the taxiway and away from the terminal.

"Delta 1989, taxi left onto taxiway Bravo and wait there," the controller further instructs.

Looking out the cockpit window at the approaching taxiways, Dunlap doesn't see any taxiway Bravo. He glances down at the airport diagram he has clipped on the board next to him and quickly finds it, noting that the taxiway leads to a very remote part of the airport, far away from the terminal. He feels a lump rising in his throat. The sense of relief he felt upon landing turns to dread. As much as he wishes this nightmare were over, clearly it's not.

Captain Werner stops the aircraft where directed and sets the parking brake. The pilots stare blankly at each other, neither knowing what to say or do. So they wait.

"What are we supposed to tell our passengers?" Dunlap finally asks, breaking the long silence.

"I have no idea," Werner responds.

While the captain collects his thoughts, Dunlap tries to get a call through to his wife. He gets the answering machine and leaves a message letting her know that he is on the ground in Cleveland. Thankfully, their baby is allowing her to sleep in this morning and she will hear his voice before ever turning on the television. Next he calls his dad. "Hey, Dad," he says, "I just wanted to let you know that I'm safe on the ground in Cleveland."

"Good for you, son," comes a blasé response. His father is completely unaware of the day's events.

"Turn on the TV, Dad," Dunlap responds before hanging up the phone.

Air Force One, 10:15 a.m.

Air Force One pilot Col. Mark Tillman has just taken off with the president and his entourage out of Sarasota, Florida, and is planning to return to Andrews AFB. But there already appears to be a threat against the aircraft. A phone call has come in saying "Angel is next," the caller referring to Air Force One, using the relatively unknown code name for this aircraft.[5] Tillman thinks that his best option is to climb: climb fast and climb high. The passengers can't help but notice the aircraft's unusually fast take-off and steep climb. It seems as though the plane is flying straight up.

There hasn't been time to coordinate fighter escorts, and Tillman racks his brain to think of ways to protect the president. He requests an armed guard placed at the cockpit door while the Secret Service double-checks the identity of everyone on board.

Air traffic control now reports that a suspect airliner is dead ahead. Tillman pushes the thrust levers full forward and pulls the nose of the 747 upward into an even steeper climb. It's the only choice he can make: get where they cannot go—high!

Somehow Tillman needs to hide this monstrous 747. He is no longer comfortable using his radio. He knows that hijackers are on the frequencies and able to hear transmissions, so he uses his telephone to call air traffic control.

"We have no clearance at this time," he tells them. "We are just going to fly across the United States."

As the rest of the morning's drama unfolds, air traffic controllers working the various centers continue to pass off Air Force One as it crosses their airspace, issuing the same warning on each hand-off: keep the route a secret.

"Okay, where's he going?" a controller asks on one such hand-off.

"Just watch him," the previous handler instructs. "Don't question him where he's going. Just work him and watch him. There's no flight plan in and right now we're not going to put anything in. Okay?"

Although the president expresses his desire to return to Washington, Vice President Cheney strenuously objects: there are still too many planes unaccounted for and feared hijacked. It is simply *not safe*. Air Force One spends the morning flying without a destination until it's finally decided that the plane should land at Barksdale Air Force Base in Louisiana. En route, the 747 is met by several F-16 fighters, providing a military escort to the president for the first time in history.

CHAPTER 15

Shoot-Down Authority

102nd Fighter Wing, Otis Air National Guard Base,
Cape Cod, 10:20 a.m.

After escorting another airliner into New York's JFK Airport, Otis
F-15 pilot Duff tells the NEADS controller that he is going to go
take a look at the North Tower. But as soon as he arrives over the
city, he's advised of a fast-moving target coming down the Hudson.
He pushes his F-15 into afterburner and dives down to 1,500 feet
over Manhattan and then Central Park.

His target turns out to be a corporate aircraft, and he intercepts
it and turns it away, then heads back to check on the North Tower.
He witnessed the shocking collapse of the South Tower and,
although he's no architect, he figures he can certainly get a decent
idea of the second tower's structural integrity.

"There's no way they can do a rescue operation," he calls to the
NEADS Weapons controller.

With all the fire and smoke, he doesn't see how they could possibly get any rescue aircraft to the roof. He flies directly over the blaz-
ing building to see if it appears to be leaning or twisted—anything
that would indicate that it's at risk of falling. But as he looks down,
the tower looks perfect. The square of the roof seems perfectly
aligned with the rest of the building. There doesn't appear to be any
tilt or twist. He's relieved and feels confident that the fire will just
burn out the top floors and they'll be able to save the building.

"The building looks structurally really good," he calls to NEADS. But no sooner does he finish his sentence than he notices that the top of the building appears to be moving away from him. He can't comprehend what he's seeing—it makes no sense.

When he sees a plume of smoke come out of the bottom of the structure, he understands that the building is falling away from him. And it's not just falling—it's imploding. Stunned, he realizes that if *he* thought the structure had looked good from the air, then surely so did the people on the ground. *What about all those firefighters?* he thinks.

Taken off his game by the sight, Duff has to make an intense effort to focus on the task at hand. *No emotion, focus right now!* he scolds himself.

**121st Fighter Squadron, DCANG, Andrews AFB,
Maryland, 10:25 a.m.**

When Billy Hutchison turns toward the capital after his unsuccessful attempt to locate an inbound hijacked airliner, Washington Approach controller Dan Creedon is still in the TRACON. Secret Service has just called to say that the target Hutchison had been sent to take down is gone. It's no longer a threat. That's only so much comfort for Creedon, though, who is concerned about planes and helicopters that are taking off and landing all over the city, mostly flights evacuating government officials according to the Continuity of Government protocol. Many medevac helicopters are also flying in and out of the area of the Pentagon. He recognizes some of the larger aircraft, like the one circling over the White House, but he doesn't recognize most of the other planes. *People are already freaking out,* he thinks as he watches. *Why are you flying right overhead?* Few flights are talking to him, only adding to the confusion. The ones that are, are getting blanket departure clearances: "Altitude/heading at your discretion. Released!" Never in his career has he given such clearances.

"We have more contacts!" he calls to Hutchison, advising him of more suspect aircraft in the area.

"Roger that. I'll investigate," Hutchison says. He looks down at his fuel gauge and tries to determine just exactly how much longer he can stay airborne. He's only a few miles from Andrews at this point, and although he has less fuel than he is allowed to fly with, he can't bring himself to leave while there are still threats—or until some other fighters can get there to relieve him. He doesn't know that the Langley fighters are now also protecting the capital, although at much higher altitudes.

Hutchison tries to check out the targets that Creedon has called, but he keeps losing them in the ground clutter on his radar screen. The flights are too close to the surface and, from what he can see, appear to be mostly helicopters flying medevac from the Pentagon. There are no commercial airliners in sight, but there's a whole lot of smoke.

What the hell has happened there? he wonders, still having been given no explanation of the events.

Hutchison had seen that the Pentagon was on fire when he approached Andrews at supersonic speed a half hour earlier and figured some kind of bomb had exploded. The scene reminded him of the fires he had witnessed from the oil wells over in Iraq: billows of heavy, dark smoke.

He decides it's time to investigate. Pointing his F-16 toward the earth, he descends to a mere 150 feet above the ground and knife-edges over the top of the burning Pentagon in a steep, counterclockwise circuit. Down below, where firefighting efforts have been suspended due to reports that another airliner is incoming, one firefighter has evacuated to the center courtyard, where he is waiting for the second plane to crash into the building. He hears the furious roar of engines overhead and braces himself, certain that the attacking plane has arrived. When he looks up to see an American jet fighter sweep just overhead, he is relieved beyond words.

Hutchison dodges the helicopters and makes a full circle around the burning complex and over the buildings of neighboring Crystal

City. The air traffic controllers at National Airport watch the F-16 fly past with a surge of relief.

"Our boys have arrived," one comments.

Pentagon staffers evacuating the building and aiding the wounded look up to watch the fighter scream right over their heads. Although he is flying low only to get a glimpse of what has happened, the reassuring sight of the F-16 offers an immeasurable sense of comfort and protection as they confront the death and destruction around them. They know that the area is now secure.

Meanwhile, down in the windowless TRACON, Dan Creedon is already calling out another contact for him to check out.

Back at Hutchison's base at Andrews, the other pilots of the 121st Fighter have been grabbing their gear and uploading flight data onto discs; these contain all the navigational waypoints, maps, and frequencies that they will need once airborne. A report now comes into the White House from the FAA that there are three planes unaccounted for, and the Secret Service determines it needs fighters up *now,* and again calls the DCANG.

Squadron Commander Sass Sasseville decides that he and his wingman will launch with hot guns only. They can't wait any longer on the missiles. They'll have only their 20 mm guns, which means they will need to be in significantly closer striking proximity to take out targets, but at least they will be there.

"Let's go!" he calls out to his young wingman, Lt. Heather "Lucky" Penney Garcia, who has been busy uploading discs with information they may need for their mission.

A third-generation pilot, Lucky caught the bug of flying, the love of the smell of jet fuel, and the brotherhood of the Air National Guard from her father. An Air National Guard pilot, he had taught her to fly in high school, then handed her off to a certified flight instructor to get legal. Her dream of flying fighters finally came true just months earlier, in January 2001, when she was hired as the first female F-16 fighter pilot with the DCANG. Having completed basic training and then pilot training at Sheppard Air Force Base in

Texas, she has just recently returned to the DCANG, fully qualified to fly her F-16.

All morning she has felt merely along for the ride as the senior officers around her became quickly occupied with the business of war—a business about which she knows very little. She has tried to keep track of all the names flying around in the conversations. *Colonel who? General who?* Most of them are unfamiliar, officers too high-ranking for her to have heard their names before. She has stayed busy reprogramming flight data discs, which still contain all the Nellis data from the Red Flag training exercise they just returned from. She hurries to gather all of her discs when Sass calls out to her.

"Lucky, you're with me! Igor, you're with Razin," he calls. "Let's go!"

All Sass can think of is Pearl Harbor. Only two pilots got off the ground that day; many lives were lost as a result. He doesn't want that to happen to the DCANG. He wants to get their planes up there to do *something*.

Lucky runs across the ramp behind him, still fastening her G suit and trying to keep up. Neither have had the luxury of any briefing from their commander, but Sass briefs what he knows while they sprint. "I have no idea what's going on," he yells, "but we're flying! Here's our frequency. We'll split up the air as we have to. Just defend as required. We'll talk about the rest in the air!"

Lucky arrives at her jet and begins to preflight her aircraft. It's what she's been trained to do.

"JUST GET IN THE AIRPLANE AND START IT!" Sass commands, climbing quickly into his own.

She abandons her preflight inspection and clambers into her plane. She starts the engine before she even has her harness buckled to her ejection seat. The jet hasn't been started for three days, and other than the preflight from the crew chief, no one has inspected the aircraft. As a young lieutenant, she is inclined to cling tightly to procedures, but she accepts that today she has no choice. She switches on all of her radios and anticipates the customary 8-minute wait for the Inertial Navigational System to spool up. Sass calls her on the radio. "Let's go!"

"Sir, I don't even have my . . ." she begins to object.

"Doesn't matter!" he interrupts, starting to taxi. "Let's go!"

Panicked to see her squadron commander taxi away, Lucky yells to her crew chief. "Pull the chocks! I've got to go!" She moves the throttle forward, and her F-16 obediently accelerates off the flight line.

"Are you pulling pins?" she calls to the ground crews.

They're trying! While her F-16 pulls away, the crew chiefs are running alongside and underneath, doing their best to pull the control pins that lock the weapons and control surfaces.

Back in Ops, Wing Commander Col. Dave Wherley has to translate the unequivocal instructions he received from the Secret Service at the White House into something that his pilots can use. The agent said the jets must protect a 20-mile perimeter around Washington, but Wherley knows that it would be nearly impossible for an F-16 to intercept and turn away—much less shoot down—an aircraft that is already within 20 miles of a potential target. An airliner will simply be moving too fast. He comes up with meaningful military rules of engagement and quickly briefs pilots Captain Brandon "Igor" Rasmussen and Razin when they pass by the SOF area on their way to fly. "You need to establish a CAP over Washington. Intercept any incoming aircraft 60 miles out and use whatever force necessary to keep it from targeting buildings downtown."

"You will be weapons-free," he adds. "Just be careful."

Such shoot-down authority is highly unusual for NORAD and the Air National Guard, which are generally "weapons-tight," firing only at the explicit instruction of commanders. Although the DCANG's pilots have flown weapons-free overseas while in combat, they are not part of the Air Defense Mission of 1st Air Force. They have no experience flying armed—much less weapons-free—as part of America's air defense. Colonel Wherley knows that his pilots fully recognize the enormous responsibility this authorization carries and the critical judgment they are being expected to exercise.

"YOU are the Capital Guardians," he reminds his pilots. "And YOU are in charge of this CAP!"

NEADS, Rome, New York, 10:15 a.m.

NEADS receives word that United 93 has crashed at 10:15, when Tech Sgt. Kelley Watson calls Washington Center to give them a report on the flight, which the ID techs are still unable to locate. Watson's initial reaction is relief, thinking the plane has landed. But the controller quickly corrects her.

"He did not land," he clarifies.

"Oh, he's down? DOWN?" she asks, startled by more tragic news.

Nasypany's thundering voice echoes across the command floor of NEADS: "Did we shoot down that plane?"

As news of the crash spreads, similar questions abound at the White House and throughout the echelons of NORAD. Yet because of the heroism of the men and women aboard United 93, no American—and no fighter pilot—will have to live with the legacy of having shot down an airliner full of innocent civilians on this day. Had the plane not crashed, it would have arrived in Washington at approximately 10:25 to 10:30. NEADS would have had approximately 20 minutes to prepare for its arrival after first learning of its approach at 10:06, and the Langley fighters would have been in position to intercept and shoot down the flight, although Hutchison probably would have gotten to it first.

No sooner has the word about United 93 come into NEADS than attention is refocused on a group of unidentified planes that have just been spotted by the Canadian border. Air Force One is requesting escort. Officers at CONR headquarters are making calls to find any available jets to provide escort, regardless of branch of service. As a result, a call comes in from a colonel from the 1st

Fighter Wing at Langley. He explains that they would love to help, but that the "three star" (general) at Air Combat Command has told them to stand by since, technically, the wing belongs to Air Combat Command, not NORAD. In times of war, commanders can waive a significant amount of the military bureaucracy and make such decisions, but they are assuming an enormous personal responsibility if they do so and something terribly wrong happens. This morning, as they do their best to create a national air defense suitable to this attack, NEADS is continually reminded of the military bureaucracy governing orders and authorizations. Fortunately, it turns out that fighters from a unit at Houston's Ellington Air National Guard Base, among others, will be able to provide the president's escort.

On the NMCC teleconference, a lieutenant colonel now notifies the NMCC that the vice president has cleared fighters to engage inbound aircraft if they can verify that the aircraft is hijacked. When this information makes it to NORAD and then down to CONR headquarters, a message is sent out via the chat log to all three sectors (Western, Northeast, and Southeast): "10:31 Vice President has cleared us to intercept tracks of interest and shoot them down if they do not respond, per CONR CC [General Arnold]." [1]

On the NEADS Ops floor, the information creates confusion. Maj. Steve Ovens, a major in mission crew commander training, sees the chat message and, with Nasypany's concurrence, immediately draw Foxy's attention to it.

"You need to read this," he says, showing the order to Foxy. "Region Commander has declared we can shoot down tracks if they are not responding to our direction. Copy that?"

Ovens is not convinced that the message has been understood, so he reads it again. "Okay?" he asks.

"Okay. Copy that, sir," Foxy responds.

"So if you're trying to divert somebody and he won't divert—"

"DO [director of operations] is saying no," Foxy cuts him off. The Director of Operations, Col. Lanny McNeely, is indicating "no." He had understood that the battle staff wanted to keep shoot-down authority in the battle cab. The commanders were not prepared to pass such authorizations to airborne fighters.

"No?" Ovens thunders. "It came over the chat log. You got a conflict on that direction?"

"Right now, no, but—"

"Okay!" Ovens retorts, showing him the message. He needs assurances that his crew will cooperate if a shoot-down becomes necessary. "Okay, you read that from the vice president, right? Vice President has cleared . . ."

"Vice President has cleared us to intercept traffic and shoot them down if they do not respond, per CC." Foxy reads. "Okay, I'll pass it to Weapons." It doesn't take long for the information to get out.

Since they launched over Ohio, the F-16s from Toledo's 180th Fighter Wing have been having difficulty contacting NEADS on the frequency they have been given. The NEADS Weapons officer has been communicating with them via Cleveland Center. With this new and critical information, he gets on the phone to the Cleveland controller to make sure the fighters have these new rules of engagement. In the battle cab, though, Marr is not aware that any blanket authorizations are going out.

F-16 pilots Gus Rinke and Scooter Reed from Toledo's 180th Fighter Wing—who are not tasked for an alert mission but have responded to NEADS's urgent call nonetheless—wouldn't have thought things could get stranger, but they do when they get their next radio call from Cleveland Center. "Sting 1-1, Cleveland Center, do you know what your ROE is?" the controller asks. Scooter is surprised to hear a civilian controller use the military acronym for "rules of engagement."

"Sting 1-1, no," he responds simply.

"Would you like to know?" the controller asks.

"Well, sure . . . yes!" Scooter says, realizing that this day is even stranger than he thought.

"Sting 1-1, if you have a nonmilitary aircraft moving toward a population center, you are clear to engage." The controller has been given his instructions from one of the NEADS Weapons controllers because NEADS has not been able to bring up the fighters directly on their UHF frequency. The NEADS techs have resorted to relaying instructions through air traffic control. It's the best they can do.

"Did he just say what I think he said?" Gus asks.

"Cleveland Center, Sting 1-1, please confirm ROE," Scooter calls.

"Sting 1-1, if the airplane you are vectored against does not comply with your instructions, you are cleared to engage." Scooter is shocked; he's just been given clearance—from a civilian controller—to shoot down a commercial airliner.

Boston Center, Nashua, New Hampshire, 10:20 a.m.

Boston Center controller Colin Scoggins is still listening to the FAA headquarter's hijack net, and it appears that the attack is escalating. An Iberian airliner has been reported hijacked off the coast of Spain, and there is also a report of a hijack or possible crash at Camp David. Most worrisome to him, however, is a large, slow-moving target he sees on his screen, approaching his own sector from the east. It's just off the coast and is heading directly for Boston.

He gets on the phone with Giant Killer, the Navy-operated air traffic controller for waters off the East Coast, to find out more about this suspect target.

"We have a large, slow-moving target approaching Cape Cod and heading for Boston," he announces. "Do you have it? What is it?"

"We're looking. We've got a fleet of ships heading toward the northeast and an Aegis cruiser on the way," the Giant Killer controller reports in the meantime, referring to a high-tech warship capable of performing search, tracking, and missile guidance functions simultaneously for over 100 targets.

That's wonderful, but Scoggins is concerned that they're not able to specifically identify the target he's seen. It appears to be heading straight for Boston Center's facility, and Scoggins can understand why. *If I wanted to use airliners to attack a country*, he thinks, *I would take out their air traffic control facilities!*

As he continues to watch the unidentified aircraft, he learns from a colleague that a large tractor-trailer has parked directly in front of the controller's facility on New Hampshire's Route 3. The staff is becoming increasingly anxious. When the regional FAA office in Burlington, Massachusetts, calls to report that an unidentified aircraft is heading for their facility, all hell breaks loose. Managers immediately order the closure and evacuation of the building, declaring "ATC Zero"—a complete shutdown of the center's airspace. Workers run out of the building while managers try to determine which, if any, personnel will remain.

To make matters worse, in the midst of the mass confusion, a bomb scare call comes in to the child care facility. Managers quickly decide that *everyone* must evacuate. Scoggins stays behind to make two calls. First he dials Gander/Moncton Center, the Canadian air traffic control facility that handles arriving flights from over the Atlantic. "Yeah, Boston Center here," he announces, his voice cracking. "We're going to ATC Zero and evacuating." He checks himself, aware for the first time of the incredible emotional burden he is bearing. He's alone in the building now. His next call is to NEADS.

"I wanted to let you know," he begins, his voice again breaking, "Boston Center has declared ATC Zero and we are evacuating due to an airborne threat. It's approaching Martha's Vineyard and it's coming our way." He gives NEADS the airspeed and coordinates of the approaching aircraft and then hangs up to get out of the building. By the time he gets outside, SWAT and FBI teams are surrounding the facility.

At NEADS, the information is quickly passed on. A Weapons controller makes an urgent call on the scramble line to Otis Air

National Guard base. There is little doubt in his mind that this target is going to get shot out of the sky.

"Get everything you've got in the air!" he directs. "NOW!"

102nd Fighter Wing, Otis Air National Guard Base, Cape Cod 10:20 a.m.

At Otis, the pilots who have returned from their aborted training missions—and those who have just arrived at the base from their homes—are fixated on the television in the break room. Lt. Col. Jon "Tracer" Treacy, their squadron commander, gathers them in front of the Ops desk. "This is what we know," Tracer begins. "This is clearly a national emergency. Two aircraft have been hijacked and flown into the World Trade Center. The Pentagon has been attacked. We need to get all our jets ready to go because we're not sure where this is leading. We have information that there are more coming.

"You must be prepared to meet any surprise," he continues. "You have had years of training and preparation. This is not what I expected, and certainly not what you expected either. If it comes down to it, look into your hearts and do the right thing. You may be taking out an airliner. You must engage. You cannot fail. Our nation is relying on us." The room falls silent. "Good luck. Godspeed. God bless America."

There is nothing more he can say to his men. He must give them their assignments now. He looks at them carefully. "Are you ready for your missions?" he asks.

"Yes, sir!" they respond in unison.

"You're flying. You're flying," he begins, pointing to each airman and looking each directly in the eye.

"You're going home," he says to the next. The words seem to him like the hardest he's ever uttered.

"I don't *want* to go home, sir." the pilot objects.

"You *must* go," Tracer responds, "because in 10 hours I need you to come back and be rested because then *you're* going to be the guy in that cockpit protecting this country."

This will be one of the many challenges faced by guardsmen all around the country as they transition to this new 24/7 mission: they must hand over the fight—the watch—to another so that the operation can be sustained in full force. Every airman is reluctant to leave his or her post for fear of missing something. Each yearns to be on the front lines in battle, and the desire spans all ranks. Many of the most experienced fighter pilots sit in command positions. They're unable to be the guy at the tip of the spear. Instead, they must use their experience to guide the battle. From the officer to the enlisted, it's not easy for any of them.

Just when Tracer finishes briefing his pilots, someone comes into the room yelling. NEADS has called with orders to launch everything they've got.

"We have to get everything we have airborne now!"

The confused pilots look to Tracer for guidance, but there is no time for questions or explanations. "Go, go, go!" he yells, his hands in the air as if to push them out the door. The astonished airmen run to their jets. It hasn't yet occurred to them that, since they taxied in less than an hour before from their aborted training missions, there has not been time to do much more than fuel their jets. Most of the fighters are still unarmed. Despite the furious pace of the weapons handlers, only a handful of jets have been uploaded with some armament.

"You and I are pairing up," Robert "Bam Bam" Martyn says as he grabs fellow pilot Dennis "Doogie" Doonan. "I'm 1, you're 2, and I'm locking first and I'm shooting first!"

Doogie is shocked. When in combat, tactical standards call for the wingman—the number 2—to lock on a target and fire first. But Bam Bam is the unit's newest weapons officer and he's just returned from the prestigious Fighter Weapons School with all the latest combat tactics, so Doogie is not going to argue with him.

"Go for it," Doogie responds. "If you want to be the first guy to shoot down a civilian airliner with 300 people on it, be my guest."

Bam Bam stops dead in his tracks and swings around, staring in shock at Doogie. He hadn't stopped to think yet about what his target is. He stands frozen for a moment, a confused and twisted expression on his face while he processes the realization. Then, without saying a word more, he turns and runs to his jet.

Doogie and Joe "Rosey" McGrady turn out to be the first pilots to start their F-15s and taxi off the flight line, so now they are paired. They don't know who is supposed to fly lead, and Rosey radios Tracer for clarification.

"Just go!" Tracer orders. This is a time to dispense with formalities.

Doogie moves out in front, adrenaline racing through his veins. He takes a mental inventory of his jet and quickly realizes that he is unarmed. He is being sent into combat with no weapons. He urgently calls to Rosey on the radio.

"I'm Winchester!" he cries, using the code for having no armament.

Rosey also has no weapons, and he is instantly on the radio again with Tracer. "We're Winchester, SOF! We're Winchester!" he calls in a panic.

"Just go!" Tracer responds. "You need to get airborne NOW!" Tracer has never so powerfully felt the weight of his command. These are his comrades—his friends—and he is having to send them into battle unarmed. The thought of doing so—and of their courage in following his order—will haunt him for years to come.

The two pilots taxi for takeoff with no idea of where they are going or what they will be doing. All they know is that if they have to take out a target, they will do so with their own airplanes.

"Fly 090 for 100 to intercept," the Weapons controller commands as they race into the sky, ordering them to fly due east for 100 miles.

Oh God! Rosey thinks. His mind is racing, trying to work out how he'll take out the target. *Do I take out the rudder and then try to eject? Do I just crash into the cockpit? I'll only have one chance.*

He thinks about his wife and their four children. This morning is the 6-week checkup for their newborn twins.

While he streaks toward the target, he yells out to himself with all his might and fury, screaming for no one to hear: screaming out of rage for the lives lost and all the evil in the world and in anguished acceptance of his fate. As he closes in on the target, he takes turns screaming, praying, reciting Hail Mary's, and then screaming again.

To his huge relief, when he and Doogie get within range of the target they discover that it's a convoy, a U.S. KC-10 tanker and four A-10 fighters. The five aircraft are on their way from the Azores off Portugal to Barksdale Air Force Base in Louisiana. They're still out of radio range and have no idea of the day's events. *All right*, Rosey thinks, letting the realization sink in, *they have no idea what's going on.*

After he and Doogie have radioed to the A-10 flight lead, giving them diversion instructions, they are told to fly to Boston and set up a CAP over the city.

"You're coming with me," Doogie radios to the tanker pilot. He's decided to commandeer the tanker to assist with the CAP.

"What's going on?" the KC-10 pilot asks, surprised and concerned by this sudden and unconventional change of events.

"It's serious shit and you're coming with us," Doogie responds simply. He's not going to discuss it further, and the tanker pilot doesn't ask any more questions.

Combat Air Patrol over Washington, D.C. 10:30 a.m.

Still patrolling over the Washington, DCANG pilot Billy Hutchison is running dangerously low on fuel. After he took his low pass over the Pentagon, he climbed back up to establish patrol, and he is still unaware that the Langley F-16s are on the scene and are circling 4 miles overhead. Although Hutchison can't see the Langley fighters, they see him. NEADS, who has not been informed that Hutchison is over the city, has called his plane out as a target and the Langley flight lead Dean Eckmann has managed to type and ID Hutchison without his even knowing.

"Some other F-16 is out here," Eckmann reports to the NEADS Weapons controller, "but he is flying low and apparently talking to someone else."

Hutchison is still talking only to Dan Creedon at Washington Approach Control. The Secret Service agent who had arrived at the tower is there to monitor air traffic around Washington and issue whatever orders may come from the White House.

Creedon has been calling out potential targets to Hutchison, and Creedon's voice is betraying the stress he's feeling. Hutchison is determined not to abandon him, but he is now so low on fuel he doesn't know if he'll even be able to make it the few miles back to base. When he hears fellow DCANG pilot, flight lead Sass, radio Approach Control to say that he and Lucky are airborne, he calls the controller right away. "I've got to go," he says, glancing down at his fuel gauge. It is now pegged at the lowest level it can indicate: 400 pounds. "Two others are on their way," he adds. "I'm sorry."

Turning toward Andrews AFB, he's well aware that he has played it too close. *Just don't let me flame out!* he wills his plane. He points the F-16 toward the Andrews runway, tunes his radio to the Andrews tower frequency, and is shocked by what he hears: "Attention all aircraft monitoring Andrews tower frequency. Andrews and Class Bravo airspace [the highly controlled airspace surrounding Washington, D.C.] is closed. No general aviation aircraft are permitted to enter Class Bravo airspace. Any infractions will be shot down."

Then he hears DCANG SOF Dog Thompson on the frequency telling Sass that he and Lucky are weapons-free. *Weapons-free?* Hutchison thinks. *What is going on!* He radios Dog and finally hears a brief accounting of the morning's alarming events.

He doesn't have enough fuel for the standard overhead approach into Andrews, which involves flying over the runway at 2,000 feet, then doing a "break" into a 180-degree turn for a downwind leg and then a steep 180-degree descending turn to realign with the runway, setting up a final approach one mile from the touchdown zone. Instead, he improvises, aiming his jet right for the end of the runway, then turning away at the last minute to give himself room to make the 140-degree left turn he needs to line up.

Thank God, he thinks as he touches down at 10:35.

He's marshaled in to park next to the other fighters and barely has time to shut down and open his canopy when a crew chief climbs up his ladder and hands him a cell phone. "You need to call your wife," he says. "She's been calling and she's frantic. The only thing we've been able to tell her is that you're still in the air."

Hutchison somehow manages to get through to her on the first try, and she breaks down sobbing when she hears his voice.

"I'm okay," he tries to assure her. "But once I get refueled and reloaded, I've got to go back up."

"*Please* don't go!" she begs. "There must be someone else who can fly!"

"They're not shooting back," he says, offering her the only consolation he can think of. "I'm the only one with weapons and we only have so many guys here now. Most of our pilots are back at their jobs. I need to. I'm sorry." It pains him to think that he is letting her down, because if there's one thing Hutchison feels strongly about it is that. But he's a fighter pilot first, and today he has to be more concerned about not letting down his country.

He'll just have time to get a drink of water and a briefing before he takes off again to join the CAP over Washington.

CHAPTER 16

A Tightening Grip

Combat Air Patrol over Washington, D.C., 10:45 a.m.

As the military begins to close its grip over the nation's capital, confusion ensues among the jets from different bases—speaking to different controllers—joining the airspace. Langley flight lead Dean Eckmann is flying in the high CAP the Langley jets have established over the city when he's called to investigate two fast movers heading toward the capital. He points the nose of his F-16 downward and does a radar sweep of the area, quickly locating the two aircraft on his radar.

"It's two F-16s off of Andrews," he reports back to NEADS. "They're probably coming up to help."

Eckmann's radar lock sets off a warning in DCANG pilot Razin Caine's cockpit. He knows it's not a DCANG F-16 locking on to him. Unlike the alert fighters, the DCANG F-16s aren't equipped to interrogate aircraft this way. "Who was spiking me?" he radios, but he gets no response.

"Approach, do you have any other tactical aircraft in the area?" he radios to Washington Approach Control.

"I don't know," Approach controller Dan Creedon replies. "You're the only fighters I'm talking to! Hang on a second." He picks up the direct line to Washington Center.

"Hey, target at 2-5-0 turning northbound . . . are those your Quit flight?" he asks the Center controller.

251

While the two controllers coordinate, Razin is still getting spiked. He looks on his data link to see if anyone has a radar lock, but doesn't see anything. *There are other fighters here,* he realizes. Up to this point, the DCANG had thought they were alone.

"Aircraft with a radar lock, say call sign," he radios, attempting to make contact on the common frequency. Getting no response, he switches over to the Guard frequency. "Aircraft spiking F-16s over DCA, come up on DC Approach frequency 125.65."

But Eckmann hasn't heard the request. He's turned down the volume on the emergency frequency. There's so much congestion on it that he can't hear critical transmissions from Washington Center and NEADS.

"Are you talking to those guys?" Razin asks Creedon impatiently.

"Yeah," Creedon answers.

"Well tell 'em to stop spiking me!" Razin barks.

"These guys are on Center frequency and calling themselves Quit," Creedon responds, "They're communicating with NEADS and they'd like to talk to you."

At the direction of DCANG flight lead Sass Sasseville, Lucky Garcia switches over to the frequency that the Langley F-16s are using. She talks to Langley pilot Lou Derrig, and they work out that they've both been ordered to fly a CAP over the city. "We'd better get on the same sheet of music," Eckmann radios to Creedon. He'd like a little more coordination.

Sass too now comes up on the Washington Center frequency. "This is Caps 0-1, checking in."

"Copy, say load," Eckmann replies, inquiring as to their armament.

"Who are you?" Sass asks. He doesn't want to divulge potentially classified information unnecessarily and wants to verify whom he's talking to.

"We're three F-16 ADFs out of Langley," Eckmann replies, indicating that they are air defense fighters for NORAD, and adding that they are armed with hot guns, AIM-7 Sparrows, AIM-9

Sidewinders, and AIM-120 Amraams: fully armed and very dangerous. In addition, they're equipped with an IFF (Identify Friend or
Foe), an interrogator that allows them to immediately locate a
specific transponder code. Sass responds that he and Lucky are with
DCANG, and Eckmann is happy to know that there are other
armed fighters taking up the fight.

"Listen, we're showing up on your doorstep," Eckmann
responds. "We'll take the high CAP."

"Okay, we'll take the low CAP," Sass answers.

Creedon immediately directs the DCANG fighters to an area
west of Washington to check out a suspicious aircraft. "You're
cleared to block altitude, surface to 2-3-0," he tells Sass, granting
him full access to all airspace from the ground to 23,000 feet.
Such an enormous allotment of airspace over a metropolitan area is
astonishing, and Sass radios, "Verify we're in a state of national
emergency."

Creedon's not sure why he's asking or what the implications of
the question are, and he hasn't had any official briefing saying
"Dan, we're formally in a national emergency now." That seems
blatantly obvious.

"Yes!" he blurts out. If that's what he needs to say to get their
full cooperation, then so be it. *If this is not a national emergency, I
don't know what is!*

Creedon is kept wildly busy calling out unidentified radar tracks
for the fighters to check out, but the fighter pilots are having
trouble following his nonmilitary style of giving them target
information.

"Listen, I'm not a radar interceptor kind of guy," Creedon says
to Razin about the problem. "What do you need?"

*This is as good a time as any for a lesson on military target inter-
ception,* Razin figures. "There's a common spot we're gonna call a
bull's-eye," Razin explains, "and I want you to call bearing and distance from that for every target you see."

Creedon thinks for a second. "Let's use the Washington VOR,"
he offers. The acronym stands for "VHF omni range." It's the

navigational aid right there at the airport. Razin agrees and quickly radios the other fighters with the coordinates. Creedon starts calling out the targets in the new format, and the new system works beautifully.

After he calls out one track coming inbound at low altitude from the west, several fighters quickly descend to intercept it. It's a flight of three Night Hawk helicopters. The pilots are talking excitedly to each other on the Guard frequency, alarmed by the jets, while the fighters fly circles around them, spiking them with their radar to identify them. Creedon figures they are coming from Camp David or trying to pick up or evacuate some high-level officials. Apparently it didn't occur to the pilots that they should be talking to anyone before trying to fly toward Washington. Creedon thinks to himself that anyone flying into D.C. right now without talking to controllers must have a death wish.

He quickly spots another target: "Bull's-eye, 338, 25 miles, southbound, 1,400, unknown." Simultaneously, the fighters are calling out targets they have identified as friendly, such as a tanker plane that's just arrived nearby.

Creedon realizes that there are so many low-flying targets that there's no way the fighters can intercept them all. "Alex," Creedon calls to the tower controller, "we can't intercept all these guys. You tell them they've got to stay below a thousand feet and they gotta stay slow if they want us to consider them friendly!"

Lucky Garcia feels a bit sorry for the uninformed and unsuspecting pilots who are simply out for a morning flight around Washington. She knows that if the flares she's dropping aren't startling them enough, the effects of her jet wash as she tries to turn them away—the horizontal tornado-like wind currents coming off her wings—sure are.

All the fighters have been cleared by the president, via the Secret Service, to shoot down any aircraft that cannot be determined friendly. It hits Lucky hard to realize that she and the other fighters will be the ones doing the shooting. Never in her wildest imagination has she envisioned herself flying armed and weapons-free over her own country. With every interception, she asks herself, *Will this be the one?* The tension is palpable, and the self-restraint shown by the pilots is enormous.

The skies over Washington are now under guard, but more suspicious flights are being added to the FAA's list all the time, not only over the United States but a number coming from abroad.

CONR headquarters, Tyndall Air Force Base, Florida, 11:10 a.m.

One civilian aircraft has been getting a great deal of special attention this morning. When Air Force One first launched, the president was intending to go back to Washington, but with several suspect flights still airborne—and Washington clearly targeted—the vice president had encouraged him to go elsewhere. Leaders had eventually settled on Barksdale Air Force Base in Louisiana. The Secret Service has asked General Arnold at CONR headquarters for a fighter escort for Air Force One. Actually, they've asked for it, then determined that it's best to forgo it, then asked for it again. (Air Force One has never been escorted; there is no protocol in place for this kind of coordination. Will it draw too much attention to the president's aircraft?) Fighters are now on their way, and soon two F-16s from Ellington Air Force Base's 147th Fighter Wing in Clear Lake, Texas, meet up with the president's plane. "Air Force One, you've got two F-16s at about your—say, your 10 o'clock position," the air traffic controller calls to the presidential pilot, Col. Mark Tillman.

Approaching Air Force One to set up an escort are Texas Air National Guard pilots Shane Brotherton and Randy Roberts. They have been pulled off a training mission and have been given no idea what their new mission is; all they were told was where to fly to. When they asked about their target, their commander had responded simply, "You'll know when you see it." [1]

The passengers aboard Air Force One are surprised to look out their windows and see fighters flying just off the wingtips of the

747. They gather to look out at the unprecedented event. Several take pictures. The president, a former Air National Guard fighter pilot at Ellington, gives the flight lead a brisk salute. In response, the pilot tips his wing, fades briefly off, and then returns to position.

In the cockpit, Tillman is not appreciating the fighters' close proximity. He trusts them, but not *that* much. All in all, he'd be more comfortable with a little more space. Within hours, there will be six F-16s escorting Air Force One and securing an 80-mile clear-zone around its perimeter. At least one civilian plane in the skies has no worry at all anymore that harm will come its way this day.

FAA Command Center, Herndon, Virginia

Ben Sliney is continuing to be bombarded with calls coming in from air traffic control facilities around the country. Fighter jets and other government aircraft are taking off from bases and just busting into the airspace without clearances. It's driving the controllers—who thrive on control and order—nuts. They're still trying to get the last planes on the ground. Soon requests to fly start coming in.

"We've got a Texas Ranger that needs to fly out to a highway to pick up an accident victim," one of his specialists tells him.

"A C-17 transport in Big Sky, Montana, needs to get FEMA personnel to New York and Washington," another adds.

Next, there's FBI staff in San Francisco needing to fly back east, and a two-seater F-16B from the 119th Fighter Wing in Fargo, North Dakota, that wants to fly Ed Jacoby, New York's emergency management director, back to New York. The list continues to grow.

Sliney is doing his best to field these messages and approve or reject each one as fast as possible. He wants and needs to respond to all these requests, but he's most concerned at the moment about some transoceanic flights. A US Airways flight, inbound over the Atlantic, is feared hijacked, and bomb threats are coming into the airlines for several other international flights. Also, a Korean Air Boeing 747 en route from Seoul to New York, currently west of Alaska, is now a suspected hijack. The flight recently sent a typed message through ARINC to Korean Airlines headquarters that included the letters "HJK," a code for hijacked. Alaskan NORAD Commander Lt. Gen. Norton Schwartz has already dispatched two F-15s from Elmendorf Air Force Base near Anchorage to intercept and shadow the aircraft. Sliney is working desperately to keep track of all of these developments; he's running purely on adrenaline.

The FAA teleconference that began this morning has expanded and now includes every U.S. airline and nearly every major foreign carrier. He's juggling this teleconference and updating FAA head-quarters as needed. All the calls about planes wanting special clearances are threatening to overwhelm him.

FAA Gulfstream IV, Milwaukee–Washington, D.C.

In support of the president's literacy program, this morning Attorney General John Ashcroft was on board one of the FAA's Gulfstream IVs heading to Milwaukee to read to some schoolchildren. He and his staff were relaxing around the aircraft's conference table, and Ashcroft was enjoying the opportunity to look out the window and show off his geography skills. "There's Lake Erie, look at that! Yep, that's Cleveland right there along the lake's edge," he had called out in a steady stream. His staff were less than amused, but they humored him.[2]

The flight was nearing Lake Michigan when instructions for Ashcroft to immediately call the Justice Department Command Center came in. He was briefed on the attacks and requested that the plane head back to Washington right away.

But the plane didn't have enough fuel to make it back, so the pilot landed in Milwaukee and refueled. By that time, the FAA had issued the national ground stop, and the pilot was told by air traffic control that the plane would not be allowed to take off for

Washington. Ashcroft insisted, and the pilot was eventually able to convince the controller to let them leave.

Unfortunately, the man in charge of the airspace, Ben Sliney, was not brought into the loop about Ashcroft's flight. When he hears that a corporate jet has taken off despite the ground-stop order, he is livid. He gets on the phone immediately to Cleveland Center and directs them to order the plane to land.

"They're telling me to land outside of Detroit," the pilot relays to Ashcroft.

But Ashcroft is not going to be stopped. The pilot chooses to ignore the controller and continues toward Washington.

The Cleveland Center controller reports to the Command Center that the pilot is not responding and not complying, and Sliney notifies NEADS. Before long, two F-16s from a nearby Air National Guard base, undetected by the plane's pilot, intercept the flight. By that time, the pilot has started to broadcast "in the blind"—to no controller in particular—that he has the attorney general on board and that they are returning to Washington.

The F-16s report back to NEADS that the aircraft is a private corporate jet with no markings. It's heading straight for Washington and doesn't seem to have any intention of landing. They also report that the aircraft's pilot is broadcasting in the blind that he has the attorney general on board and is returning to Washington.

Given all that is happening around him, Sliney can't believe this. He asks, "Can you GUARANTEE me that it is indeed John Ashcroft on that plane?"

"No sir, we cannot," the NEADS officer replies.

"Then get him out of my sky!" Sliney bellows.

NEADS forwards orders to the F-16s that if the plane won't voluntarily come down, then it must be taken down. As the jet continues its trek toward Washington, the F-16 flight lead calls Washington Center to have a controller send word to the plane's pilot that if the plane won't divert and land, it will be shot down. Finally Ashcroft relents, and the plane is diverted to Richmond.

This is not the last that Sliney will hear about Ashcroft as the day unfolds.

Delta Flight 1989, Boston–Los Angeles, Cleveland Airport

Dave Dunlap thought he would feel better once he was on the ground, but things don't seem to be improving. As they sit, as directed, at the farthest possible point from the terminal, Captain Werner talks to the passengers while the ground controller tells Dunlap to contact his company Operations. He does so, only to have Ops tell him to call Ground Control. The roundabout continues, with neither party very forthcoming with information about what the pilots should do now. Eventually, one offers something definitive, although it's not exactly what Dunlap would like to hear. "Just sit and wait," the ground controller instructs.

Dunlap feels his anxiety rising again. He sees "delay tactics" written all over this. No one is giving him straight answers, and ground controllers and people at Ops keep asking him odd questions.

"Are you broadcasting in the clear?" the controller queries.

"That's affirmative," Dunlap responds emphatically, "Delta 1989 is broadcasting in the clear." He looks over to the captain. "What the hell is *that* supposed to mean?" he barks. Werner simply shrugs his shoulders and leaves the flight deck to go brief the flight attendants.

Dunlap hasn't managed to convince the controller that his plane is not hijacked. A few minutes later, the controller calls again: "Are you sure you can talk freely?"

"Yeah, we're fine," Dunlap answers calmly, although he would just as soon scream. The insanity is getting to him, and more than anything, he just wants to get off this airplane. As far as he can see, the only bad option is staying on the plane. He has never felt so helpless or vulnerable. The captain is spending his time coming into and out of the cockpit trying to keep the flight attendants and passengers calm. Dunlap is thinking that they should just shut the cockpit door and leave it shut!

He starts to think about his training, to make sure there isn't anything else he is supposed to be doing. Pilots are trained to react, to *do* things; this waiting is driving him crazy. Then he recalls that pilot training instructs that in the event of a hijacking, the crew should try to escape. It's hardly his inclination as a pilot, though: "Okay, I've got all these people in my charge and at the first opportunity I'm going to run like hell!" But as he thinks about it, the policy makes sense: the pilot can fly the airplane, but if the pilot leaves, the airplane cannot fly.

He isn't sure of much, but as he sits in his cockpit waiting—and thinking about all he has learned this morning—he is damn certain that pilots didn't fly those airliners into buildings this morning. *No way*, he thinks. *If someone is going to kill me and everyone else on my plane anyway, we're going into the Hudson River.* No, he knows those pilots had to be dead or incapacitated.

So what do I do? he thinks. He scans the control panels that surround him, deep in thought. Finally he devises a way to disable the airplane if the need arises and then opens up his cockpit window. He figures he can grab the escape rope and be out in about 10 seconds.

The captain, attempting to make an announcement to the passengers while Dunlap makes these preparations, is increasingly distracted by Dunlap's sudden busyness. He asks his first officer, "What are you doing?" interrupting his announcement in midsentence.

"If anyone tries to get into this cockpit," Dunlap answers, "I'm going out the window!"

The captain's initial reaction is to chuckle, but then he thinks about it and realizes Dunlap is right. He puts down the microphone and cranks open his own window.

The two pilots sit there on one of the nicest days Dunlap can remember, with a cool breeze now blowing through the cockpit, and while they listen to reports on the radio about the attacks, they watch men in white shirts and black pants gather along the periphery of the airport.

They watch for several minutes before calling the lead flight attendant to request her presence on the flight deck. It's about time, they figure, that they fill her in on what's happening—even though they're less than certain themselves.

Just as she arrives, Dunlap looks out his cockpit window to see a small fox walking across the grass. He quickly points out the cute little critter to the others. It's a nice diversion on this hellish day. They stop talking to silently watch it traipse across the field. Suddenly, the fox springs up into the air and comes down on a large rodent and proceeds to tear it into bloody chunks. The crew winces at the gruesome sight. "I didn't need to see that," the captain says, and Dunlap silently nods his head in agreement. Could this day get any stranger?

After the flight attendant leaves the flight deck, they lock the cockpit door.

Conditions begin deteriorating in the cabin. Passengers are on their cell phones, and some are now doing the math about a bomb with a timer on it. They're not stupid, and it has long since occurred to them that there is something grossly wrong with this flight. They want off the airplane!

One young woman, a Delta employee, is completely distraught. Her mother was on board American 11. The two of them were heading to Los Angeles, and since her mom worked for American, they agreed that they'd each use their own pass privileges, which would increase the chances of them both getting there. The flights were scheduled to arrive around the same time. The flight attendants are doing their best to comfort her and also keep the other passengers calm.

While the tension rises behind his locked cockpit door, Dunlap is pushing hard for someone to come and deplane them. He's worried that a passenger is going to blow an escape slide and then they will *really* have a mess on their hands. Because there is no air stair, the crew, in accordance with federal aviation regulations, has kept all the plane's exits armed. If any door opens, a huge escape slide will inflate. Dunlap knows that it will take only one exasperated passenger to make that happen.

He feels helpless, useless, trapped, and threatened, all at once. Desperately trying to keep his wits about him, he finds himself staring intently at a ladybug that has taken up residence on the dash above his flight controls. He's thankful for the diversion; it's keeping him sane right now.

CHAPTER 17

The Longest Day

Combat Air Patrol over Washington, D.C., 11:25 a.m.

As yet more military aircraft arrive in the skies over Washington, pilots' flying skills and judgment are being put to a daunting test. Pilots are calling on all of their training to improvise solutions and to reach past their comfort zone to attend to the demands of this unprecedented crisis.

Langley F-16 pilot Borgy Borgstrom is now running out of fuel. His flight lead, Dean Eckmann, directs him to a refueling tanker plane that has been positioned just off the coast. When Borgy arrives at the tanker, his eyes widen to see the immense aircraft in front of him. *Oh shit!* he thinks. The plane is a KC-10 jumbo jet, the military version of a DC-10, and he's never refueled on one before; he's used to refueling on the much smaller KC-135 plane.

"Hey, Otis," he calls in a panic, using Eckmann's military call sign. "It's a 10!"

"Yeah, so?" Eckmann responds, not quite sure what the problem is.

"I've never tanked on a 10 before!" Borgy urgently replies.

"It's okay," Eckmann reassures. "Here's what you're gonna do . . ."

He coaches his wingman through the process, which is somewhat trickier than refueling on a KC-135. Borgy is learning on the fly, quite literally, today.

Several minutes later, he rejoins the CAP with a call to Eckmann.

"That thing's *huge*!" he exclaims, enormously relieved to have succeeded at the tricky maneuver.

Soon, F-18s from the 321 Marine Fighter Attack Squadron of Andrews AFB join the air defense over Washington, adding further confusion to the mix. When NEADS Weapons director Smurf Murphy tries to authenticate one of the Marine pilots—giving the authentication code that demonstrates that he is who he says he is and that his orders are legal and lawful—the pilot does not respond with the appropriate authentication; the code he comes back to NEADS with has too many letters. *What the hell is he talking about?* Smurf wonders. He tries again to authenticate the pilot.

"Dude, I don't know what you're trying to tell me," the pilot responds. It quickly occurs to Smurf that he has an unexpected challenge on his hands: these fighters, who are not normally part of NORAD, do not have NORAD authenticators. Instead, they have authenticators from Air Combat Command. They don't match! *Shit!*

Smurf knows that this problem is going to be repeated frequently as increasing numbers of non-NORAD fighters take to the skies. Searching for a solution, he directs fellow Weapons controller Animal Julian to help him call the various squadron commanders of the nonalert jets launching to patrol the Northeast in order to resolve the problem. Doing so is of critical importance. The authentication system is set up to ensure that a pilot knows he is being given a valid order, and a pilot cannot legally comply with an order unless he can authenticate it first. Smurf gets on a secured line to their unit, the 321 Marine Fighter Attack Squadron at Andrews AFB.

"We use this authenticator," Smurf announces. "Are you using the same one?"

"No."

"Uh . . . okay! Here's what we're gonna do." He improvises a plan of action, and soon faxes are fired off over secured lines to every squadron launching aircraft to make sure that everyone is on the same page.

Meanwhile, the Marine pilots already in the air over Washington waiting to be checked in are doing some of their own improvising. They know of only one way to solve their authentication problem: voice recognition. Smurf is a Marine buddy of some of the pilots, and they know his voice. The Marine pilots decide that they will accept orders from him and him only.

"No, no!" one pilot objects when another Weapons controller tries to give him instructions. "Smurf's voice only! That's all I want to hear."

Smurf gets on the radio to check him in. "All right! Devil 1-1, Smurf, I authenticate. . . . You're in the CAP. Here's your mission. . . . I'm turning you over to my controller."

"Roger that!" the pilot responds, and one by one, Smurf checks in all the Marine fighters.

But having these fighters is helpful only if NEADS can communicate with them, and right now radio reception is nonexistent below 20,000 feet over Washington. The NEADS radio transmitter, like all radio transmitters, operates by line of sight. This means that the radio signals, which travel in a straight line, require an unobstructed path between the transmitter and the jets. Given the curvature of the earth and the distance to Washington, the fighters' radio receivers cannot pick up the NEADS signal when they descend below that line of sight. What's needed is an AWACS plane, which has the capability to provide both radar and radio coverage over a citywide area.

Smurf gets on his radio to an AWACS from the 552nd Air Control Wing of Tinker Air Force Base in Oklahoma. Earlier this morning, the aircraft had been in the D.C. area for a training mission, but in the immediate confusion after the attacks it had been directed to return to its Oklahoma base. Smurf calls for it to turn right back around.

"Here's the deal," he announces. "We need you to cover the NCA [National Capital Area]."

"Roger that," the pilot responds. "Where do you want us?"

"No, no," Smurf answers. "You're the one with the big jet with the rotor-dome on it. *You* tell *me* where you need to go to get me a surface to infinity look at that area."

The problem of radar and radio coverage over D.C. has been solved. For Smurf, it's right on to the next task.

As the skies over the nation's capital become ever more dense with military aircraft, DCANG pilot Razin Caine is concerned by what he's seeing. There's no real communication between the units, and even less coordination. It's as close to complete chaos as he's ever seen in the skies. Some fighters are talking to Approach Control, others to Washington Center. Some are taking orders from NEADS, others from the Secret Service. Differing rules of engagement are only adding to the confusion. Flying low and weapons-free over Washington, the DCANG pilots are unaware that they are the *only* fighters in the country flying with weapons-free shoot-down authority.

Communication is cumbersome at best. The fighters are having to deal with multiple, uncustomary frequencies. They're using both VHF and UHF radios to talk to each other, to NEADS, to their bases, and to air traffic controllers. They're also relaying messages back and forth between NEADS and the controllers so that everyone stays on the same page with respect to targets.

The air traffic control facilities do not have direct connections to NEADS. Before today, they've never needed direct contact. Controller Dan Creedon at Washington Approach tries to find a phone number for NEADS, but has no luck. He asks the fighters, but the best they are able to do is to give him NEADS's discrete radio frequency. He tunes in the frequency on an extra transceiver, and then he can at least hear what NEADS is saying to the fighters. The pilots will no longer have to relay to him such things as "Huntress wants us to investigate a target here" or "Huntress is wanting us to go refuel here." Now he is able to be more careful about not talking to the fighter pilots when he hears them communicating back and forth to NEADS on the military frequency.

As Razin watches fighters peel off in all directions to intercept targets, descending on them like bees to a hive, he realizes that the chances of a mishap are high. There is simply no existing protocol for a combat air patrol like this over an American city, where the threat might be coming in at any altitude and from any direction and where the air defenses are a collage from various bases and branches of the military. He radios his SOF, Dog Thompson, to see if he can call the various units to find out their taskings and radio frequencies so that they can at least develop some semblance of coordination.

When the DCANG asserts its authority over the operation, however, it causes some tension. Dog, the SOF of the D.C. Guard, gets on the phone to the SOF of the 177th Fighter Wing in Atlantic City, Lt. Col. James Haye. "We've got airplanes running all over the place!" Dog snaps. "We've got to coordinate here or someone is going to end up shooting someone down!"

Haye is not pleased with what he's hearing. "Wait a minute," he objects, "no one should be shooting at anyone. This is getting way out of control!"

A spirited discussion follows. Dog repeatedly asks for the radio frequency that the Atlantic City jets are on and the details of their mission over the capital. Being there in Washington, one of the Capital Guardians, he feels a natural inclination to take the lead in bringing order to the situation, but Haye is agitated. He is not even sure of all the answers to the questions Dog is asking, and it doesn't take a brain surgeon to understand that the D.C. Guard pilots are operating under different rules of engagement than are his own fighters. Those rules of engagement—flying weapons-free—are not sitting too well with Haye. Firing weapons is a very serious matter, and the insinuation that "someone is going to get shot down" unless something changes is simply unacceptable.

"Listen, I have airplanes down there, and you have airplanes down there," Haye growls, "and nobody is talking on the same frequency! If you guys have a target, I strongly suggest that you be sure to make visual identification before shooting!"

Tensions between the D.C. Guard and Atlantic City will run strong for days to come.

Over Washington, Razin knows that he has the ability to bring order to this CAP. Having just completed Fighter Weapons School—the highest level of training for a fighter pilot—he knows how to develop a strategic plan to best utilize and organize these planes, and he needs to do that right here, *right now.*

While the fighters around him work to identify and intercept targets of interest, he moves into an orbit right in the center, directly over the National Mall. He begins to jot notes and make diagrams on the paper clamped to his kneeboard. He's going to organize the melee. And if, in the interim, a hostile aircraft makes it to the center of the city, he'll be the one to deliver its fate.

Razin manages to gather the capabilities, radio frequencies, and armament of the various fighters over the city. He then works to organize them to provide maximum intercept and strike capabilities, determining what areas and altitudes each will cover, what frequencies they will communicate on, and where a tanker will be positioned. When he has finished, he shares the plan with the others. To air traffic controller Dan Creedon, listening on the frequency, it sounds like they're arguing. Yet Razin would say that it is military coordination at its finest, and the DCANG is taking the lead. Despite being from different squadrons, their years of training and common military language allow them to quickly synchronize their efforts.

For NEADS Battle Commander Bob Marr, that's just fine. Building an air defense for the entire Northeast out of what was three hours earlier just four aircraft from two units is no easy task. With the D.C. Guard managing the CAP over Washington, he has one less city to worry about.

NORAD Command Center, Cheyenne Mountain, Colorado, 11:30 a.m.

The 3-foot-thick, 25-ton steel blast doors at Cheyenne Mountain have closed for the first time in history. Locked inside NORAD's command center, Gen. Ralph "Ed" Eberhart has been participating in the NMCC's teleconference. His chief of air defense operations now wants to implement SCATANA, short for Security Control of Air Traffic and Navigation Aids. SCATANA is a plan that was developed in the 1960s to clear the skies in the event of a confirmed missile attack from the Soviet Union. The plan shuts down all the navigational aids in the country and closes the airspace so that bombers, missiles, airborne command posts, and support aircraft can operate unencumbered.

General Eberhart is not sure that the order is appropriate. With new hijackings still being reported, however, he knows he must take action. He issues a modified SCATANA order known as ESCAT, Emergency Security Control of Air Traffic. The order allows for the continued operation of navigational aids, and also selective approval for specific and necessary flights. The order won't ground everything, but it will give the military what they need for the current circumstances.

Notice is sent out to all civil and military air traffic control facilities: the skies now officially belong to NORAD. Across the country, airport facilities begin broadcasting alerts to all aircraft that the airspace is closed and that violating aircraft will be fired upon. For the 30 aircraft still airborne, that is nerve-wracking news.

At 12:16 the FAA Command Center announces that the airspace has been successfully shut down. There are no commercial airliners flying over the United States. Ben Sliney is hopeful that the madness is over; there have been no new attacks for hours now. The military has taken firm control of the skies and fighters have moved into position escorting the last two suspicious international flights headed toward U.S. airspace.

Delta Flight 1989, Boston–Los Angeles, Cleveland Airport, 12:20 p.m.

While the last of the straggling flights over the United States is landed as the nation's skies are cleared, First Officer Dave Dunlap's saga continues, despite his being safely on the ground.

At 12:20, Dunlap and Capt. Paul Werner are advised that SWAT teams and the FBI are coming out to their aircraft. An air stair has arrived. Upon hearing the news, the captain immediately jumps out of his seat and goes to the cabin to make an announcement. In a time like this, he figures, it can be comforting to have a face with a voice. By now, the crew is confident that if there's a threat to their aircraft, it's *not* from one of their passengers. Dunlap stays in his seat, still staring at the busy ladybug crawling on the dash above his flight instruments.

When Werner returns to the cockpit several minutes later, he cracks his head on the overhead circuit breaker panel. On the 767, the panel is located exactly where the pilot's head needs to be when doing the advanced yoga position required to get into the pilot's seat.

The SWAT teams approach the aircraft and Werner, blood running down his face, leans out of his window to give the "all clear" signal. The agents do a double take when they see the bloodied captain waving his arm out the cockpit window. They seem perplexed, at the very least, by this new development. After regrouping momentarily, they head up the air stair to the main cabin door.

As the SWAT team boards the plane, an officer enters the cockpit with his gun drawn. Never in his life can Dunlap remember being happier to see a gun. He realizes with a new degree of appreciation just how vulnerable he has felt for the past few hours. It's hellish to know that you cannot protect yourself.

The FBI instructs everyone to gather their belongings, cell phones included, and line them up on the tarmac. Dunlap had completely forgotten about his phone. He quickly turns it on to see if his wife has returned his call, discovers he has 17 messages waiting. He has no time now, though, to respond to them. He regretfully turns the phone back off and places it in the growing pile. The SWAT teams—wearing body armor and brandishing automatic weapons—corral the crew and passengers onto nearby busses while bomb-sniffing dogs board the aircraft.

Washington Approach Control, 12:30 p.m.

Washington Approach controller Dan Creedon hasn't had a break since he stole a moment to call his wife, who works in the city. That was when he heard United 93 was headed their way. "There's more shit coming," he warned. "Get out of the city *now*! Just leave! Go home and get in the basement!"

He can't remember ever being on duty for so long without a break. *But why take a break?* he figures. *By the time I explain to someone else all they need to know, my break will be over!* The controllers are finally finding their rhythm. One is in charge of everything off of Andrews, another is working traffic into and out of the area, and Creedon is working the fighters. For a while, Creedon had tried to keep track of which fighters are in charge of each area of the sky, but that got overwhelming.

"I'm just gonna call the targets to you," he finally said to Razin. "*You* assign the resources."

Creedon tries to coordinate traffic flow with one of the other controllers, but it's getting too confusing. The fighters are not on set headings and their altitudes are changing all the time. The number 2 manager, a very "by the book" kind of guy who had been at a conference this morning, walks in just as Creedon comes up with a solution. "Hey Terry," he yells across the room to another controller. "Descend through me! No rules! I'll call out the traffic to the fighters!"

"Okay, I'll miss ya!" Terry responds, clearing his aircraft to descend down through the CAP.

Creedon radios the fighters: "Friendly, bull's-eye 222, 15 miles descending."

The manager who has walked into this can't believe what he's hearing. "Jesus!" he exclaims. He knows not to say anything more. They've got the TRACON under control and it's best to just stay away. He turns around and leaves the room. *Good decision,* Creedon thinks.

The line from Washington Center rings and Creedon picks it up to be told, "Hey, we've got November 2 out here. He wants to land at DCA. There's some concern and they want a fighter escort."

"What?" Creedon asks, confused by the request for an escort.

"Well, they said they want fighter escort," the Center controller explains. "They said they don't want any misunderstandings."

Attorney General John Ashcroft has not given up trying to get into D.C. After his aircraft was diverted to Richmond, he called the Justice Department Command Center for assistance. With some high-level coordination, one of the Secret Service agents on board convinced the pilot to try once again to enter the city. The pilot, however, is less than enthusiastic; he really doesn't want to get shot out of the sky.

Creedon recognizes the N-number of the aircraft. "Yeah, November 2 is based out of Washington," he says.

He knows the tag belongs to one of the FAA jets. When the aircraft carries the transportation secretary, it's called Transport 1; the FAA Administrator, FAA 1; and so on. When it's not holding any of those people, it just goes by its N-number: N2. Controllers elsewhere, Creedon realizes, might not recognize it as a government aircraft.

"Hang on a second," he says. He calls up Razin, managing the CAP over the city: "Bull's-eye 270, 75 miles, November 2, land Washington. Wants an escort."

Razin hesitates for a moment. He just finished organizing this CAP and getting everyone on the same page. Now he's being asked to give up two of his fighters. "Any idea who's on board?" he asks.

"I don't know," Creedon answers. "My assumption is FAA-1 or DOT-1." He's guessing Jane Garvey or Norman Mineta. He has no idea that it's Ashcroft—not that he wouldn't send an escort for Ashcroft, too.

"Okay," Razin answers. "Quit 2-5 will handle it."

"He can have *one*," Eckmann responds when Razin forwards the request. He directs his wingman Lou Derrig to intercept the aircraft.

Creedon finally needs a bathroom break. "Let me steal a cigarette," he says to one of the other controllers. The guy stares back at him with a confused expression; he knows that Creedon doesn't smoke. "Just give me a fuckin' cigarette, Tom! Jesus!" The pressure has built up to the boiling point.

He takes a two-minute break and smokes a Merit Ultra Light before returning to his station.

Combat Air Patrol over New York City, 12:30 p.m.

While Duff and Nasty, along with several more F-15s from Otis, secure the airspace over New York City, civilians down below wait in lines that stretch for blocks for boats that will take them out of Manhattan. Others are walking over the bridges; some will walk many miles to get home. Helicopters are launching in huge numbers to assist in rescue efforts, and copters from the 150th Attack Helicopter Battalion have just gone in search of protective breathing equipment. Meanwhile, in the Newark tower, the few remaining controllers watch as a truck drives across the ramp; workers jump out to paint large X's where more helicopters can land. Liberty State Park, just across the Hudson from the city, is becoming the marshaling point for the rescue operation.

The Otis fighters have now sucked up every drop of fuel the KC-135 can offer, and the tanker diverts with only enough fuel to make it to McGuire Air Force Base in Burlington County, New Jersey. There the 108th Air Refueling Wing immediately sends a KC-10 to take its place. Duff and Nasty are finally given orders to return to their base.

When Duff and Nasty arrive back at Otis—a mere 5 hours after their departure—it's a significantly different base from the one they left. They departed on a quiet Tuesday morning, blasting past the six fighters getting ready to launch on routine training missions. They return to find rows and rows of the unit's fighters lined up near the runway. The jets are surrounded by perhaps a hundred maintenance personnel working furiously in tag teams, preparing the planes for battle. *It looks like war*, Duff thinks, bringing his F-15 to rest on the flight line.

Commanders and subordinates alike are working feverishly to execute the well-developed response plans that will guide the base's transition to its new combat mission. Duff and Nasty immediately go to work to help organize the 24/7 schedules that will be needed to support continuous flight operations. Otis is nearly doubling in staff size in a matter of hours as the unit's members, some as far away as Florida, call up to announce that they're on their way. While ammunition stocks are assessed and day and night shifts assigned to pilots and flight line and aircraft maintenance personnel, arrangements are made to house and feed the influx of staff. No one knows what's going to happen next, but they're working together to prepare for the worst.

Guard units all over the country have called their full-time and reservist personnel to base. Reservists are getting no pushback from employers as they leave their civilian jobs. The only opposition they are facing is the logistical nightmare of trying to get where they're going with no flights taking off and the highways snarled.

Steve Miller, US Air/Air National Guard Pilot,
en Route to Atlantic City, 12:30 p.m.

Pilot Steve Miller has been furiously trying to make his way to the Atlantic City National Guard base since managing a deft emergency landing at LaGuardia Airport. He had flown out of LaGuardia in the early hours of the morning, so, unlike other crews, had a car waiting when he returned. He intended to take the Brooklyn-Queens Expressway to the Verrazano-Narrows Bridge and then head down Staten Island, taking either the Goethels or Outer Bridge Crossing to head into New Jersey. That would have taken him to the Garden State Parkway on a straight shot down to the 177th Fighter Wing at Atlantic City's airport.

But the Brooklyn-Queens Expressway was a logjam. He threw his Bonneville into reverse and backed down the entrance ramp, then worked his way through the back streets and alleys of Queens and Brooklyn, listening to the shocking radio coverage of the unfolding disaster. He was tuned to shock-jock Howard Stern, who this morning was all business, giving a pretty good real-time accounting of the breaking news.

He is desperately trying to get through to his wife on his cell phone, but the circuits are jammed. She often had to cope with worrying about him when he was in the Navy. He had been airborne in the Persian Gulf one time and witnessed a midair collision between two Hornets in his air wing. He knew his wife would hear about the accident from news reports and not know whether he had been involved. By the time he had landed on his aircraft carrier, the USS *George Washington*, outgoing communications had been shut down due to security concerns and he couldn't get word to her that he was all right. He hated the next few hours before he could get through to her, watching CNN report the story, knowing what kind of hell she must be going through. When he was finally able to talk with her, she said she was okay, that she knew it wasn't him, but he figured that was more a defense mechanism than true intuition.

Being married to a naval aviator deployed to fight wars is one thing; being married to an airline pilot is quite another. Miller knows her defenses have come down since he started flying for the airlines, so he kept trying and trying to get through to her. Finally, he switched his effort to trying to get through to the base, but again he couldn't get a connection.

When he arrived at the Belt Parkway on the south end of Long

Island, between JFK Airport and the Verrazano-Narrows Bridge, he found it empty and realized the highway had been closed. Then he saw a police officer blocking the entry ramp. He tried to convince the officer to let him through, but the guy wasn't budging.

Not easily dissuaded, Miller then took a road parallel to the highway and made his way to the next entry ramp. He had better luck with the cop there, who gave him the go-ahead, and he flew down the Parkway toward the Verrazano Bridge. But he didn't get far before he encountered a traffic backup approaching the bridge and realized the bridge had been closed.

No matter. Where there's a will, there's a way, and today Miller had plenty of will. He crossed the median and drove west on the vacant eastbound side of the closed Parkway, plowed onto the bridge up the off-ramp and flew across the span as fast as his purple '94 Pontiac Bonneville would take him, all the while pressing "redial" on his cell phone. About midspan, a call finally went through to the squadron, answered by the supervisor of flying. Sure enough, the base was calling for all pilots to report for duty. The SOF was glad to hear from him and told him he'd be in the rotation to fly when he showed up.

Miller flew down the Garden State Parkway, blaring his horn, noticing that the farther he got from New York, the more the other drivers seemed unaware that a national emergency was in the works. In the New York area, drivers had moved right out of his way; the drivers on the Parkway were less responsive and he had to weave back and forth, maniacally switching lanes.

When he finally arrives at the 177th he learns that the jets have been armed and the squadron has already been flying combat air patrol over New York, Philadelphia, and Washington. The base is drastically short of pilots, though; with the majority of the base's pilots working full time as airline pilots, most have been unable to get there. Miller is one of only 10 who will make it. He is eager to get into a jet and up in the air, but the SOF greets him with the words "You're being put into crew rest." After what he's been through to get there, Miller can hardly believe what he's hearing. *As if I could sleep!* he thinks. But he knows that this could be a long operation, and the guys in the air now are going to need to be relieved.

119th Fighter Wing Alert Detachment, Langley AFB, Virginia 12:30 a.m.

Langley flight lead Dean Eckmann is on a tanker refueling for a second time when the order comes in for him, Lou Derrig, and Borgy Borgstrom to return to base. Lou and Borgy immediately turn their fighters toward Langley, flying as a two-ship, while Eckmann finishes refueling.

When Borgy lands, he's astonished to see at least a dozen missile-laden trailers lined up near the runway.

"What else did they get?" he urgently asks his crew chief when he parks his F-16 and opens the canopy. The crew chief fills him in on all the horrible details of the attacks.

The driver of the refueling truck notices that one of the fighters has returned with no weapons—no missiles are hanging from the wings—not knowing that Borgy went up in the spare jet, which had not been loaded up. He knows that United 93 has gone down and now he surmises who took it down. The following day he will voice his concern to Borgy, and Borgy will clear the issue up with him. But in the interim, a rumor is started that makes its way onto the Internet and will haunt the pilots for years to come.

FAA Command Center, Herndon, Virginia, 2:00

The tension of the day isn't quite over yet for Ben Sliney. At 2 o'clock, one of the two suspicious international flights, Korean Air Flight 85, finally reaches radio range of Alaskan airspace and makes contact with Anchorage Center. The flight had used a code for hijacking in an ARINC message, but Sliney is confident that that must be a misunderstanding, which will now be quickly resolved. The controller queries the pilots as to the status of their aircraft, including in his transmission the code word "late"—the way of asking pilots if they are in a hijack situation—in case the crew is unable to speak freely.

To the controller's amazement, rather than offering assurance that the flight is secure, the pilot switches his transponder to the hijack code. He has just confirmed hijacked status.

At the Command Center, Sliney stares up at the Traffic Summary Display to see the hijack code flashing off the Alaskan coast. He can't believe what he's seeing. *No! This has got to be a mistake!*

NORAD's Alaska region commander, Lt. Gen. Norton Schwartz, directs air traffic control to turn the flight away from Anchorage and the oil facilities of Valdez.[1] He wants it diverted to Whitehorse, in Canada's Yukon Territory. But Sliney is urging officials to allow the flight to continue. His staff is in contact with Korean Air headquarters, who are emphatically maintaining that they have received *no* indication that the flight is in jeopardy. They also don't think that the aircraft has sufficient fuel to reach Whitehorse, a full 500 miles beyond the flight's scheduled refueling stop of Anchorage.

Sliney urges his controllers to continue to seek clarification from the pilots while the flight continues toward Anchorage. Less confident than Sliney that the flight poses no threat, Alaska's governor orders an evacuation of the Trans-Alaska Pipeline, as well as all large hotels and the federal buildings in Anchorage.

To Sliney's dismay, each time controllers query the aircraft, the pilots offer no reassurance that they are not, in fact, hijacked. Sliney knows that the military will have the final say in this matter, and before long General Schwartz has had enough. He orders air traffic control to turn away the aircraft and warns that he will shoot it down if the plane refuses to divert and continues on its course. Canadian officials agree to allow the flight to divert to Whitehorse, and a whole new wave of evacuations begins.

The airliner, accompanied by fighters and still squawking the hijack code, finally lands at Whitehorse at 2:54 (EST). The pilots are escorted off the aircraft at gunpoint for interrogation. Only then are officials able to determine that the flight was never hijacked. The crew had simply been trying to relay to controllers their awareness of the hijackings on the East Coast. It was an odd idea for the pilots to have, and contrary to their training. But for whatever reason—perhaps because of some language or communication barrier, or some training failure—they made a very dangerous bad call. In the aftermath of the attacks, whole new procedures would be put in place to guarantee that pilots would not do any such thing in the future.

Finally, at 3:30, Sliney is relieved to be able to announce that the last of the flights inbound to the United States has landed. From his post, he watches a new, military-directed air traffic control system emerge under NORAD's ESCAT order. The Command Center works in coordination with NORAD according to a strict protocol. Any flight requesting to fly is evaluated closely by NORAD to determine if the flight is necessary and if it conforms to the military restrictions in place. Under the new military rules, only certain planes will be given takeoff authorization: those flying combat, those flying in support of the combat mission, those on life-saving missions, and select others. If NORAD issues approval, then the Command Center takes over and issues the flight a security control authorization, a clearance with a narrow takeoff window. If the pilot misses that window, he or she can forget about flying.

One of the first nonmilitary aircraft allowed to take off after ESCAT is enacted is a United Airlines Boeing 757 carrying FBI agents and equipment from San Francisco to Washington, D.C. The approval has come from NORAD headquarters, and United 8811 takes off from San Francisco in the late afternoon with 75 FBI agents and 14,000 pounds of equipment. For Capt. Barry Nance, it is the strangest flight he will ever fly. No sooner does he take off than he is cleared "direct" across the country. En route, he hears a total of three other aircraft on the frequency, all of them fighters.

Sliney looks up at the air traffic display at the front of the Command Center. For the first time in American aviation history, the nation's air traffic control system has been shut down. The president, who is now at Offutt Air Force Base in Sarpy County, Nebraska, and has just convened a teleconference with his senior staff and the National Security Council, has ordered that commercial air traffic be resumed by noon tomorrow. Sliney wonders how in the world that's going to happen. Shutting the system down has been hellish, but starting it back up is going to be the really hard part.

EPILOGUE

By early evening, President Bush is on his way back to Washington with a fighter escort. A new air defense mission for the United States has been born. The 103rd Air Control Squadron from Connecticut—a radar squadron—is linking their radar picture into NEADS. Refueling tankers from McGuire are landing at Andrews to refuel so that they can continue to feed the fighters over Washington. AWACS are circling over the country and battleships have arrived off the East Coast. None of these operations are the result of orders from a central authority; they have been improvised due to the initiative and courage shown by so many individuals.

Air National Guard commanders all over the country are busy preparing for combat operations. By 6 p.m. Atlantic City has 13 fully armed F-16s either in the air or ready to fly. Otis Air National Guard has 21 of its 24 F-15s airborne. In total, over 150 fully armed fighter aircraft are protecting U.S. cities. The number would be greater if more pilots were available.

The grounding of commercial aircraft has left Air National Guard pilots scattered around the country, desperately working to get back to their bases in any way they can. In another impressive improvisation, DCANG commanders have come up with a creative solution for getting their pilots back to base; the DCANG's 201st Air Lift Squadron, which normally flies business jets for government officials, is using one of its planes to fly around the country and pick them up. The Boeing 727 receives Priority 2 flight approval: Forces being deployed, or in direct support of combat operations against the enemy. Col. Linda McTague is at the controls, and she is struck by the almost complete silence on the normally busy VHF frequencies; all but for one transmission that is repeated every 30 minutes as the plane makes its way around the country: "WARNING! We are under a national emergency. The United States military has control of the airspace. Any aircraft squawking an unauthorized code will be launched upon!" The announcement gives McTague the chills every time she hears it.

At NEADS, Bob Marr and his team are continuing to ramp up for war operations. Troops had started arriving at the base almost immediately after the attacks began and, as the day progressed, the background din of intense activity had become a roar. Bob Marr calls for all staff who had arrived during the day to gather in the conference room across from the Command Post for a Battle Brief, and he tells them the nation is at war. When he then tells those who had been hard at work since the morning that they should leave and get some rest, few do so. Finally he sends out an unequivocal order; the day shift must leave.

Some of the first fighter pilots to launch are finally returning home. Others are staying to work. When Otis F-15 pilot Duff finally arrives at his house, he sits down to speak with his oldest sons. "Are you all right?" he asks. "Well yeah, Dad," they tell him, "We know you're taking care of it."

When Billy Hutchison takes off again just after midnight—this time with his night vision goggles—the air traffic controller tells him, "The sky is yours. Go where you need to go."

At the FAA Command Center, on the traffic summary display at the front of the operations floor, the dots of fighter aircraft can be seen circling over cities all over the country. A lone United 757 makes it way across the country filled with FBI agents and equipment. Unfortunately, despite the extensive ESCAT protocol that's been put in place for flight operations, there are kinks in the system. When United 8811 approaches Washington just after midnight, news of an incoming airliner causes agents at the White House to quickly whisk the president and first lady into the emergency bunker.

Epilogue

As the night progresses, the government and the airlines will settle on a whole host of changes that will eventually accompany the reopening of the skies: a high-visibility display of law enforcement at all large airports, security sweeps of all airports before they can reopen, expanded use of Federal Air Marshals on commercial flights, more rigorous airport screening, no more off-airport check-in, and no passengers without paper confirmation of a ticket allowed past security. And that's just the beginning.

The next morning, rows of phones are set up in the glass-enclosed conference room in the corner of the Command Center to handle all of the requests for takeoffs. New air traffic control methods and defense measures are quickly being crafted, and when the skies reopen on a very limited basis three days later Americans will realize that air travel has forever changed.

Those stranded overseas the day of the attacks will experience an outpouring of sympathy. The crew of American Airlines Flight 53, which had reversed course and returned to Glasgow after being turned back from U.S. airspace, is invited by the city to a memorial service. At the service, pilot Mike Jefferson and the rest of the crew are given an American flag, and they are deeply touched by the dozens of Scots who approach them after the service to express their deep-felt sorrow. The following day, when the crew departs their hotel for the flight back home, the entire hotel staff lines up to wish them well.

As commercial flights return to U.S. airspace, slowly at first, fighter jets continue to police the skies, still under weapons-free orders to take out any confirmed threats. All the pilots now thoroughly understand their shoot-down authority, and each has signed a document indicating he or she understands the new rules of engagement. The country will live in fear of further attacks for many days yet.

Two days after the attacks, when Midwest Airlines Captain Gerald Earwood gets the word that his flight is cleared to leave New York's LaGuardia Airport, armed guards meet him and his crew as they arrive at the entrance to the airport. They enter a vacant terminal and must pass through an extensive screening before being escorted to their gate, where two Port Authority police officers accompany Earwood down to the aircraft. He's been given a security checklist and must perform a "walk around" of the plane with the law enforcement officers. When the crew is permitted to board, they get busy looking beneath every seat and in every overhead bin for anything that should not be there.

Unbelievably, as they are preparing to take off, Earwood receives word that a bomb threat has been called in about the plane. His announcement of the news to the crew is met with stunned disbelief. As the crewmembers file calmly out onto the runway, several begin to cry. After another meticulous inspection, the plane is cleared to leave, and after Earwood disengages the parking brake and the aircraft begins to push back, he hears applause from the cabin.

While taxiing out, two F-15's from Otis fly a low pass over the runway. They've gained Earwood's full attention. As he pushes the thrust levers to full power, he wants the world to know that a U.S. commercial plane is flying again.

"V1, rotate," the first officer calls out, and Earwood lifts the nose of the aircraft for takeoff.

"Let 'em hear you, Midex, and safe flight!" the controller calls out as the plane heads skyward.

AFTERWORD

*"If everyone would just turn off CNN, there wouldn't be a
threat from Osama Bin Laden."*
> —Remarks made to Maj. Gen. Arnold
> by Vice Admiral Martin J. Mayer,
> Wednesday, August 22, 2001.

I am Major General (retired) Larry Arnold, and on September 11,
2001, I was the commander of 1st Air Force and the Continental
U.S. North American Air Defense Command (CONR) Region
located at Tyndall Air Force Base near Panama City, Florida. I
was responsible for the lower 48 states, and my boss was General
Ed Eberhart, who was commander of NORAD. It would be General Eberhart who would declare *SCATANA*—Security Control of
Air Traffic and Navigational Aids—in response to the attack on
September 11, 2001, by which the military took control of the airspace over the United States. The person who would implement
SCATANA would be me.

Lynn Spencer's book about the terrorist attack on 9/11 and the
military response to it had to be written. Lynn has dedicated three
years of her life to this effort and for this I am glad. In some cases
the facts published in this book, as told to her in interviews with airmen and airline pilots who were involved, differ markedly from the
account in *The 9/11 Commission Report,* as well as from the depiction in the movie *United 93.* The corrections to the record are
important, and I'm glad our people in the military were able to tell

her their stories of the events of that tragic day. Lynn does not have a political agenda, as the 9/11 Commission clearly did. She understands the clear professionalism of the men and women of the United States Air Force and Air National Guard in performing their duties that day. No less, she is intimately aware of the dedication of the men and women of the FAA in accomplishing their jobs that morning.

The terrorist attack came without warning and in a way that we had not imagined. It was an asymmetric attack, by which the terrorists exploited the weaknesses within the United States' air surveillance and air defense system; a system that was designed to look outward, away from our shores, to detect aircraft or missiles approaching our borders. Nonetheless, our outstanding weapons controllers at the Northeast Air Defense Sector and the pilots in their F-15s, F-16s, AWACS, and tanker aircraft quickly adapted to the situation. We believe we could have shot down the last of the hijacked aircraft, United 93, had it continued toward Washington, D.C. the 9/11 Commission said we could not have done so. After reading this book, you decide.

Many people in the military at that time considered NORAD to be a relic of the Cold War, one which had outlived its usefulness with the demise of the Soviet Union and the Warsaw Pact. NORAD was created in 1958 when the Cold War was boiling hot, and was responsible for bomber and missile attack warning, as well as air defense of North America. But the collapse of the Soviet government didn't obviate all danger from the many intercontinental ballistic missiles the Soviets had controlled, which are now possessed by Russia. In addition, China had developed ICBMs, and North Korea would soon have these weapons of mass destruction as well. You can argue whether or not a nuclear power in today's world would unleash these weapons, but missile attack warning for the United States is still a vital military mission. Nonetheless, air defense capability to guard against the threat from enemy bomber aircraft had been seriously cut back by the time of 9/11. We had become sort of the border patrol in the sky.

Just within CONR, we had gone from over a hundred squadrons of air defense fighter aircraft in the late 1950s to only 10 Air National Guard squadrons of fighters, and all had an overseas mission as well as air defense. In the continental United States, we had only 14 aircraft on immediate alert status and it had become a budget battle every year to keep these aircraft on alert. Immediate alert status means the aircraft are loaded and cocked with live munitions and can be launched within minutes to respond to an unauthorized intruder flying into our airspace. In the days of the Soviet Union, this could mean flying several hundred miles out to intercept a Soviet Bear aircraft which flew along our coast line to gather intelligence, just as we did along the borders of the Soviet Union with our intelligence-gathering aircraft. By the time of 9/11, we mostly scrambled our fighters to intercept aircraft that had failed to file a flight plan properly or, when requested, to intercept a suspected drug smuggling plane and follow it until customs could get one of their own aircraft into position to apprehend the smugglers.

That didn't mean that we might not be called on at any moment to defend against a serious threat. The world was changing fast, and I had a great fear about what that threat might be. In 1999, the U.S. Commission on National Security for the 21st Century, commonly known as the Hart-Rudman Commission, issued a report stating that the greatest threat to the United States would come from independent or state sponsored terrorists. In January 2001, in the commission's third and final report, the bottom-line conclusion was that the primary national security challenge the United States would face in the next 20 or 30 years would be an attack by an adversary on the American homeland, which could produce thousands of casualties. Many of us in the military shared the commission's view.

Before 9/11, then–Marine Corps Commandant General Charles Krulak said in an interview for the *Wall Street Journal* that ". . . the one thing that keeps me awake at night is concern about a terrorist detonation of a weapon of mass destruction over the United States." I later told a reporter during an interview that I lay awake worrying about such a weapon being delivered through the air. It was the job of my command to detect, intercept, and shoot down anything in the air determined to be hostile and to threaten the United States. Everyone in my command took our job seriously. We planned for it; we exercised our capabilities; we fought the bureaucratic battles for more resources; and we were good at what we did. But our capabilities had dwindled to the point that our previous NORAD commander, General Richard Myers, had told the secretary of defense that he could provide only nominal air sovereignty—meaning tight command over United States airspace— at best.

Our air defense had atrophied to three command and control facilities watching our borders. Those forces had limited radar coverage and could scramble only fourteen alert aircraft at seven remaining alert locations. Congress had wanted to limit the forces even further. The Congressionally directed Quadrennial Defense Review of 1996 completed by the Air Force and Department of Defense said we only needed four alert locations. They used a basketball analogy of "four corner defense," which might be okay for basketball, but was totally useless for the air sovereignty and air defense of the United States. We in military command fought hard to keep ten locations and ended up with the seven. We had an expanse of nearly 1,500 miles between two of our locations along our southern border; we had no response capability at all along the northern border; and there were 500 to 1,000 miles between alert locations on the east and west coasts.

We had only 44 radar machines along the periphery of our borders to monitor incoming traffic, with about the same number of radios available for us to talk to our airborne fighters with from our command and control facilities. The computer command and control system that allowed us to display the radar returns on scopes for our weapon controllers could not accept any more radars or radios. When a Russian general officer visited the Southeast Air Defense Sector at Tyndall AFB, Florida, nearly eight years after the collapse of the Soviet Union he said, "Okay! Now show me the real facility." Our preparedness was that limited.

The fact that we had any air defense capability on that tragic day in September is only due to dedicated people like Maj. Gen. Phillip Killey, Gen. Howell Estes, and Gen. Richard Hawley, who was the Air Combat Commander during my tenure. They listened and asked the tough questions when others wanted to shut down the remainder of the air defense system. In fact, the secretary of the Air Force, James G. Roche, stated that he and the then chief of staff of the Air Force, General John Jumper, had decided to withdraw funding for air defense, and they had made that decision on September 7, 2001, four days before the terrorist attack.

Just two weeks before September 11, 2001, I had met with Vice Admiral Martin Mayer, the deputy commander-in-chief of Joint Forces Command located in Norfolk, Virginia. He had informed me that he intended to kill all funding for a plan my command had been working on for two years, that would defend against a cruise missile attack by terrorists. While I convinced Admiral Mayer to continue his funding support, he told me in front of my chief-of-staff, Colonel Alan Scott; Navy Captain David Stewart, the lead on this project; and my executive officer, Lt. Col. Kelley Duckett, that our concern about Osama Bin Laden as a possible threat to America was unfounded and that, to repeat, *"If everyone would just turn off CNN, there wouldn't be a threat from Osama Bin Laden."*

Much has been done to improve our defenses in the aftermath of the 9/11 attack. In an ongoing operation known as Noble Eagle, NORAD forces remain at a heightened readiness level, with pilots flying irregular air patrols over metropolitan areas and critical infrastructure facilities. They have flown more than 42,000 mishap-free sorties over the U.S. and Canada since the attack, and NORAD has scrambled or diverted aircraft more than 2,100 times in response to potential threats. An integrated air defense system has been deployed to defend vital assets and personnel in and around the U.S. National Capital Region, and a Visual Warning System

(VWS), which alerts pilots straying into the National Capital Region Air Defense Identification Zone (NCR ADIZ) and not in radio contact with ATC was also introduced, achieving Initial Operational Capability (IOC) 21 May 2005.

We have also stepped up our training and greatly improved our communications. NORAD has conducted more than 100 Command-level exercises to test these rules of engagement and to train designated authorities since 9/11. NORAD also partnered with the FAA, Transport Canada, and NAV CANADA to enhance our ability to monitor air traffic within the interior of the continent, linking FAA radars into the NORAD air picture. The disconnect in communication between NORAD and the FAA that was brought into glaring light on 9/11 has also been corrected for. A FAA sponsored telephonic call network, called the Domestic Event Network, has been set up, which broadcasts 24/7 and connects all of the FAA's major air traffic facilities in the U.S. The FAA has also placed representatives within NORAD command and regional operations centers. NORAD reviewed air defense alert facility locations to ensure timely response to threats to critical infrastructure throughout the U.S. and Canada. NORAD has developed and fostered close working relationships with many interagency government partners to significantly improve air security.

In the immediate aftermath of 9/11 we had to hook up to FAA radars throughout the country, install compatible radios for nationwide coverage between our command and control agencies and our airborne assets, and purchase a new command and control computer system to integrate radar and communications. The initial investment was for $75 million, and this number has grown to nearly $200 million. To put this in perspective, Saudi Arabia spent $1.2 billion during the 1990s to upgrade their system and they have contracted to upgrade their system again this year for a similar amount of money.

I believe Al-Qaeda is planning another attack that will make 9/11 pale in comparison. The Hart-Rudman Commission report of January 2001 predicted the following: "We should expect conflicts in which adversaries, because of cultural affinities different from our own, will resort to forms and levels of violence shocking to our sensibilities. America will become increasingly vulnerable to hostile attack on our homeland, and our military superiority will not entirely protect us. Therefore, the United States should assume that it will be a target of terrorist attacks against its homeland using weapons of mass destruction. The United States will be vulnerable to such strikes." Though we have taken many important steps to guard against this threat, we are still vulnerable, and we have much work to do to further strengthen our defenses.

We do not know how the attack might be carried out, and defending ourselves will not be easy, but we must try.

—Larry Arnold, Maj. Gen.,
United States Air Force, Retired

NOTES

PRELUDE

1. Unless otherwise noted, all quoted conversations in this book are from interviews and correspondences with one or both participants in the conversation.

CHAPTER 1

1. Transcript of American Airlines Flight 11, *New York Times*, October 16, 2001.
2. Ibid.
3. T. Brokaw, "The Skies over America: The Air Traffic Controllers on 9/11 Saw the Nightmare Coming," *Dateline NBC*, September 9, 2006, http://www.msnbc.msn.com/id/14754701
4. "America Remembers: Air Traffic Controllers Describe How Events Unfolded As They Saw Them on September 11th," *Dateline*, NBC, September 11, 2002.
5. Ibid.
6. Transcript of United Airlines Flight 175, *New York Times*, October 16, 2001.
7. Unless otherwise noted, all airline headquarter conversations in this book are from "Borders, Transportation, and Managing Risk," seventh public hearing of the National Commission on Terrorist Attacks Upon the United States, Washington, D.C., January 27, 2004.
8. S. Carey and S. McCartney, "American, United Watched and Worked in Horror As September 11 Hijacking Unfolded," *Wall Street Journal*, October 15, 2001.
9. "Borders, Transportation, and Managing Risk."
10. Carey and McCartney, "American, United."
11. "Borders, Transportation, and Managing Risk."
12. M. Ellison, " 'We Have Planes. Stay Quiet'—Then Silence," *The Guardian*, October 17, 2001.
13. Unless otherwise noted, references to conversations from the Ops floor of NEADS are from personal interviews or from audio tapes obtained from NEADS.

CHAPTER 2

1. http://www.archives.gov/legislative/research/9-11/staff-report-sept2005.pdf (Subject to Classification Review, Staff Report, August 26, 2004.)

293

2. Carey and McCartney, "American, United."
3. Transcript of United Airlines Flight 175.
4. "America Remembers."
5. Michael Bronner, *9/11 Live: The NORAD Tapes: Politics and Power,* VanityFair.com. Bronner, *9/11 Live.*
6. "America Remembers."

CHAPTER 3

1. "9/11 Recordings Chronicle Confusion, Delay," CNN.com, June 17, 2004.
2. G. Johnson, "Probe Reconstructs Horror, Calculated Attacks on Planes," *Boston Globe*, November 23, 2001.
3. Unless otherwise indicated, references in this chapter to controller transmissions are from Transcript of United Airlines Flight 175.
4. "America Remembers."
5. Ibid.
6. Bronner, *9/11 Live.*
7. Carey and McCartney, "American, United."
8. Ibid.
9. National Commission on Terrorist Attacks Upon the United States. *The 9/11 Commission Report: Final Report of the National Commission on Terrorist Attacks Upon the United States* (New York & London: W. W. Norton, 2004).

CHAPTER 4

1. Unless otherwise noted, all conversations involving air traffic control come from the National Transportation Safety Board (NTSB) report, *Air Traffic Control Recording—American Airlines Flight 77*, released by the *New York Times* on December 21, 2001.
2. National Commission on Terrorist Attacks Upon the United States, "Improvising a Homeland Defense," Staff Statement No. 17 (June 17, 2004), www .msnbc.msn.com/id/5233007.
3. S. Carey and S. McCartney, "American, United Watched and Worked in Horror As September 11 Hijacking Unfolded," *Wall Street Journal*, October 15, 2001.
4. Ibid.

CHAPTER 5

1. *The 9/11 Commision Report*, 22.
2. Ibid.
3. "America Remembers."
4. Ibid.
5. A. Levin, M. Adams, and B. Morrison, "Part I: Terror Attacks Brought Drastic Decision: Clear the Skies," *USA Today*, August 11, 2002.

Notes

CHAPTER 6

1. *The 9/11 Commission Report*, 23.

CHAPTER 7

1. S. Adcock, "A Loss of Control," *Newsday*, September 10, 2002.
2. Murphy, Tom. 2007. *Reclaiming the Sky: 9/11 and the Untold Story of the Men and Women Who Kept America Flying*. New York: AMACOM, p. 18.
3. Transcript of American Airlines Flight 77, *New York Times*, October 16, 2001.
4. "Grounded on 9/11" The History Channel, A&E Television Networks, 2002.

CHAPTER 8

1. Clarke, Richard. 2004. *Against All Enemies*. New York: Free Press, 2004, p. 2.

CHAPTER 9

1. *The 9/11 Commission Report*, 37.
2. *The 9/11 Commission Report*, 36–38.
3. NTSB, *Air Traffic Control Recording—United Airlines Flight 93*, December 21, 2001. These materials are reproduced from www.nsarchive.org with permission of the National Security Archive. http://www.gwu.edu/~nsarchiv/NSAEBB/NSAEBB196/index.htm
4. *The 9/11 Commission Report*, 11.
5. NTSB, *Air Traffic Control Recording—United Airlines Flight 93*.
6. T. Brokaw, "The Skies over America: The Air Traffic Controllers on 9/11 Saw the Nightmare Coming," *Dateline NBC*, September 9, 2006, http://www.msnbc.msn.com/id/14754701
7. NTSB, *Air Traffic Control Recording—United Airlines Flight 93*.
8. Russ Kick, "Air Traffic Control Recording of 9/11 Flight 93," http://www.the memoryhole.org/911/flight93-air-traffic.htm, 2002.
9. Ibid.
10. Carey and McCartney, "American, United."

CHAPTER 10

1. *The 9/11 Commission Report*, 37.

CHAPTER 11

1. Kick, "Air Traffic Control Recording of 9/11 Flight 93."
2. *The 9/11 Commission Report*, 29.

Notes

CHAPTER 12

1. Carey and McCartney, "American, United."
2. *The 9/11 Commission Report*, 29.
3. 9/11: Interview by Peter Jennings, ABC News, September 11, 2002. http://s3.amazonaws.com/911timeline/2002/abcnews091102.html

CHAPTER 13

1. A. Levin, "Voices from the Air Traffic World," *USA Today*, September 11, 2002.

CHAPTER 14

1. Conversations as reported by those in the DCA control tower.
2. http://en.wikipedia.org/wiki/United_Airlines_Flight_93.
3. Ibid.
4. From personal interview with Bob Marr. The information had come from a phone call between the White House and the NMCC, also referenced in: 9/11: Interviews by Peter Jennings, ABC News, September 11, 2002. http://s3.amazonaws.com/911timeline/2002/abcnews091102.html
5. All references to Air Force One, unless otherwise indicated, are from "The President's Story," *60 Minutes II*, CBS News, September 10, 2003. http://www.cbsnews.com/stories/2002/09/11/60ll/main521718.shtml.

CHAPTER 15

1. D. Balz and B. Woodward, "America's Chaotic Road to War," *Washington Post*, January 27, 2002, p. A01.
2. *The 9/11 Commission Report*, 42.

CHAPTER 16

1. "The President's Story," *60 Minutes II*, CBS News, September 10, 2003. http://www.cbsnews.com/stories/2002/09/11/60ll/main521718.shtml.
2. Information regarding Mr. Ashcroft's flight was obtained from his office via e-mail, which attached chapter eight from his book *Never Again* (Center Street, Oct 3, 2006); from an e-mail obtained from controller Dan Creedon, written by Ashcroft's pilot and dated 9/14/2001; and from various interviews.

CHAPTER 17

1. A. Levin, "Korean Air jet may have narrowly missed disaster," *USA Today*, Aug 8, 2002. http://www.usatoday.com/news/sept11/2002-08-12-koreanair_x.htm

ACKNOWLEDGMENTS

I thought myself a pilot, not a writer, but this project called to me in a way that I could not ignore. While I gathered the names and the places and the stories, I became increasingly aware of the importance of these accounts. I am exceedingly grateful to those whose contributions made this book a reality. It has been a rewarding and humbling experience.

Ultimately, the names of those responsible for this book fill the preceding pages, and I am most grateful to them. They entrusted their stories to me despite my unproven writing ability and their discomfort in revisiting a very emotionally charged day. To the countless others whose names do not appear, I am indebted to you for the stories and the information you graciously shared, providing me a better understanding or leading me to other contacts. The experience of meeting each of you was the most rewarding part of writing this book. It was an honor and privilege.

My children—Caroline, Brigitte, and Chase—shared their mother with a demanding multiyear project. I am grateful for their patience and encouragement, and I will honor my promise that any subsequent books will be written during school hours. My parents never doubted my ability to see this project through—or if they did, they didn't show it—and for that I am appreciative. I thank Don, Andrea, and Gregg for being tolerant of their distracted sister.

I could not have accomplished this project without the assistance of the Air Line Pilots Association, the Allied Pilots Association, and the National Air Traffic Controllers Association, who spread the word to their memberships. Heartfelt thanks to all their members who generously shared their stories.

It has been a pleasure and an honor to work with NORAD and the Air National Guard, whose units and members were tirelessly forthcoming with information and personal accounts. Thank you to the men and

Acknowledgments

women of NEADS, the 177th Fighter Wing, the 113th Wing, the 119th Fighter Wing and the 180th Fighter Wing, and to Lt. Col. Roberta Neidt of the New Jersey Department of Military and Veterans Affairs, who was kind enough to make my first military introductions. A special thanks to the 102nd Fighter Wing, whose members not only shared their stories, but also gave me the opportunity to fly in an F-15. In doing so—and retracing the flights paths of the Otis fighters as well as American 11 on that fateful day—I gained an invaluable understanding and perspective. You all are the best!

I am especially indebted to Paul Worcester and Don Shepperd, who graciously opened the doors of the aviation and military communities. Their encouragement, guidance, and tireless introductions made this book possible. I am deeply grateful for their "you can do it and you'll do it right" attitudes, which motivated me to reach deeper within myself to achieve more than I thought I could.

Several individuals deserve special thanks, including Colin Scoggins, Larry Arnold, Ben Sliney, and Joe McCain for their prompt replies to my myriads of e-mail and phone questions that arrived at all hours of the day and night asking for information and explanations. Thanks also to Paul Olechowski, Harvey Siegel, Sandy Niedzwiecki, and Kerri Cole of the 102nd FW, James Hambrick at the FBI, Thomas Territt at NEADS, and authors Loree Lough, Rick Newmann, Carol Jose, and J. Carson Black. Your input, advice, and guidance were much appreciated. Thank you, Gen. Myers, for the time you gave me over cups of coffee at Starbucks.

I knew I could fly, but I was not as sure about writing, and I owe a debt to those who helped with reading and editing the manuscript: Paul Worcester, Rose Shepperd, Ann Levy, and Jordan Genest. Your assistance enabled me to pull everything together and produce a readable manuscript for my wonderful editor, Emily Loose. I was awed by Emily's quick grasp of the intricacies and complexities of this project, her patience, and, above all, her insightful and creative editing. It was a delight to work with her. My heartfelt thanks to everyone at Simon & Schuster for helping me make this dream a reality.

And finally, a huge thank-you to my agent, Jane Dystel, who took a chance on a pilot who had no writing experience. She believed in the stories and my ability to share them, and offered invaluable guidance and assistance every step of the way, never once making me feel foolish for my ignorance of the publishing business. I will always be grateful for the opportunity and her faith in me.

INDEX

Index

Applegate, Curt, 47
ARINC (air-ground radio
communications), 72
Arnold, Larry, 285–91
and American Flight 11, 31, 38–39
and authorization to intercept, 83, 86,
111
gathering information, 178, 187
and scrambled jets, 111, 112, 140, 178
and shoot-down orders, 140–41, 225,
240
and United Flight 175, 83
Arpey, Gerard, 35, 52, 65, 107–8
Ashcroft, John, 257–59, 272–73
ATC (air traffic controllers), see air traffic
controllers
ATC Zero:
at Boston Center, 243–44
and FAA/Sliney, 68–69, 126–27,
128–31, 160, 170, 171, 185–86,
223
at New York Center, 68–69, 70, 79,
80–81, 91, 95, 99, 111, 129, 130,
145
use of, 68
Atlantic City ANG:
F-16s at, 29, 34, 57, 99, 120, 281
military threat conditions at, 120–22
mission of, 121
177th Fighter Wing, 58–60, 99,
120–22, 267–68
scrambling jets from, 33–34
supervisor of flying (SOF) in, 58–59,
120
AWAC communications, 265

Baker, Gerald, 208–11
Ballinger, Ed, 103, 132, 134, 161
Barksdale AFB, Louisiana, 231, 247, 255
Belger, Monte, 69, 88
Biggio, Terry, 79–80
Bin Laden, Osama, 285, 289
Borgstrom, Craig "Borgy," 115–19
and battle stations order, 117–18,
141–42
flying, 118–19, 148, 151–52, 181–82,
222–25, 227
as Langley SOF, 116, 118, 119, 148
refueling, 263–64
RTB (return to base) order to, 277
and shoot-down orders, 223, 224
Boston, CAP over, 247
Boston Center, New Hampshire:
and American Flight 11, 11–17, 52,
137

and American Flight 77, 150
approaching threat, 242–43
and ATC Zero, 243–44
functions of, 6–8, 49, 174
Scoggins in, see Scoggins, Colin
stopping all departures, 98–99,
130
teleconferencing, 45–46, 79–81, 88
and United Flight 175, 80, 82
Boston Logan Airport, 6–7
flights leaving the gate, 8–11
hijacked aircraft originating in, 128,
130
Bottiglia, Dave, 24, 36–37, 47–49, 53,
55, 74
Brotherton, Shane, 255
Bueno, Dan, 16, 22, 24, 27, 33, 49
Burlingame, Chic, 62–63
Burnett, Tom, 221
Bush, George W.:
in Air Force One, 230–31, 255–56
in Florida schoolroom, 109,
124
and resumption of commercial flights,
280
return to Washington, 281
and Secret Service, 123, 230
in White House bunker, 282

Caine, Daniel "Razin":
and airspace congestion, 271
as Andrews SOF, 123–24, 156–57,
183, 217
and Ashcroft's flight, 273
suiting up to fly, 184, 237
and Washington CAP, 238, 251–54,
266–68
Callahan, Greg, 78, 94, 95
Camp David, rumors about, 242
Canada:
and international flights, 196–97
NORAD partnership with, 290
Operation Yellow Ribbon, 197
CAP (Combat Air Patrol):
no protocol for, 267–68
over Boston, 247
over major cities, 189–90, 267,
281
over New York, 111–14, 152, 213–14,
273–74
over Washington, D.C., 148, 180–82,
184–85, 218, 234–39, 247–49,
251–55, 263–68
Carty, Don, 52, 89, 107–8, 186
Charlebois, Dave, 62

301

Index

Index

ABOUT THE AUTHOR

Lynn Spencer is a pilot for ExpressJet Airlines as well as a certified flight instructor. She has been a commercial pilot for eleven years, and in that time has held the coveted position of Instructor for the airline. She graduated from Duke University with honors, before following her dream to become a pilot, and she completed her high-altitude training at NASA's Johnson Space Center in Houston. She lives in Arlington, Virginia, with her three children.